My GLORY AND THE LIFTER OF MY HEAD

A STUDY OF THE
BOOK OF NUMBERS

CHRISTY VOELKEL

Copyright © 2020 by Christy Voelkel

Scripture taken from the New King James Version®. Copyright © 1982 by Thomas Nelson. Used by permission. All rights reserved. Unless otherwise noted, all Scripture cited in this study is from the NKJV.

Scriptures passages have been copied from the online Bible reference source, Blue Letter Bible (www.blueletterbible.org) using its copy feature.

Strong's Hebrew Lexicon definitions from Blue Letter Bible. Web. 7 May, 2018.

Table of Contents

Introduction	i
Lesson 1: The Lifter of My Head	1
Lesson 2: Wilderness of Sinai	11
Lesson 3: Taberah	45
Lesson 4: Kibroth Hatta'avah	53
Lesson 5: Hazeroth	85
Lesson 6: Kadesh	103
Lesson 7: Wilderness of Paran: Consequences	127
Lesson 8: Wilderness of Paran: Korah's Rebellion	147
Lesson 9: Wilderness of Zin	175
Lesson 10: Into Enemy Territory	195
Lesson 11: Into Enemy Territory: Final Battle	205
Lesson 12: On the Plains of Moab by the Jordan	243
Conclusion: Glorification	263

About This Study

I developed this study of the book of Numbers for a 12-week overview class I presented at my church in the winter of 2017-2018. As I began to read through the text and draw out a theme to tie the lessons together, it became apparent that I would have to present much more than just an overview of the main events! All parts of the book were significant. The names, the numbers, even the laws that seemed like interruptions in the narrative flow, all provided necessary context and connective tissue for understanding the events themselves. There was simply no way to go through the main events without discussing these other elements, and it was a challenge to boil the text down to something I could present coherently within 12 weeks. Hence, the reason for this book. It is my hope here not only to capture the research and content I presented in my lecture (before I forget it), but also to explore relevant passages that I was not able to cover in the study.

This study is an exegetical commentary on the book of Numbers with topical discussions that complement the main text. It is meant to accompany a reading of the Scriptures, not replace it. I encourage you to read through the Numbers' chapters before reading the chapter studies. This is not a typical Bible study with application questions at the end of each chapter. Instead I have reserved the final chapter for self-assessment questions which I hope will help you look at your own journey and assess your progress in learning how to see God as a glorious God and give Him glory in your life.

Introduction

When my friends heard I was teaching a class on the book of Numbers, most of them gave me a look of disbelief and said, "What is there to teach? It's just about, well, numbers." I asked my class on the first day how many had read the book of Numbers in the past year, and no one raised their hand. I asked if any had read the book of Numbers sometime in their life, and only a few raised their hand. The general consensus was that Numbers was just another book of the Law made up of dry, boring lists of names and numbers, statistics and details that have no application or relevance today. I set out to change their minds.

I think the name, Numbers, gives this book a bad rap because it sets up that expectation of a lot of dry facts. But the book of Numbers is about numbers only in the sense of an accounting. There is an accounting of people in two censuses. There is an accounting of places that the Israelites (and we the readers) travel through. There is an accounting of materials, plunder, and divisions of inheritance. Mostly it is an accounting of failings and deaths. If you focus on the numbers, however, you will miss the point of this book.

I think the original Hebrew title, *Ba'midbar*, "in the Wilderness," is much more appropriate. The wilderness journey is what the book is truly about and *that* is as relevant to us today as it was to the children of Israel back then. The shoes of those children of Israel have yet to wear out, and we can get as many practical lessons out of walking in those shoes as they did.

The Structure of This Study

The book of Numbers is about a physical journey, so it makes sense to focus on the places and events presented in the narrative. I have divided the book into chapters aligned with the geographical places we visit, and in each place I discuss the events that happen there, why they happen, their outcome, and their significance and impact for the children of Israel.

The physical journey is also a reflection of the spiritual journey—the sanctification journey—which is what we as believers identify with. Paul tells us in 1 Corinthians 10:1-12 that the physical journey was meant for our admonition that we might not fall short in our relationship with God as the children of Israel did, and yet how many of us ever bother to study the physical journey? All of the physical events, and the physical relationships between people, places, and things, teach lessons about the spiritual relationship. With each place we come to, I discuss the principles, spiritual lessons and New Testament teachings that correspond to the physical event.

The final aspect that I will cover in this study are the pictures of Christ that appear in the narrative. The Gospel truly is portrayed in detail through and through this journey, as are the events of the End Times and Christ's second coming. As many of these as I have been able to identify, I will explain.

Standing in Their Shoes

When I study the Scripture, I try to study from the perspective of the people in the narrative. I always try to find a pair of shoes to stand in. The shoes that I have picked for the beginning of this study are the first generation adults that come out of Egypt (20 years old and over at the first census).

We are going to step into their sandals and walk their walk. We are going to consider their failings as if they are our failings. This is tough to do because they fail a lot in this journey—spectacularly at times. But so do we. So before we judge these people too harshly, we're going to pick the plank out of our own eye first, as Jesus warned us.

In Numbers 14, the adult generation refuses to enter the Land. Since the first generation does not finish the journey, I asked my class at that point in whose shoes we should continue the journey. Everyone voted to walk with Joshua and Caleb. We continue the journey with our kinsmen, suffer with them, fight alongside them, but from the eyes of elders watching a younger generation continue in their relationship with God beyond their parents' experience.

Conclusion

When I finished the 12-week class, I asked my students again if they still thought of the book of Numbers as being only about numbers. Unanimously, they all agreed that it was nothing like what they had thought and they were all able to take away lessons that were relevant to their own lives. I hope that readers of this study will also be able to take away something that they can apply to their own lives, but more than that, I hope that they come to a deeper understanding of how to experience God's glory in their own lives and how to live for that glory.

LESSON ONE

The Lifter of My Head

The book of Numbers is the fourth book in the Law of Moses (the Pentateuch), and it gives a detailed account of the second half of the Exodus journey, from Mount Sinai to the plains of Moab on the Jordan River across from Jericho. It covers only a portion of the overall physical journey, and yet the narrative is presented in such a way as to create a self-contained picture of the spiritual sanctification journey that we can experience in this life, from the point of salvation to glorification, just short of entering the Glorious Kingdom.

I've titled this study *My Glory and the Lifter of My Head* because of the opening command in the original Hebrew phrasing of Numbers 1:2 to "lift the head of the children of Israel." This theme of glorification and "lifting" runs through both the physical and spiritual journey depicted in the book. In terms of the physical journey, the reason God brings His children out of Egypt and through the wilderness is to give them a deep understanding and experience of *His* glory and to glorify *them* as His people. His end goal was always to bring them into the Glorious Land that He has prepared for them. In terms of the spiritual journey, the purpose is to move us through the experience of sanctification toward glorification. Entering a state of glorification is the common goal for both journeys.

When the children of Israel made this journey, most of them failed to gain a mature understanding of God in His glory. They failed to understand what their own glorification was meant to look like and how it was to be achieved. As a result, many faltered in their faith and failed to enter into the Glorious Land. We face the same challenge in our own spiritual walk with the Lord. We know about God's glory, but that knowledge often fails to translate into the *experience* of His glory. We lose sight of what He is trying to accomplish in us through this journey, and many of us fall short of achieving a full understanding of God in His glory, a oneness with Him, and the full glory of that reward waiting for us in the end.

The purpose of this study is to learn from the example of the children of Israel what are the pitfalls and obstacles along the journey that get us off track and keep us from fully realizing God's glory in our lives.

Before we get into the Book of Numbers, I want to talk a little about this theme of glory that runs through the wilderness journey. If we are going to navigate this journey successfully, we need to keep a few things very clear in our mind.

1. What a glorious God looks like
2. How God reckons His own glory
3. How we give glory to God and take glory from God
4. What our own glorification looks like
5. What is God's definition of glorious life

If we do not have a good grasp on the goals of this journey, we will falter along the way. So let's explore these one at a time.

What a Glorious God Looks Like

It is God's great desire that we know Him as a glorious God, and so it seems logical to begin by asking what makes God a glorious God? How do we define God's glory? One lady in my class answered that to her God's glory was His awesomeness, not just in His power but in His mercy, His graciousness—the great totality of who He is. That is a pretty good description.

There are many Hebrew words in the Old Testament translated as glory, and their definitions include beauty, splendor, honor, and majesty. They communicate the weightiness of God—like the heaviness of a kingly garment. He is the great Creator. His physical creation reveals His glory, and yet nothing in the physical realm can encompass it.

God in His glory is untouchable, distant, and so highly lifted up in cleanness and holiness as to be fully separated from us in our sinful state. Such glory is impossible for us to comprehend, let alone relate to.

I believe God is even more glorious than this definition. He is the all-powerful judge of sin, and yet His power is tempered by His love. He is removed from us, and yet dwells among us. When we are unfaithful to Him, He is still faithful to us. All of these are assets of His glory not included in that definition of "heaviness." If we limit our understanding of His glory to the definition of the word, we will not have a complete picture of Him.

What we know of God's glory can only be understood by our experience of Him. It is a picture that is built from experiences happening over time. Realizing that picture requires a lifetime journey.

The picture of God as a glorious God is built through a history of experiences. One of the main reasons the children of Israel failed to realize

God's glory in their lives is because they forgot their history of experiences with Him. We can make the same mistake in our own spiritual journey. The trick to knowing a glorious God is to find a way to keep that history and that expanding picture of Him present in our minds in the daily walk.

How God Reckons His Glory

Understanding God's glory begins with the understanding that He is a sovereign God. As a sovereign God, His glory demands acknowledgement. He does not give His glory to another (Isa. 42:8), nor does He tolerate anything that rivals His glory. He will be glorified by the praise of His people, or He will be glorified by putting down His enemies. One way or the other, every knee will bow and every tongue confess His sovereign kingship in the end.

It is important to understand how God reckons His glory, because He does it very differently than the world does. In general, the world reckons glory by numbers.

The glory of a king is counted by how many people he rules, how much territory he has conquered, his nation's wealth, its resources, its military strength or even the number of its allies. The glory of an army rests on how many troops it can deploy, how many weapons it can muster, how many casualties it inflicts, and how much plunder it takes from the conquered enemies. What is true of kings is true of masters. Masters glory in the number of slaves they own. Employers glory in the number of workers they employ and the profit they have from them.

Even today, the world has taught us to reckon our glory by numbers, from material wealth to social media standings—how many "friends" or "likes" we have on Facebook, how many connections we have on LinkedIn, how many views our webpage gets. Billions of dollars of advertising are spent each year by companies trying to boost their numbers.

We live in a world of numbers, and we glory in numbers. The problem with numbers is that it reduces people to nameless, faceless quantities. Everything is turned into a statistic. Individual identities get aggregated into a group identity. Individuality is eroded by the demand for group conformity. Behavior is driven by trends. Personal relationships are sidelined.

We are a people enslaved to our numbers. Our journey with the children of Israel begins with learning how to throw off that bondage. Let's view this from their perspective for a moment.

When we were slaves in Egypt, we got used to being faceless, nameless pieces of property. We understood our value was based on our works—how many bricks we could make a day. But we have been brought out from under our Egyptian masters, and we are now being called to serve this new master, God.

God is not going to count His glory by the number of slaves He owns, the number of troops under His command, by the lands He conquers or the wealth He possesses. He is the sovereign God, the Creator. All that is already His, and it is countless. When you own all the gold in the world, however, gold ceases to have value and becomes a meaningless way of reckoning glory.

God is going to reckon His personal glory by the one thing He does not own and cannot take by His own will. That is the praise of His people. It is a glory that must come spontaneously from the heart of His people, out of their personal understanding of who He is as their God and what He has done for them. It is the free-will offering of praise and thanksgiving that He covets. He has been and always will be a God who glories in gifts freely given, whereas the world attributes glory to the cost and the level of effort it takes to achieve their glorification.

The glory God seeks, He can only gain from a personal relationship with His people. He can't have a relationship with a nameless, faceless slave, which is why the first thing our new master does is identify us individually and give us a new identity anchored in Himself. Our identity is tied to His identity. Our glorification is tied to His glorification. Our glorification is going to be reckoned by our praise and faithfulness to Him.

How We Give Glory to God and Take Glory from God

The New Testament teaches us a number of ways we give glory to God:

- Through our praise and worship (Rom. 15:6).
- Through our good works and our "fruitfulness" (Matt. 5:16, John 15:8).
- By treating our bodies as His dwelling place (1 Cor. 6:18-20).
- By bearing reproach for His sake (1 Pet. 4:14).

What is true for us today was true for the children of Israel on their journey. The ways God receives glory from His people haven't changed a bit. We can, and will, fail to do these things just as the children of Israel did. On this journey, we will fail to praise and worship God as we should. Our progress will be marred by a lack of good works, and we will often complain about the lack of fruit in our lives. Many of us will forget that our bodies are His dwelling place, and our sin will cause us to suffer sickness and corruption. Even in the strongest of us, pride will override humility in moments of weakness, and we will refuse to submit to reproach when it would be glorifying to God that we do so. Many of us will not finish well.

Every failing in the book of Numbers and every judgment that falls on God's people during this journey will happen because we failed to give God glory when and where it was due.

Taking Glory From God

We take glory away from Him when we try to lift ourselves up instead of letting Him lift us up. From the beginning, He made us in His own image for His glory and praise, and it has always been His great desire to be the one to lift us up as His people. But He needs to be the one to do the lifting, not us. So often we try to take the glory for ourselves by our own judgment, our own will, our own words and actions. When we do that, we make ourselves rivals to Him by lowering His authority and place in our lives. His glory tolerates no rivals. In spite of His desire to lift us up, He must answer that rivalry with judgment for His glory's sake.

We take glory away from Him by giving it to others and making them His rivals. We have a natural tendency to lift others above the realm where God has put them and give them a place in our life that should rightly belong to God. We look to people in our lives to be our providers, our protection, and our problem-solvers—all things that God should be in our lives, and we credit them with God's work—by praise when things work out to our benefit or by blame when things go wrong.

In this journey, we are going to learn the hard way what happens when we lift others up in place of God. We will become disillusioned when they fail to meet our unrealistic expectations. Their failure is really a result of our failure when we glorify a man instead of giving God the honor of being those things to us.

The goal of this journey is to know God in His glory, so it stands to reason that by knowing what is true, we should recognize counterfeits. We take glory away from God when we fail to identify counterfeits and deceptions, especially late in the journey after a lifetime of experiences with Him. While we have a number of physical enemies in this journey, there is unseen Enemy stalking us. Throughout this journey he will throw arguments at us that distort the truth and try to lead us away in pursuit of counterfeit paths to glory.[1] When we fail to identify the counterfeits and deception, we will fall into the Enemy's hands. Our failure will be our own fault, but in the eyes of the world, it will be seen as a failure on God's part that He is unable to accomplish His purpose in us. Failing to recognize the counterfeit is a way we take glory from God, because it means we lack an understanding of Him.

We take glory from God when we are not satisfied with the provision, purpose or place He gives us in life. We deny His glory when we challenge Him to prove Himself to us over and over again. Our understanding of God's glory is built on that history of experiences and should be increasing as we progress through this journey. When we contend with Him again and again over basic lessons we should have learned already, it reveals in us a heart that doesn't really want to know Him.

Their Example is Our Warning

These are the major ways the children of Israel fell short of realizing God's glory in the journey, and they are the same ways we are prone to fail in our own journey, which is why, in 1 Corinthians 10:1-12, Paul lists five major failings of the children of Israel as warnings to us:

- Do not lust after evil things
- Do not become idolaters
- Do not commit sexual immorality
- Do not tempt Christ (challenging Christ to prove His power)
- Do not complain

We would like to think that most of the points on this list don't apply to us. We don't pursue evil things. We don't have idols in our house that we bow down to. We've kept ourselves from sexual immorality. We don't tempt Christ. And yet Paul says, *"Therefore let him who thinks he stands take heed lest he fall."* (1 Cor. 10:12)

Israel's failings on this journey are meant for our admonition. We are just as susceptible to these failings as they were. We think we don't do these things, but we don't always recognize the form they take in our lives. As we walk through this journey, we are going to see how these failings work

---

[1] There are two kinds of enemy in this journey. There is Satan, our spiritual Enemy (enemy with a capital "E") and there are human enemies (enemy with a lowercase "e"). I have used the uppercase and lowercase "e" to indicate the enemy to which I am referring as I go through this study.

themselves out in a multitude of ways. We will look at how they develop, what heart attitudes drive them, and what forms they take in modern life.

God wants us to know Him, really know Him in an experiential way, as a great and glorious God, our savior and redeemer, our provider and protector, our problem-solver and comforter. He wants the chance to put His strength and power and glory on display in our lives. He loves us fiercely, and He challenges us to pursue Him. He has promised that if we live a life that brings glory to Him, He will lift us up and glorify us in return. The point of this journey is not just for God to be glorified, but for us also to be glorified through Him as His people.

What Does Our Glorification Look Like

Our glorification is tied directly to God's glorification. Our glorification is defined by how well we identify with Him, how we align ourselves with His mission and vision, and how we live our lives in praise to Him. Our ultimate glorification comes when we achieve perfect oneness with Him.

When we think about being glorified by God, we often define our glorification in terms of having eternal life (John 17:1-3), having a resurrected and incorruptible body (1 Cor. 15:42-44) and receiving rewards or inheritance in the Kingdom to come (Rom. 8:16-18). When we think of our own glorification, we tend to think of everything that will come to us when we die and enter that future kingdom. These are most certainly promises we should rest on, but let's face it, that glorious life is quite a ways down the road for most of us. So far down the road, in fact, that it can seem almost unachievable when the daily walk begins to feel like a long slog through deep sand. If we only focus on the distant promises, we can easily lose a sense of God's presence and glory in this journey. The lessons are hard to learn and we may feel like we are covering the same ground over and over again. We can even come to the place in this life where we feel we are no longer progressing. At that point we can lose faith and falter in our walk.

Even though we know God's glory and believe His promise of a glorious life to come, that knowledge of Him has to translate into an experience of Him in this life if we are going to remain faithful through the challenges of this journey.

What God does to make this journey bearable and keep us moving forward is to give us little experiences of glorious living along the way. These are not the full-blown fulfillment of what we will have in the kingdom, but little tastes of fruitfulness as rewards for steps of faith and deepening trust. They should create in us the desire to pursue a deeper relationship with Him. But before we enter this journey, we need to make sure we understand what God's vision of glorious living is so that we will recognize it when He gives us a taste of it in this life.

God's Definition of Glorious Living

In this journey, God brings His children to a wilderness for several reasons, most of which have to do with creating distinction and separation. This time in the wilderness creates a distinction between Egypt and the Promised Land by defining a space of time where living conditions are in stark contrast to one another. There is an initial contrast between Egypt and the wilderness—from slavery to freedom, from bountiful land to the barrenness of the wilderness. The barrenness of the wilderness is then replaced by the extreme fruitfulness in the Land.

The Sabbath Theme

The wilderness experience is a Sabbath experience. Whenever you find a period of time set apart and defined by extreme contrasts or reversals like this, it has the character of a Sabbath. The Sabbath is a formal break between different periods of life. Sabbath days mark breaks between the work of one week and the work of another. Sabbath years mark breaks between periods of fruitfulness and working the land. Jubilees mark breaks between generations and systemic economic resets. Sabbaths are often thought of as single days, but they can also be bookends to periods of time where living conditions are altered or economies are changed.

This journey into the wilderness was meant to be a form of Sabbath for us. It was meant to teach us a complete reliance on God. God will lead, feed, teach, and protect His people throughout this time. It was meant to be a time of rest from work to focus on developing a deeper relationship with God apart from the distractions of the external. It teaches that life does not depend on external things but an internal relationship with God.

The Sabbath embodies God's definition of glorious living, and it is going to be a recurring theme throughout this journey.

God's Definition of Glorious Living

God's definition of glorious living may not be what we expect because we have been raised with the world's definition of glorious living. The world focuses on material wealth, power, luxury and excess. These things are physical and tangible. We achieve these by our own work, our own judgment and planning, and often at the expense of others. Our success can be gauged simply by counting up the numbers.

God's definition of glorious living is an experience of rest, peace, joy, well-being, wholeness and righteousness. These are intangible and spiritual, and more importantly, they are experiential. They are achieved through a deepening relationship with God and as a reward for remaining faithful to Him.

Learning to value God's definition of glorious living is going to be one of our biggest challenges on this journey. Rest and peace and joy are not things that the world has taught us to value. We need to learn to desire them and pursue them.

We cannot comprehend the full glory of these things until we enter eternal life, but we can get tastes of them on this journey. Have you ever had an unexpected peace wash over you in the middle of a crisis? Or felt a sense of joy, even in the midst of sorrow? Or maybe you have taken a stand on an issue of faith and come out of it the worse for wear in your relationship with the world, yet with this strange sense of well-being over having done the right thing? These are little tastes of the glorious peace, joy, rest, righteousness and well-being to come, and we can experience these even today. We get a taste of these fruits at moments when we are completely aligned with God and His vision, engaged with God in His mission, and looking to Him for help in times of need. It should be our goal to pursue these as we go through this journey.

We must keep God's vision of glorious living locked in our mind's eye, because the Enemy is going to target it repeatedly in our journey. He is going to go after anything that gives us hope or strengthens our identification and relationship with God. If he can't sway us to return to the world's value system, he will throw counterfeits in our way to trip us up and get us off the path. He will be the driving force behind the attacks of our human enemies. In this study, we are going to be looking at the tactics our Enemy uses, learn how to recognize them and keep them from becoming a pitfall for us on the journey.

Moving forward, here is what we need to keep in mind:

- What a glorious God looks like and how that glory is reckoned
- Ways we bring God glory and take glory away from Him
- How our own glorification is supposed to be achieved
- God's definition of glorious living

LESSON TWO

Wilderness of Sinai: How to Organize an Army in 20 Days

CHAPTERS 1–10:10

The book of Numbers opens with the children of Israel at Mount Sinai. Chapters 1–10 give us a detailed account of preparing the camp for the journey. What might seem like a lot of laborious accounting and instructions actually sets the context and provides a vital foundation for understanding many of the upcoming events. In this lesson we are going to establish the environment we will be interacting in for the rest of the journey.

In twenty days' time, God organizes His army and prepares it for deployment. Chapters 1–10 outline five basic tasks to organize an army or any large task force:

1. Roll call—identify your people (1–3)
2. Assigning places, including boundaries (2–3)
3. Assigning roles and duties (3–4, 8)
4. Establishing camp rules (5–6)
5. Establishing camp communications (9–10)

Before we discuss each of these tasks, let's first examine why the physical aspect of the camp is important.

From Physical Environment to Spiritual Relationship

Numbers is a book of the Law, and believe it or not, the Law teaches us about the relationship we have with God through Christ. As we work through the lessons to come, we will see different aspects of this relationship play out through the people and events in the narrative. Not only is the gospel fully presented, but many doctrinal truths are built from these passages of the Law.

Our spiritual relationship with Christ would not be known until after His death and resurrection. From where we stand in time here in the book of Numbers, that relationship is hidden behind a veil (2 Cor. 3:15). So the practical problem that the Old Testament seeks to solve is how to teach a relationship where half the relationship is still hidden. It does this by setting up physical relationships between physical people, places, and things that correspond to aspects of the spiritual relationship. What you end up with is a relational equation like this:

A is to **B** what **C** is to **D**

"A" and "B" are the physical people, places, or things in the Old Testament with a physical relationship between them. These are known.

"C" and "D" are also people, places, or things with a spiritual relationship between them. Sometimes "C" and "D" can be known even in Old Testament times, but often they represents Christ and the Church and are hidden behind the veil.

The physical relationship between "A" and "B" teaches the spiritual relationship between "C" and "D."

The book of Proverbs uses many examples of physical relationships ("A" and "B") to explain the human or spiritual relationships ("C" and "D").
For example:

> *"A satisfied soul loathes the honeycomb, but to a hungry soul every bitter thing is sweet."* Proverbs 27:7

The honeycomb is a physical thing that should be desirable but isn't. Bitter things should not be considered sweet, but here they are. The natural relationship is turned on end to teach us about conditions of the soul.

The books of the Law are no different. They are just more subtle and varied in how "A" and "B" are presented. That is why it is necessary to make a minute examination of all the various physical components being presented in a passage.

All physical relationships need a physical environment to work in. Whenever you study the Old Testament, and particularly the books of the Law, you need to be very aware of the physical environment you are moving in.

In the Old Testament, God creates a number of different environments or structures as a basis for understanding the physical relationships. He creates the environment. He places Himself in the environment. Then He places His people into that environment with Him, and they move within that environment relative to where He is. Their physical place, either closer to Him or farther away from Him, reflects their spiritual relationship. For example, the Garden of Eden was one such environment. When God asks Adam "Where are you," it is not just a question of where Adam is physically, but where he is spiritually in relationship to God in that moment. Different places in the environment can also indicate different spiritual status, such as clean or unclean, relative to a relationship with God.

In addition to a relationship between God and His people, there are also relationships between people. Who we are, where we are, our roles and boundaries—all these provide context and structure for teaching relationships in the Old Testament. If we are going to understand the lessons to come in this journey, we need to understand our environment.

The environment for this leg of the journey is going to be an army encampment and it is defined for us in chapters 1-10. We are going to work through these chapters, defining the physical environment but also discussing the many implications as it translates into a spiritual relationship with God.

Let's begin by establishing our timeline.

Timeline

Where Are We on the Overall Timeline?

> "Now the LORD spoke to Moses in the Wilderness of Sinai, in the tabernacle of meeting, on the first day of the second month, in the second year after they had come out of the land of Egypt..." Numbers 1:1

> "Now it came to pass on the twentieth day of the second month, in the second year, that the cloud was taken up from above the tabernacle of the Testimony. And the children of Israel set out from the Wilderness of Sinai on their journeys..." Numbers 10:11-12

Numbers 1:1 tells us we are in the first day of the second month, in the second year after coming out of Egypt. Numbers 10:10 marks the day we actually start the journey, which is on the twentieth of the same month. So we have a span of 20 days between Numbers 1:1 and 10:10. From that bit of information, what else do we know? Let's flesh that out a little.

We are now in the second year. That means we have had one year of separation from Egypt, one year of learning those early lessons as a child of God, one year of being taught the Law and gaining knowledge of who God is, and what a relationship with Him requires.

We are in the second month, one year out of Egypt, which means we have just celebrated the first anniversary of the Passover. This anniversary is noted in Numbers 9. It is specifically noted that some of us were excluded from that celebration because of ritual defilement (Num. 9:6-7) which is why the Lord instructs us to hold a second Passover on the 14th of the second month for those who missed it in the first month (Num. 9:10-14). It is vitally important to God that everyone begin this journey having celebrated the Passover.

Significance of the Second Passover (Numbers 9)

Numbers 9 gives instructions for keeping of the second Passover, which is supremely significant in regards to the spiritual aspect of this journey. Remember, this journey is as much about the spiritual sanctification journey as it is the physical one.

The full journey experience actually encompasses the night of Passover when we left Egypt, our passage through the Red Sea, the wilderness, and entrance into our inheritance in the Land. The Passover is the beginning point on the timeline for the entire journey.

Numbers is only a part of that journey, but it is a very specific study of one leg of the journey that corresponds to the sanctification process that believers experience. Numbers is a self-contained journey of its own, housed within the greater narrative.

Just as the Passover marked the start of the overall journey, we see very deliberate attention given to the commemoration of Passover at the start of the Numbers journey. Every person entering into this leg of the physical journey must begin with celebrating the Passover. Everyone must begin with the reaffirmation of their redemption through the death of the Passover lamb and its blood on the doorposts.

As Church-age believers, we know that the Passover is the foreshadowing of Christ's death. In the physical journey, the children of Israel identify with the Passover, but in the spiritual equivalent, we are identifying with Christ's death. Everyone entering into this spiritual journey must first identify with Christ's death.

That means that everyone who enters into this leg of the journey enters as a believer. This has a spiritual implication: it means that the salvation experience has already been accomplished before this journey begins. If you believe (as I do) that salvation once received cannot be lost, then this leg of the journey is not about receiving salvation, but moving from salvation into sanctification and then to glorification. The issue of salvation is not the focus of this journey. This is a vital foundation for future lessons.

Roll Call (Numbers 1–3)

Rooting Ourselves in a New Identity

The very first thing God addresses in the book of Numbers is who we are.

We were slaves in Egypt, but God brought us out of Egypt. He told us we are His people and He is going to establish us in another land where we will be rooted and fruitful. But right now we are wandering in this limbo. We aren't where we used to be, doing what we used to do. We aren't where we are going to be, doing what we will be doing. We have left the world we once knew. We are not yet in the land that is to come. Life in this physical journey is one of continual change and transition. For our own well-being, we need to be rooted in something, to be identified with something or someone.

In the parable of the Sower (Matt. 13), Jesus talks about rootlessness:

> *"Some [seed] fell on stony places, where they did not have much earth; and they immediately sprang up because they had no depth of earth. But when the sun was up they were scorched, and because they had no root they withered away. . . . he who received the seed on stony places, this is he who hears the word and immediately receives it with joy; yet he has no root in himself, but endures only for a while. For when tribulation or persecution arises because of the word, immediately he stumbles." Matthew 13:5-6, 20-21*

We came out of Egypt with joy, but wilderness life quickly heats up. Trials begin almost immediately. If we don't have something to root ourselves in, we will have nothing to cling to. For this reason, many of us die in the early days of this journey. Others try to revert back to the old roots as slaves in Egypt.

I think rooting has a lot to do with identity and what you identify with. A sense of identity is important in a physical journey; but in the spiritual realm, it is absolutely prerequisite for any fruitfulness at all.

During this journey the only thing that will never change is God. He is the one we need to root ourselves into. Who we are as His children will be with us wherever we go and whatever role we play in life. He is the sole constant in our changing world.

We are going to find our root in identifying with a great and glorious God.

The new identity He gives us is anchored in His own identity. He is going to be our new role model, the standard by which we judge ourselves and know our value. Our character is going to begin to mold itself to His character, His mission, His vision and values. It is going to focus on the spiritual aspects of our lives instead of the physical ones.

We were once slaves in Egypt who were counted only as numbers and our value was determined by the numbers of bricks we could produce. We are used to identifying ourselves by our physical works or physical roles. This is as true for us today as it was for the children of Israel. Too often we root ourselves in the roles of parents, spouses, employees, etc. But the problem with identifying ourselves by our physical role in life is that roles change. Children grow up, spouses pass away, jobs change.

If we root our identity in our physical works or roles, then at some point in this journey we are going to lose our identity. Our new identity will no longer be rooted in our works or roles in life. It is based solely on our relationship with God.

Our new identity will not be rooted in a physical place. Letting go of our identity with Egypt is going to be a major challenge. We are used to identifying with the physical place—where we were born, what country we live in—but the problem with identifying ourselves by our physical place is that God's purpose in our lives often uproots us and forces us to move.

If we root our identity in our physical place, then at some point on this journey we are going to lose our identity. Our new identity in this journey will not be rooted in a physical place but a relational place with God. No matter where we go, we will always be in a relational place with God, for better or worse. God is going to reinforce that understanding when He assigns us places in the camp, which we will talk more about in the section, "Assigning Places."

The Numbers

Our identity is formally established with a census. The first census of the armies is taken in Numbers 1, and includes all men twenty years old and above who could go to war. A separate census of the Levites is taken in Numbers 3.

Readers tend to bog down in these chapters because of their long lists of names and numbers presented in a strict formulaic repetition. There is, however, a significance to the army census numbers revealed after the second census in Numbers 26.

> *"To these the land shall be divided as an inheritance, according to the number of names. To a large tribe you shall give a larger inheritance, and to a small tribe you shall give a smaller inheritance. Each shall be given its inheritance according to those who were numbered of them."*
> *Numbers 26:53-54*

The point I wish to make concerns the inheritance rankings determined by the census numbers. In the course of this journey, the inheritance ranking is going to change significantly. Acts of unfaithfulness are going to result in deaths in record numbers. An entire generation is going to pass away. The generation replacing it will have different numbers.

All tribes come into the Land, but the inheritance with which one tribe begins is not necessarily the inheritance they receive in the end. The tribe of Simeon, for example, drops from the third largest allotment to the twelfth and smallest allotment at the second census. There is a signature act of unfaithfulness originating with the Simeonites that tremendously affects camp numbers, which we will study later. The second census, taken immediately after that, shows much of the land initially allotted to Simeon is annexed to Judah. The inheritance of the tribes who decrease will be taken from them and given proportionately to the tribes who have increased.

What is true of the physical inheritance has some interesting implications when we apply it to spiritual rewards. If we follow the pattern of the physical journey, the spiritual journey plays out this way:

We all entered this journey as believers, and servants to our God. He gives us a certain allotment of His kingdom initially. Over the course of a journey, that allotment can increase by a little or a lot, or stay the same, or decrease. The amount of increase or decrease is going to be determined by our acts of faithfulness or unfaithfulness.

At the end of the journey, a new accounting is taken by the Master. To those who have increased, more will be given proportionately. To those who have decreased, what was allotted to them at the beginning will be taken from them and added to those who have increased.

If this sounds like one of Jesus' parables of the kingdom, it should. It corresponds to the

Inheritance ranking at the first census
(largest to least)

Tribe	Number
Judah	74,600
Dan	62,700
Simeon	59,300
Zebulun	57,400
Issachar	54,400
Naphtali	53,400
Reuben	46,500
Gad	45,600
Asher	41,500
Ephraim	40,500
Benjamin	35,400
Manasseh	32,200

Inheritance ranking at the second census
(largest to least)

Tribe	Number
Judah	76,500
Dan	64,400
Issachar	64,300
Zebulun	60,500
Asher	53,400
Manasseh	52,700
Benjamin	45,600
Naphtali	45,400
Reuben	43,730
Gad	40,500
Ephraim	32,500
Simeon	22,200

Parable of the Talents in Matthew 25. Jesus speaks of a master who entrusts three servants with different quantities of his goods as he prepares to go on a journey. One servant is given five talents, one is given two, and one is given one talent.

The first two servants invest and increase their allotment. The servant given one talent did not increase at all. In fact, he even lost the little interest it would have accrued as a matter of course without any effort on his part. Count that as a loss of value and a decrease.

The increase of the two was attributed to their faithfulness and they were rewarded with additional allotments (governorships). The decrease of the one was attributed to his unfaithfulness or laziness. His allotment was taken from him and given to the servant who accrued the most. The unprofitable servant is then cast into outer darkness.

Both the Numbers scenario and the parable share the common elements of:

- An initial allotment given,
- An increase or decrease directly related to faithfulness or unfaithfulness, respectively, over a period of time described as a journey,
- A second accounting taken at the end of the journey, and
- The allotment is reapportioned to take land from unprofitable members and give it to the most profitable members. I return to the tribe of Simeon for this detail. Look at the map of the final inheritance allotments to the right. Simeon's holdings in the Promised Land were encompassed by Judah's holdings. Simeon began with an allotment nearly equal to Judah's, but was then annexed to Judah. The holding of the one with the least numbers was taken away and added to the one with the greatest.

There is one element in the parable seemingly without a parallel to the Numbers' scenario, and that is the poignant end for the unfaithful servant who is cast "into the outer darkness" with "weeping and gnashing of teeth" (Matt. 25:30). All the elements correspond closely to one another up to this last detail at the end, which shows up only in the New Testament parable.

If the parable is interpreted apart from the Old Testament picture, we might conclude that the unprofitable servant has lost his place in the Kingdom, which is equated with losing one's salvation. Being sent into the outer darkness would then indicate being sent to Hell.

But if the Old and New Testament pictures together were meant to form one consistent, cohesive picture of the Kingdom, there remains the question: is

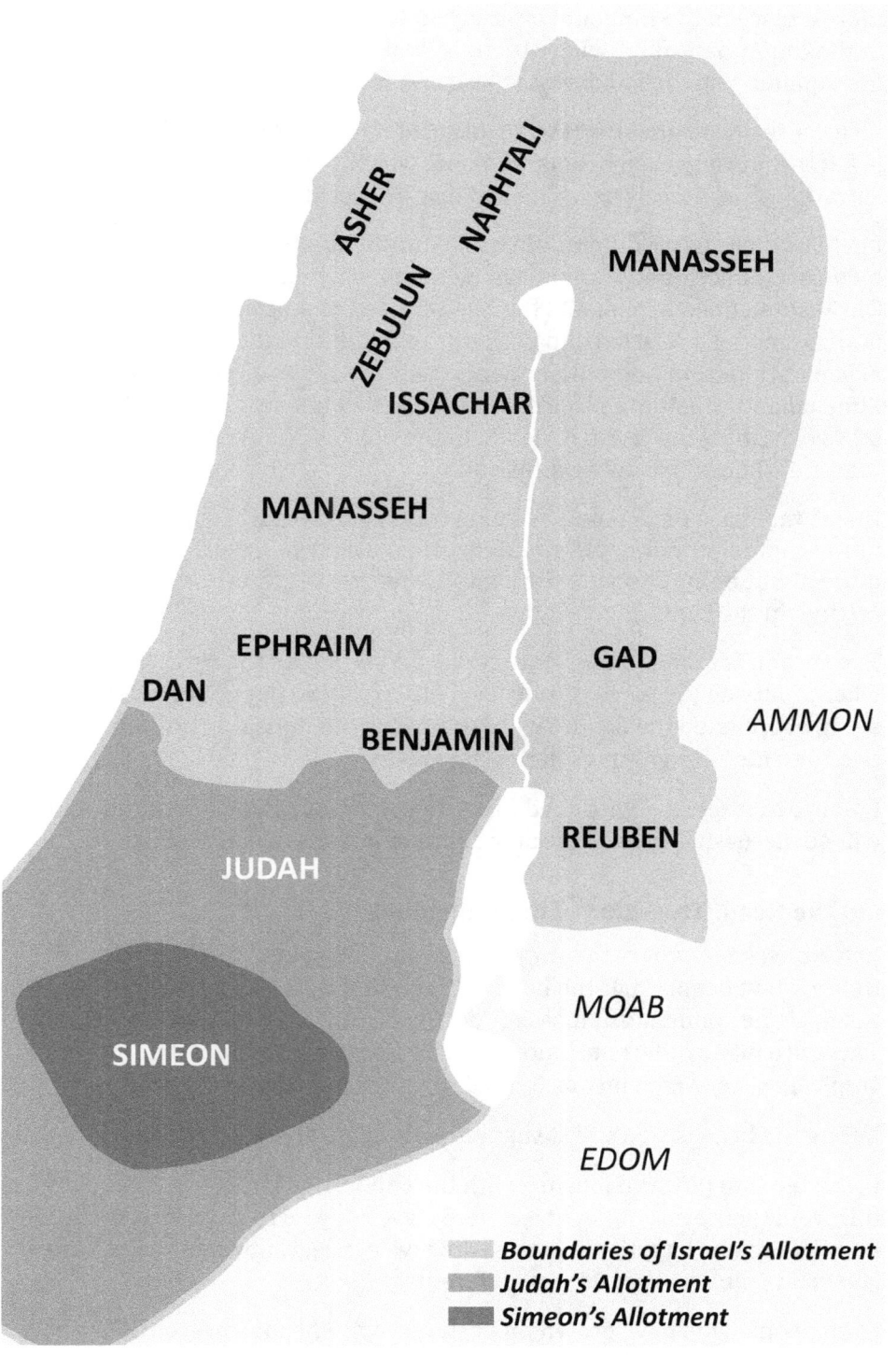

there a place in the Kingdom or attached to the Kingdom that corresponds to the "outer darkness" where there is "weeping and gnashing of teeth," but not equated with hell and a loss of salvation?

I have already posited that the act of salvation is accomplished before this leg of the journey even begins, and once accomplished, it is never lost. Salvation, therefore, is never in jeopardy or even an issue on this journey.

I believe there is an "outer darkness" equivalent found in the Numbers picture. I think this equivalent can be found in almost all of the physical Old Testament environments the Lord created as a framework for understanding a relationship with Himself. It is a relational place—a place of separation from God but not necessarily the separation associated with unbelief and hell. It is a place of separation that borders on (but does not cross over into) the realm of death. In the book of Numbers, I think the "outer darkness" has two expressions.

One is the place designated as being "outside the camp," which is relative to the camp without being equated with places like Egypt. (I will explain more about being "outside the camp" when we get to the section on setting up the camp.)

The second is found in the instructions for setting up the cities in the Land, where "outside the gates" is one level of separation but not equated with being put outside the Land. I will explore the relationship between these two "outside" designations in the last lesson.

I realize that these points need further explanation and exploration, and we will be discussing them in greater depth in lessons to come.

Lift the Head: The Value of the Individual

In Numbers 1:2, where the English translation begins "Take a census," the Hebrew text begins "Lift the heads." When God calls for the numbering of His flock, he commands Moses to "lift the heads" of the children of Israel. There are many different Hebrew words that mean to count, but this is an atypical usage, which means it is a deliberate and significant one.

Lifting the head is God's first signature act of glorifying His people.

Let's step into physical journey with the children of Israel now, and consider this from their eyes. In Egypt we were slaves. We were nameless, faceless numbers to our Egyptian masters. Now we are servants of God and this new Master is going to treat us very differently.

For a people who have grown up in slavery with heads lowered and eyes averted, being told to lift our head and give our name and family genealogy would have a significant psychological effect. This is the way free men are treated, not slaves. Having God as a master is going to be a significantly different relationship from the one we had as slaves to Egyptians.

We now have a master who values us as individuals, free men with families and histories; with choices, responsibilities, and consequences. There are some benefits, but also some serious pitfalls to being a free man.

On the benefit side, we have a certain degree of self-determinism. We have the ability to make independent choices. The journey in Numbers highlights certain individuals who make wrong choices, and others who make right choices even when it goes against the group consensus.

As individuals, we are no longer part of "the herd." We are able to withstand peer pressure, should we choose to. Those who resist peer pressure and don't run with the crowd get greater rewards. We are able to avoid destructive group behaviors, such as the madness of mobs.

On the pitfall side, being lifted up can become a heady thing. A new-found sense of self can balloon into excessive ego and selfish ambition, while at the same time narrowing our focus into extreme self-absorption. We begin to demand and take glory for ourselves and forget to give glory to the Lord. Entitlement becomes an issue. We begin demanding our rights to have the things we want, even when they aren't good for us, and the Lord has something better planned.

We are all individuals, yet still connected to each other. As we will see, one individual can be the undoing of the entire group or the redemption of the group.

A nation of "individuals" all exercising their new-found choices can be a handful to lead. Moses is going to have quite a time of it in the days to come. If this camp of individuals is going to work cohesively, a certain perspective is needed to maintain balance.

It begins with having a healthy respect for God as our King, understanding who He is in His glory and sovereignty and who we are as His servants. This was the first item on my list of things to remember as we enter the journey, and it is the first thing that we forget in the days to come.

Responsibility and accountability measures need to be put in place to maintain our relationship with God and also with other people. Self-control is going to be demanded of us. We are going to learn some tough lessons in governing our own bodies with moderation. We have individual responsibility for ourselves and our decisions, but the results of those choices are going to affect the entire camp. Everything that happens between the first census and second is going to be a result of individual choices that impact the entire group. Accountability will feature heavily in the camp rules we will discuss shortly. Understanding our place and, more importantly, respecting our boundaries is vital. We will discuss this more when we get to assigning places.

The Names

The value of the individual is communicated in the meticulous recording of names in Numbers. In Numbers 1:2, we begin with the census taken of all the congregation of Israel "by their families, by their father's houses, according to the number of names, every male individually." This command communicates the Master's desire for people to be known individually, but also in the context of relationships to family and the congregation as a whole. In Numbers 3, there is a separate census taken of the Levites with the same emphasis on family details.

In Numbers 1:4 a circle of leadership is established in relationship to Moses and Aaron. One man from each tribe, a leader in his father's house, is called, making a total of twelve. In Numbers 1:5-15, the leaders of the tribes are recorded by name, including his father's name. The same names recur in chapter 2, where they are identified as the leaders of the armies. The same list recurs again in chapter 7 where their offerings for the dedication of the altar are noted. Chapter 7 is the longest chapter in Numbers (89 verses), but 71 of those verses could easily be summarized in five verses by saying "All the leaders of all the tribes each brought . . . [the list]." But that is not how it is written. There is this meticulous accounting of what each of the twelve leaders brings, and every single leader who brings something is acknowledged by name. *Hint:* every time an individual glorifies God, that individual gets personally acknowledged in return.

When God calls out specific people, as He does the leaders in chapter 1, the names are meticulously recorded because they often paint a picture or have significance in their meaning. In this study, we are going to pay close attention to the meaning of names. I have listed the names of the leaders from verses 5–15 along with their meanings.

These names are not in order according to tribal ranking or place in the camp. Their order seems random, and yet when you look at the meanings of these names, placed in this order, a structured picture begins to appear.

Here at Mount Sinai, in this opening passage where the Lord begins the lifting up of His people, He identifies this group of men whose names reflect His own glory. Verse 5 opens with a son identified with God. Behold a son. God is his kinsman. God is a Rock, casting forth fire, almighty, praised, and noble.

He gives recompense to one brought low, who becomes exalted by the Father's strength. The names in verse 10 run with the promise of fruitfulness, reward, and the forgetting of toil. A majestic God has heard his people. He is the Rock who ransomed them. The names in verses 5-10 begin and end with allusions to God as the Rock, creating bookends to that glorious picture.

The names in verses 11-15 strike a much more somber note. Opening again with an allusion to a son (son of my right hand), the picture turns to God as almighty judge, "my hewer." There is a brief note of hope in help from a brother, but then this "happy event of God" becomes "troubled." "A troop God has added, a troop known by Him"—that is the calling by name of the armies described here. Then wrestling ensues. From the wrestling emerges a second picture of the brother. In contrast to the brother who helps, this brother is evil of eye.

The meanings of the names listed in chapter 1 speak of a journey that begins gloriously with a glorious God and the promise of reward, then sinks into judgment, and ends with an army wrestling with inner conflict. That is the narrative of Numbers in a nutshell. This study will take us through that

Leaders Names (Numbers 1:5-15)

Reuben	"Behold a son"
Elizur	"my God is a rock"
Shedeur	"casting forth fire"
Simeon	"hear"
Shelumiel	"friend of God"
Zurishaddai	"my rock is almighty"
Judah	"praised"
Nahshon	"diviner"
Amminadab	"my kinsman is noble"
Issachar	"recompense"
Nethanel	"given of God"
Zuar	"brought low"
Zebulun	"exalted"
Eliab	"God is father"
Helon	"strength"
Joseph	"Jehovah has added"
Ephraim	"I shall be doubly fruitful"
Elishama	"God has heard"
Ammihud;	"my kinsman is majestic"
Manasseh	"causing me to forget my toil"
Gamaliel	"reward of God"
Pedahzur	"the Rock has ransomed"
Benjamin	"Son of my right hand"
Abidan	"my father is judge"
Gideoni	"my hewer"
Dan	"judge"
Ahiezer	"my brother is help"
Ammishaddai	"my kinsman is almighty"
Asher	"happy"
Pagiel	"event of God"
Ocran	"troubled"
Gad	"a troop"
Eliasaph	"God has added"
Deuel	"known of God"
Naphtali	"wrestling"
Ahira	"my brother is evil"
Enan	"having eyes"

Lesson 2: The Wilderness of Sinai

glorious beginning into the trouble and wrestling of an army plagued by inner turmoil and external enemies. The final battle we will study will be precipitated by the grand deception and betrayal of one we considered a brother.

Names of people and places are important in Numbers. They are significant in the narrative and relevant in the spiritual lessons we will be discussing.

The first thing God does is establish who we are. The second thing He does is assign us places in the camp.

Assigning Places in the Camp (Numbers 2–3)

Chapter 2 is about setting up the camp. Where we are placed in camp reflects our physical relationships with God and kinsmen, our roles, and authority levels. More than that, the physical environment reflects a spiritual relationship. As we go through this journey, where we find ourselves in the camp will place us nearer to God or farther from Him, in a state of cleanness or uncleanness. Boundaries become very important.

Placement of the Armies and Levites

In chapter 2, the congregation is divided into four armies (North, South, East and West), each composed of three tribes. We are given their leaders' names, their census numbers, and where they are placed in the camp. In chapter 3, one family of Levites is designated for each of the four armies. The roll call begins with Judah in the army of the east and moves clockwise.

The census number of each tribe is given a second time, but now they are grouped in threes. Adding them together gives you the total for each army. Look at the numbers for the armies noted in the chart to the right.

The army of the east is very large whereas the army of the west very small. The army of the north is nearly the same as the army of the south. These numbers paint a picture. To see the picture, I have laid out gray bars around the camp according to the census numbers, each representing 10,000 men of war (not including women and children). The camp would not have been so rigidly laid out as my bars are, but you get a sense of volume and the shape the camp might have taken.

Imagine looking down on them from a distance. They would appear roughly shaped like a cross (with the Tabernacle right where Christ's body would be).

Boundaries

With place assignments come boundaries. Maintaining boundaries is going

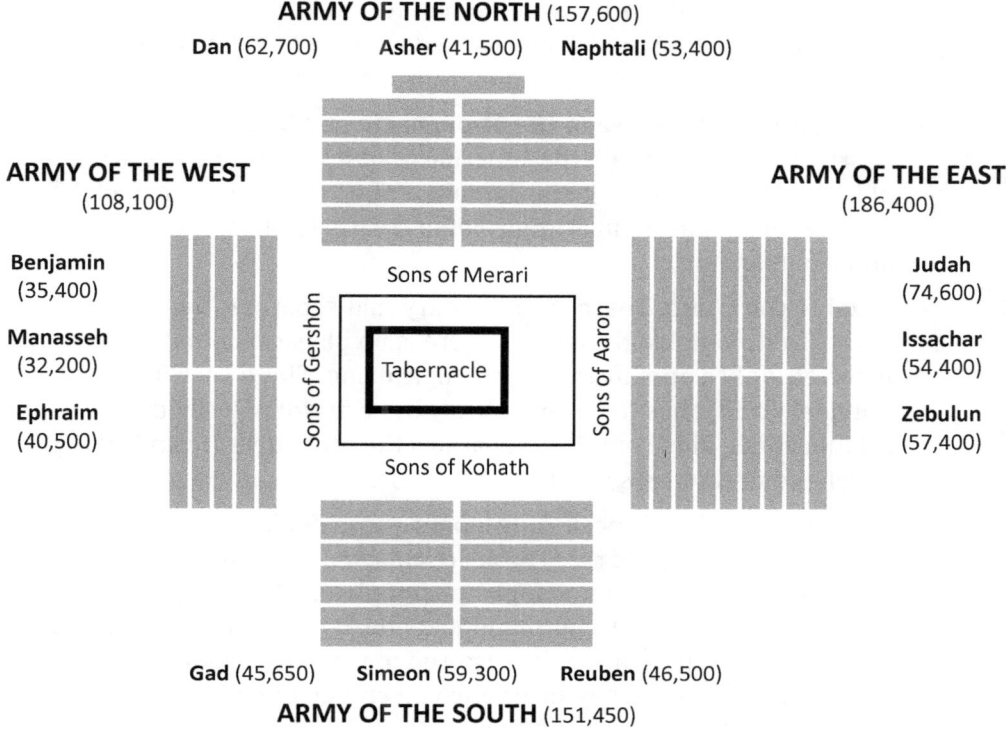

to become very important in the lessons to come, so these need to be defined. Within the camp, beginning with where God is, the boundaries are:

- **Veil between God and Priesthood:** Within the Tabernacle, there is a veil that divides the holy of holies from the rest of the Tabernacle. The veil is a physical barrier that stands in the gap between God and the people, and it is a type of something that stands in the gap. Later on in this journey, the Lord is going to present us with a picture of a man who stands in the gap and is associated with this veil. He is the High Priest.

- **Tent walls between Priesthood and Levites:** The sons of Aaron, the priesthood, could go into the Tabernacle, but the other Levites served outside the Tabernacle. These walls are a physical barrier while we are camped, but that physical barrier disappears during the walk. When the camp prepares to move, the walls will come down, so the priests are responsible for veiling the holy things inside for the Kohathites to carry.

The physical boundary is replaced by a human boundary. It is the responsibility of the priests and Kohathites to keep the holy things of the Tabernacle from being approached by outsiders during the course of the walk, in the absence of the physical boundaries.

- **Courtyard fence between the Tabernacle and Tribes:** The courtyard walls separate the Tabernacle compound from the armies of Israel. The courtyard is the domain of the Levites, and they pitch their tents outside along its perimeter, creating both a physical fence and a human fence.
- **Outside the camp.** There is a boundary that separates "inside the camp" from "outside the camp." There is no physical boundary involved, only a human and psychological one. This a very fluid boundary and it has to be kept purely by restraint of individual relationships. This boundary separates the "outsiders" from Israel. It is defined in Numbers 5:1-4 as a place for:

    - Unclean people, specifically lepers, those defiled by a corpse, and those with a discharge. These are children of Israel in a state of separation from God, though not completely disassociated with the camp. It can be a permanent abode, but if healing is granted, the affected person can be restored to the congregation. In the course of this journey, everyone will end up outside the camp for uncleanness at some point or another.

    - Gentiles and the "mixed multitude." Exodus 12:38 mentions that a mixed multitude came up with us from Egypt. No place is made for the "mixed multitude" in camp. In the Old Testament, anything described as mixed in nature has the taint of uncleanness about it. They are relegated to outside the camp. The only time a Gentile is allowed a place in the camp is if they are married into a tribe. There must be a marriage covenant involved.

    Outside the camp is a place of uncleanness and death. It is farthest from the Tabernacle and God, both physically and spiritually. It is a place attached to the camp, having a relationship with the camp but at the same time representing a separation from God. When I spoke earlier of a place equivalent to the "outer darkness" of Jesus' parables, I think "outside the camp" is one equivalent.

You will notice that all these boundaries have a physical presence for a time, but during the daily walk, the physical boundaries disappear and are replaced by human counterparts. This illustrates the transition from a physical relationship into a spiritual one. In the spiritual relationship, there are no physical boundaries in place. There is no longer a veil, a tent, or a courtyard. All boundaries must be maintained physically and psychologically by the restraint in human relationships and by individual and self-control.

Wherever you have boundaries, you have changes of status and relationship. Crossing boundaries will cause changes in our status for better or worse.

Wherever you have boundaries, you have points of conflict. Not everyone is content with the place God has given them in the camp. Each one of these boundaries is going to be challenged at some point in the journey.

Many people will value themselves based on their position in the camp. They will see their place as a reflection of how much status or influence they have or how close to God they are. These people who put value on status and rank among the congregation will cause conflict trying to attain what they consider to be a more glorious place in the camp.

Following the assigning of places, there are the assigning of roles and duties within the camp.

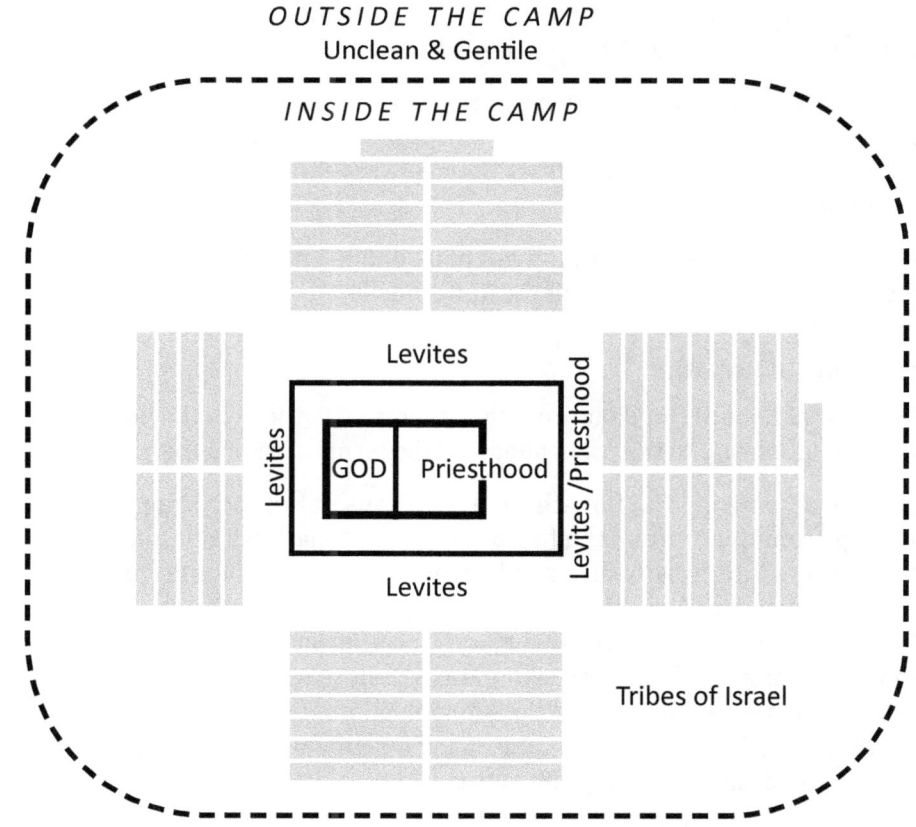

Lesson 2: The Wilderness of Sinai | 27

Assigning of Roles and Duties (Numbers 3–4)

Every camp has housekeeping duties when deployed. These duties involve the practical tasks of moving camp from one place to another and setting up headquarters again in each new place. In the book of Numbers, the housekeeping duties fall to the Levites.

Where Leviticus dealt heavily with the role of the priesthood, Numbers focuses instead on the duties of the second-level Levites who served the priesthood. Chapter 3 opens with the identification of this task force by census, a general description of their duties and assigned places in camp, as well as their dedication in place of the firstborn. I won't go into those in depth. Chapter 4 outlines the very specific duties of the sons of Kohath, Gershon, and Merari.

Duties of the Sons of Gershon and Merari (Numbers 4:21-33)

The sons of Merari are charged with transporting the Tabernacle structure (wood panels, metal fittings, etc.). In Numbers 7:2-9 we read that they are given four carts and eight oxen to carry these items. This is heavy work, so the term of their Tabernacle service is limited to ages 30-50.

Similarly, the sons of Gershon are charged with the transporting the Tabernacle curtains (with the exception of the Veil) and they are given two carts and four oxen to carry these. Their term of Tabernacle service also has the same age limit.

The sons of Merari and Gershon are placed under the authority of Ithamar the priest for their handling of the Tabernacle.

The Sons of Kohath

The sons of Kohath stand out from the other two divisions in the nature of their family relationship to the priesthood and the terms of their Tabernacle service.

The priesthood and the Kohathites are all sons of Kohath. The priesthood springs from the Amram, the firstborn son of Kohath who begets Aaron, Miriam, and Moses. No other children are mention as coming from Amram. His first born son, Aaron becomes the High Priest. After Aaron's sons Nadab and Abihu are killed by the Lord for offering profane fire, his other sons, Eleazar and Ithamar, step in to take their place. Little is said of the priesthood's general duties in the book of Numbers with the exception of the priesthood preparing the Tabernacle for moving, giving the Aaronic blessing, and Aaron tending the lamps.

The other sons of Kohath are Izhar, Hebron and Uzziel. When Numbers speaks about the service of the Kohathites, it is understood to be speaking of the sons of Izhar, Hebron, and Uzziel, not the priesthood. They are of the same family as the priesthood, but they do not have the same rights or privileges as their priestly cousins, not being descended from Aaron. This family dynamic will be one of the catalysts for Korah's rebellion in chapter 26.

Duties of the Kohathites (Numbers 4:1-20)

The Kohathites were tasked with carrying the most holy things of the Tabernacle, things that only the priesthood was allowed to see and touch. These things had to be veiled by the priesthood as the Tabernacle was being taken down before the Kohathites could approach them. If the Kohathites touched or even looked at the holy items, the Lord would kill them. Once the holy things were veiled, the Kohathites were to carry the furniture and vessels on their shoulders, not on ox-drawn carts. The sons of Kohath are placed under the authority of Eleazar the priest for their handling of the Tabernacle items.

They are the only Levites apart from the priesthood allowed to handle the holy vessels of the Tabernacle, and this requires extreme levels of accountability. They become an important model for us when we translate

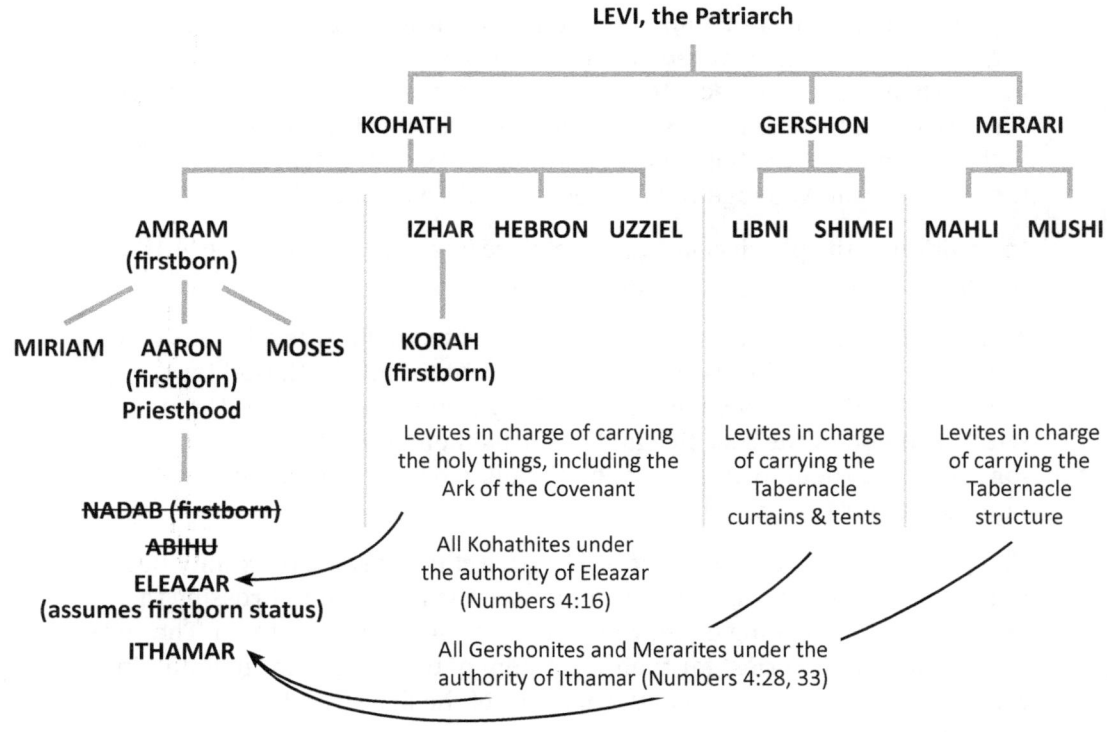

Lesson 2: The Wilderness of Sinai | 29

this into the spiritual journey. I want to walk through the physical picture of Kohathites' service presented in Numbers 4:1-20, and then discuss the implications for us.

As the armies begin to move out, the Tabernacle has to be taken down. The physical boundaries of the courtyard, the Tabernacle tent, and the Veil come down. This would leave the holy vessels on display for all the camp to see and approach unless steps are taken to maintain the holy, set-apart status of the vessels while on the daily walk. So that is the physical problem: how to maintain the vessels' holy, set-apart status.

Paul tells us we are holy vessels. In this journey, we should know how to possess our vessels in sanctification and honor. We are to maintain our set-apart status as we mix with the world around us on our daily walk, in the absence of physical boundaries. The physical challenge now translates into a spiritual challenge.

The Physical Accountability Model (Numbers 4)

Let's consider the physical solution first. The way the holy vessels maintain their set-apart status in the absence of physical boundaries is for each piece to receive two layers of protection. Numbers 4:5-15 details how the priesthood is to veil the holy items with two layers—a layer of red, blue, or purple cloth and layer of animal skin for waterproofing and protection. The order of the layers gets mixed and matched, perhaps to help identify the items when veiled, but each item receives two layers of physical covering. The Ark of the Covenant is a special case because it is first wrapped in the Veil that separates the holy of holies from the rest of the Tabernacle, and then the Ark and Veil together are covered with a layer of skin and cloth.

In addition to the physical layers, each piece also received two layers of people protection: the priest and the Kohathites.

The priest is the first level of defense. He has the highest level of intimacy, greatest amount of liberty and greatest accountability with God for the holy vessels. He can touch and see the holy items. He sanctifies them with the blood of the sacrifice and cleanses them. He is responsible for preparing them to go out among the people and establishing their boundaries for the Kohathites.

The second layer is the Kohathites. They are allowed some proximity but with boundaries. They can carry but not see the holy things. Crossing the veiled boundary—going under the covers—meant death for them. They are accountable to the priest for their treatment of the vessels, for maintaining the purity of the holy vessel in the absence of the priest, and restraining "outsiders" from coming close.

That is the physical solution. Let's translate that into the spiritual model.

The Spiritual Accountability Model

We are holy vessels. Unlike the Tabernacle's holy vessels, we are people possessed of will and able to make choices; therefore, we are able to maintain our own purity to a certain extent. God gives us accountability measures to help us with this, but overall, we are responsible to God for maintaining our purity as His holy vessels.

We are given two layers of physical protection: a skin and clothes. Our skin is our fleshly body, which Paul reminds us continually is the dwelling of the Holy Spirit and must be kept sanctified and holy. Great emphasis is placed on how we treat our bodies in our walk, and we are particularly admonished to abstain from sexual immorality (1 Thes. 4:1-5). The second layer is cloth which speaks of how we clothe ourselves as believers, both physically in modesty and spiritually in humility, girding ourselves with truth, etc.

In addition to our own responsibility, we are also given two layers of human protection to help us. Those two layers are represented in both a physical and spiritual relationship.

In terms of a physical relationship, our inner circle is our spouse. For women like myself, my husband is my first layer of help and accountability when it comes to keeping my purity. My vessel is for his eyes and use only. He has the highest level of intimacy with me, greatest amount of liberty, and greatest accountability to God for helping me keep my person undefiled (Eph. 5:25-27).

Wives act as veils for their husbands as well. That inner-circle accountability help men establish and maintain boundaries at work and socially, and give them a reason for withdrawing from inappropriate advances. Wives are given to men to help them maintain their vessels in purity. Paul speaks on this extensively in Ephesians 5.

Our spouses are responsible for helping establish and maintain the boundaries for our "Kohathites." Our Kohathites, our outer circle, include our family, friends and our congregational community. These have contact with us but with boundaries. Inappropriate sexual relationships are strictly forbidden (1 Cor. 5). Our Kohathites are accountable to our spouses for their treatment of us, and they are responsible for helping maintain our purity in the absence of our spouses.

In addition to helping us maintain physical boundaries such as sexual purity, our spouses are the veil we put up when Kohathites or "outsiders"

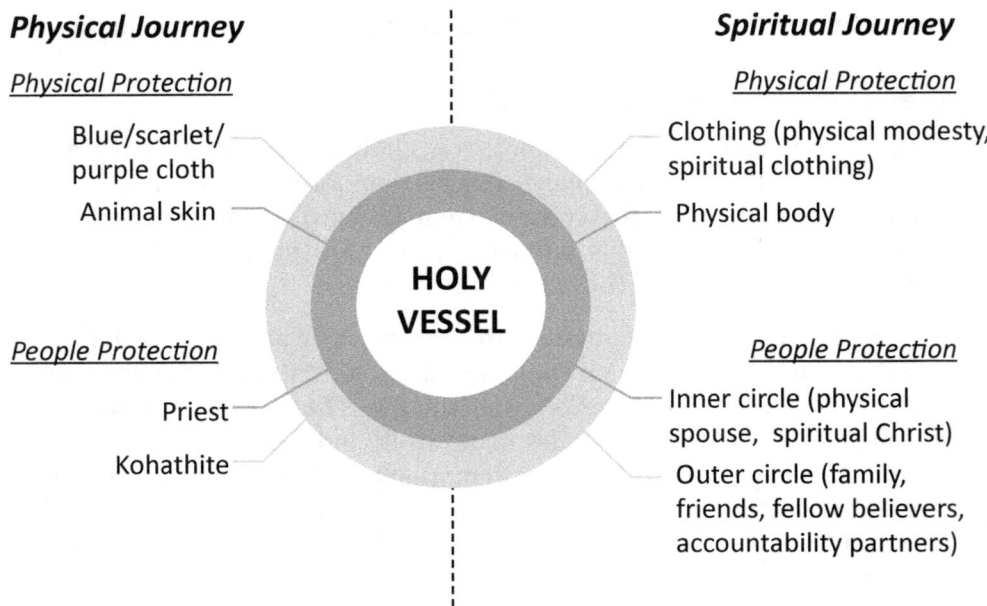

exceed their relationship boundaries—when they try to assume levels of authority or handling of our lives to which they have no right. What married woman does not know the value of playing the "husband card" when pressed to do something she feels will compromise her? We rely on our husbands to back us up and intervene when relationship boundaries need to be reinforced. I remember hearing one woman in my church weep after a confrontation with another member, saying they would not have treated her that way if her husband had been standing there. No woman should ever have to experience that in her dealings with other believers, but it happens. Just as we are accountable to God for maintaining our own purity, we are also accountable to the people in our inner and outer circles because we are part of the greater body, and there are consequences for them if we are defiled.

In terms of the spiritual relationship, our inner circle is Christ, our High Priest. He corresponds to the "husband" level of relationship, and His Bride, the Church, is set apart for His use only. We experience the highest level of intimacy, greatest amount of liberty, and greatest accountability in our relationship with Christ and the Holy Spirit (2 Cor. 3:17). He sanctified us with His sacrifice, cleanses us with continual washing, and is responsible to the Father for keeping us undefiled (Eph. 5:25-27).

He establishes our boundaries for the "Kohathites" (other believers) and the outside world. Because we are betrothed to Christ but not yet living in His presence, He gives us His Spirit to help us maintain our purity, but also places a greater responsibility on our "Kohathite" community to guard us until His return.

As Kohathites, we have contact with each other but with boundaries. We help each other stay accountable and bear one another's burdens. We intercede when a believer's purity is on the line and there is a cry for help. We are accountable to Christ for our treatment of each other.

This is the accountability model that springs from Numbers 4. The spiritual and physical models are remarkably parallel. We will come back to this model when we discuss Korah's Rebellion in chapter 26, but I wanted to lay the foundation here.

Other housekeeping duties crop up along the journey, but these are the basic duties covered in chapters 1–10, and they have rendered a rich relational model for us.

We have established who we are, where we are physically in camp and in the timeline, and a rough understanding of our roles. We have an identity rooted in God and in relationship to our family, our congregation, and our leadership. We have our places defined by physical boundaries which are also relational boundaries. To keep all these relationships working and in their proper place, we are going to need some camp rules for the journey.

Camp Rules (Numbers 5–6)

These laws presented in chapters 5-6 seem out of place. Why weren't these laws included with the rest of the laws in Leviticus, or even Deuteronomy? The conclusion must be that these laws were put into the Numbers narrative because they are somehow relevant to it. Additionlly, if we look at these laws with an understanding of a relationship with Christ and a background of New Testament teachings, they are going to make a lot more sense as to why they are here.

Chapters 5 and 6 present a series of laws that create some ground rules for camp life at the start of the journey. Additional laws will come up along the way, but we will start with these.

These laws govern this particular environment. Without a Tabernacle or Temple or a working priesthood, these laws cannot be practiced as God commands here. We as believers today are not called to recreate this environment or return to the practice of these laws. That being said, these laws working within this environment create relationships between people and places and things that teach us about a relationship with God. What I want to take from these laws are the relationship principles relevant to the physical journey and to our spiritual walk.

The camp rules are:

Camp Rule #1: What gets us put out of camp (5:1-4)

Camp Rule #2: Accountability between one another (5:5-10)

Camp Rule #3: Accountability between husbands and wives (5:11-31)

Camp Rule #4: Accountability between the individual and God (6:1-21)

Camp Rule #5: The priestly blessing (6:22-27)

Looking at these laws, we should note the progression toward intimacy with God. The first begins outside of camp and then levels of relationship progress in intimacy until we reach the point of priestly blessing.

Camp Rule #1: What Gets Us Put Out of Camp

We have already defined "outside the camp." Numbers 5:1-4 defines the conditions that get you put out of camp, which are forms of defilement, including leprosy, defilement by the dead, and ritual uncleanness from discharges

It is important to note that while we strive to maintain our cleanness and holiness in this journey, everyone ends up outside the camp at some point. Ritual uncleanness is a common condition that everyone suffers at some point in life. For this reason we will need continual washing.

Leprosy is visited on a person as a consequence of sin and unfaithfulness to God. Leprosy in Old Testament times is incurable, so unless the Lord provides healing, the leper's permanent abode will be outside the camp until he or she dies. We will talk about leprosy more when we get to chapter 12.

Defilement by contact with death is going to become a grim reality on this journey. Death will ravage the camp as a result of our unfaithfulness and rebellion to God and will defile all of us at some point. This defilement happens when a person dies near you and you come in contact with a dead body. It happens when you help move or prepare the body for burial. It happens just from being in the same room as a dead person, like at a funeral. It most certainly happens on the battlefield.

Uncleanness and defilement by contact with death happen to all of us at some point. All women will end up outside the camp on a monthly basis for their menses. Men will also suffer uncleanness at times. Natural death of relatives happens to all of us and is a source of defilement all face. Soldiers on the battlefield are defiled. Anyone who has to clean up the dead after a battle or outbreak of death in the camp will be defiled. All these instances defile you, and on this journey, no one escapes them.

There is a specific way to be cleansed from this defilement before we can be allowed back in camp as we will study in chapter 19. In short, someone must come outside the camp to cleanse us because once put out of camp, we cannot go back in. We cannot cleanse ourselves. We need another's intervention.

Principles surrounding this passage:
- *Unfaithfulness to God results in death and defilement by death.*
- *Everyone ends up outside the camp at some point in this journey.*
- *We will need continual washing and cleansing throughout this journey.*
- *We cannot make ourselves clean by our own effort.*
- *We need another's intervention to be restored to God and fellowship.*

Camp Rule #2: Accountability between One Another

Camp Rule #2 is foundational for all our relationships with each other in this camp. I want to walk through Numbers 5:5-10 carefully to catch an important principle that is easily overlooked.

What is the sin in verse 6? Any sin committed by either man or woman in unfaithfulness to the Lord.

How do we make things right again? Confess the sin and make restitution.

To whom do we make restitution? To one who has been wronged.

Who has been wronged? The sin was unfaithfulness to God, but do we make restitution to God?

Look at the transition to verse 8. Almost in the same breath, it segues into "if the man has no relative to whom restitution may be made" and instructions for that. How did we get from an act of unfaithfulness to God to making restitution for a wrong done to another person? Interesting how those two things are expressed almost as a single thought.

There is a direct connection between our relationship with others and with God. We cannot be faithful to God and unfaithful to our neighbor at the same time. We cannot love God apart from loving our neighbor. This should not be a foreign concept to us because 1 John 4 speaks about this at length.

> *"If someone says, 'I love God,' and hates his brother, he is a liar; for he who does not love his brother whom he has seen, how can he love God whom he has not seen?" 1 John 4:20*

Note: We must make amends with the man first before going to God with our sacrifice. If we cannot find the person we've wronged or his kin to make restitution, then our restitution goes to the priest.

Principles from this passage:
- *Sin against others is counted as an act of unfaithfulness to God.*
- *Confess our sin and make restitution, to one another first and then to God.*
- *Unfaithfulness always costs us something.*

Camp Rule #3: Accountability between Husbands and Wives

Numbers 5:11-31 gives us the laws concerning unfaithful wives. Husbands and wives are the physical picture of the spiritual relationship between God and His people, and more specifically, Christ and the church. God identifies Himself with a jealous husband (Exo. 20:4-5, 34:14).

Here is a quick overview of the case of the unfaithful wife:

> The wife's unfaithfulness is suspected but not known. There is no witness of the act (v13). There is a spirit of jealousy on the part of the husband, whether it is warranted or not (v14). The husband brings her to the priest with the offering for jealousy (v15). The priest brings her before the Lord, and uncovers her head. Jewish sources say he loosens or uncovers her hair[1], signifying she has been unrestrained in her behavior (v18). A trial by ordeal is performed to prove the woman's guilt or innocence. She is made to drink the bitter waters that bear a curse (v16-26). If she guilty, over a period of time she will begin to waste away in sickness. She will become a curse among her people and she will be barren (v27). If not guilty, she is free and able to have children (v28).

There is an obvious question to ask here. Why is it only the woman who is put on trial? Jealousy is only attributed to the husband. There is no corresponding action should the woman become jealous. That is because the Law is using the physical relationship to teach the spiritual relationship between God and His people. This is also a future picture of Christ and the Church. There is never a question of God's faithfulness to His people or Christ's faithfulness to the Church. The failing is only ever on the bride's part (our part).

---

1 Jewish sources vary in the interpretation of "parah" in the text—whether it means to uncover or loosen. The following article provides an overview of Jewish sources and their interpretations: Bronner, Leila Leah. "To Cover or Not to Cover: That Is the Question Jewish Hair Laws Through the Ages." Dr. Leila Leah Bronner Bible and Jewish Studies, www.bibleandjewishstudies.net/articles/haircovering.htm.

This is a singular law where a person accused of sin is tried without the support of physical witnesses. According to Mosaic Law, in the accusation of sin, truth is established "by the mouth of two or three witnesses" (Deut. 19:15), but here the only witness of the wife's faithfulness, or lack thereof, comes by the spirit and the water. It is understood that God Himself makes the deliberation in this case, not a human judge. This is a new precedent and a shadow picture of something to come.

When Jesus begins His ministry, it is verified by the Spirit descending on Him at His baptism, with the voice of God declaring, "This is My beloved Son, in whom I am well pleased" (Matt. 3:17). The witnesses that established the truth of Jesus' identity were the Spirit, the water, and the voice of God. Not even John the Baptist recognized Him apart from these (John 1:29-34). Just as he writes in his gospel account, so John iterates in 1 John 5:6-8, *"For there are three that bear witness . . . the Spirit, the water, and the blood; and these three agree as one."* The Spirit bears witness for the Spirit is truth. The water bears witness, for those who pass through that ordeal will either die from it or be lifted up to new life. The Spirit and water are valid witnesses in establishing truth, and have an early precedent in our Numbers passage.

Something to note: In the previous camp rule, we read 1 John 4:20 speaking of loving others and loving God. Now, this camp rule illustrates 1 John 5:6-8 in regards to what bears witness of truth. The laws presented in Numbers 5 are tracking a parallel path with John's commentary in his letter.

If the woman is found guilty, she is technically guilty of adultery and should be put to death by Law. But in this case, the evidence of guilt is not immediate; therefore, death is not prescribed nor is there any call for the husband to put her away despite his jealousy. The punishment for unfaithfulness is wasting and unfruitfulness—to be barren. The passage ends with the statement that the unfaithful wife will bear the curse, but the man will be free from iniquity.

This is significant because on this journey, many of us are going to end up in a place of fruitlessness on account of our unfaithfulness to God. We are going to walk away from our relationship with Him by refusing to enter the Land, and we are going to exchange it for a barren wilderness. It will be like a curse and we will weep for the lack of fruit in our lives. The failing will be ours and we will bear the guilt of that unfaithfulness, not God. That is the picture God is setting up for the journey to come.

Principles from this passage:
- *Unfaithfulness results in unfruitfulness and wasting away. Unfaithfulness doesn't necessarily end the relationship with God, but*

brings the curse of unfruitfulness in that we will not experience the blessings and increase that we should have had from that relationship. This is true for the children of Israel and for us as believers.

- *If faithfulness is in question, it will be tested in a trial by ordeal, and it will be long, drawn-out time of testing. Our wandering in the wilderness is going to be our trial by ordeal.*

Camp Rule #4: Accountability between the Individual and God

Numbers 6:1-21 gives us the laws concerning the Nazirite vow. The purpose is to separate oneself to the Lord (v2). This act represents a high level of intimacy between the individual and God because it expresses a deep desire to be close to and aligned with God. It is an exercise of self-control and a way of rooting ourselves in our identity with God.

The conditions of this vow include:

1) **Separating oneself from wine and grape products** (v3-4) which represent the material pleasures of this world. The practice of abstinence is a key element in this law. Taking a Nazirite vow doesn't mean a permanent loss of freedom or pleasure. It is a temporary abstinence with the goal of achieving a more desirable condition. It is a delay of personal gratification for the sake of attaining a better reward.

    This is a very important point because when we start this journey and begin that process of separating ourselves from an old life, the world is going to throw this argument at us: "A relationship with God means giving up your freedom of choice." This is one of the first challenges we tackle on our journey.

    Entering into this wilderness journey is, in a sense, entering a Nazirite vow. We agreed to leave Egypt with all the material pleasure it represented. We have entered a time of separation marked by a distinct lack of material things in this wilderness. We agreed to undertake this temporary period of abstinence with the goal of entering into a better condition in the Promised Land. This act is meant to glorify God and lift us up to a more intimate relationship with Him.

2) **Not shaving the head** (v5). This time of separation is made distinct by a lack of shearing, in the same way the Sabbath year is made distinct when the grapevines go unpruned. This act is an echo of the Sabbath year which represents a higher, more glorious level of experience of God from a Sabbath day experience. The Sabbath year would be experienced by those who entered the Land, but many of us

will die here on this journey and never reach that goal. The practice of the Nazirite vow served as a taste of a more glorious relationship to come. We will discuss the levels of Sabbath experience in greater detail in chapter 14 when we talk about what it means to enter the Land and the Lord's rest.

3) **Not going near a dead body** (v6-12). Death is a form of separation from God, but it is a separation caused by sin and results in defilement. A Nazirite's separation has to be apart from sin. The Nazirite is to be holy and undefiled. The two forms of separation cannot be mingled. If defilement by death occurs, the individual must begin again.

This journey should have been like a Nazirite vow for us. Like a Sabbath, it is a time of drawing closer to God. Yet many of us fail to grasp the full significance of this vow we have taken to follow God. We come into this journey mentally unprepared for the level of commitment it requires of us, and unwilling to let go of the pleasures of the old life. As a result, many of us fail to reach that next level of intimacy with Him.

Principles from this passage:

- *The exercise of self-control is meant to be part of this journey. This isn't a requirement, but when done, it is to be done voluntarily.*
- *Abstinence is a choice. Remember this in the lessons to come.*

Camp Rule #5: Priestly Blessing

The priestly blessing marks the pinnacle of our progression in intimacy with God. Numbers 6:22-27 gives a simple blessing composed of three lines that the priesthood was to say over the congregation regularly.

"The LORD bless you and keep you . . ." The first line speaks of God's provision and protection. It should remind us of the first blessing in Genesis associated with the command to be fruitful and multiply. There is also the promise to keep us, meaning to guard and protect us or hedge us in.

"The LORD make His face shine upon you, and be gracious to you . . ." The second line refers to God's light and His grace—light that He may enlighten us and grace that we may know the fullness of His love (Eph. 3:18). This implies God's engagement with man at a higher level, beyond providing for simple needs and protection. There is an increasing level of relationship described here.

"The LORD lift up His countenance upon you, and give you peace. . . " The last speaks of peace, that is, shalom. Shalom represents the harmony and

oneness between God and ourselves and our community, and it is what ties all the other blessings together. It is the completion of all blessings and the fruition of man's relationship with God.

In all three phrases, "you" is expressed in the singular form so that they are understood to be blessings on an individual and not a collective group. This blessing is for each person individually.

There are two references to the Lord's face. The turning of the face indicates a heart attitude. To turn one's face toward someone indicates love and acceptance; to turn one's face away communicates anger and rejection. Twice in this blessing the Lord turns His face toward us. The final act is to lift up His face to us like a loving father lifting His child up above his head and smiling up at him.

Why include this blessing in the camp rules?

It is God's way of rooting the children of Israel in their identity with Him by putting His name on them and blessing them (v27). It is a way of lifting us up and reaffirming to us who He is, His love for us, and His ongoing commitment to us. This reassurance of love will be vital when the failures happen on the journey.

It is a call for the priesthood to love the people. This blessing is an expression of God's love for His people, and the priesthood is to be the conduit for communicating this love. The priest cannot give the blessing without first loving the people he is to bless. You cannot give a blessing or be a conduit for God's blessing without love. In fact, in Jewish practice, if the presiding priest was sad or grieving and could not attain the required feeling of love, another priest was required to step in and give the blessing.

So this is very much a command to love, and fits with a future aspect of our identity and ministry as part of a royal priesthood. That is why I include it in the camp rules.

Principle from this passage: Love one another and be a conduit for God's love.

Those are the basic camp rules we are going to start with, and I will refer back to them in future lessons. The last step in organizing an army will be to set up our camp communication system.

Camp Communications (Numbers 9–10)

If God is going to move His army of 600,000-plus soldiers traveling with their families and all their livestock, establishing a system of camp communications will be vital. As King and leader in this journey, God will always be the one to move first. Then we will move. We get our cue to move after 1) observing His glory lifted up in the cloud and 2) hearing the trumpet call.

Chapter 9:15-23 explains God moving in the cloud. So long as we are camped, the cloud will rest over the Tabernacle. When we see the glorious cloud lifted up from the Tabernacle to take its position the air, that is our sign to prepare to move. So long as the cloud is on the move, we are on the move. When the cloud returns to the Tabernacle, we camp and remain camped until the next time the cloud moves.

Chapter 10 describes the two silver trumpets used for in-camp communications. If only one is blown, the leaders are to assemble at the Tabernacle (v4). If both are blown, then that is a signal for the whole congregation to assemble (v3). Before this journey is done, we will be thoroughly conditioned to listen for the sounding of two trumpets. Not one but two. The second trumpet is for us—our signal to rise and be gathered.

The trumpets also sound the advance of each army in its turn as they move out on the journey, but that trumpet sound is to be distinguished from the sound to assemble (v5-7). In chapter 2, there is mentioned the basic order for breaking camp, but much more detailed instructions are given in Numbers 10:14-28. When the tribes begin to move out, the Ark of the Covenant carried by some of the Kohathites leads off, followed by the rest in order by camp placement beginning with Judah and the Army of the East.

When we come into the Land, the purpose of the trumpets will change. The trumpets will sound in times of war, that we might be remembered by the

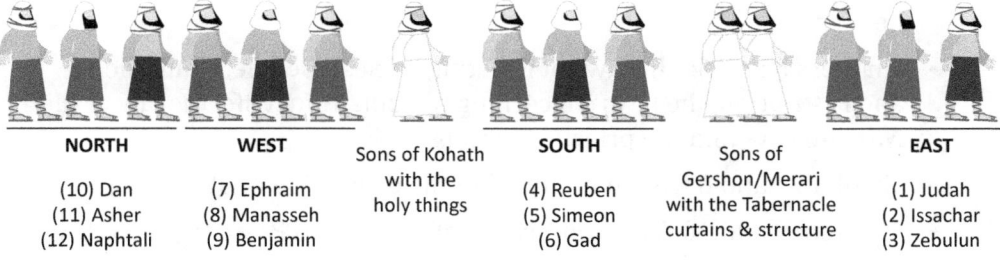

NORTH	WEST	Sons of Kohath with the holy things	SOUTH	Sons of Gershon/Merari with the Tabernacle curtains & structure	EAST
(10) Dan	(7) Ephraim		(4) Reuben		(1) Judah
(11) Asher	(8) Manasseh		(5) Simeon		(2) Issachar
(12) Naphtali	(9) Benjamin		(6) Gad		(3) Zebulun

Lord and saved from our enemies (v9) and as memorials at our feasts (v10), specifically at the Feast of Trumpets and the Day of Atonement.

Besides chapter 10, these trumpets are mentioned only two other times in the book of Numbers. First is in chapter 29 with the reminder to blow the trumpets on the first day of the seventh month, which is the Feast of

Trumpets. The other is in chapter 31 where Phinehas takes the signal trumpets with him when going into battle with the Midianites.

All of these references to the trumpets in the book of Numbers combine to create a prophetic picture of End Times events. There is the call to rise and assemble when we see the glory in the cloud—the Rapture. There is the sounding of the trumpets on the Feast of Trumpets, a day prophetically associated with the coming of the Day of the Lord and Christ's return. There is the picture of Phinehas leading the 12,000 into war against the Midianites, taking the signal trumpets with him—a picture of Christ with the 144,000 (Rev. 14) and the final battle (Rev. 19:11-21) which we will discuss more when we get to chapter 31.

The blowing of the trumpets was commanded throughout all the generations of Israel as a memorial to keep this picture alive in their minds. All God's people should live in expectation of hearing that second trumpet.

Summary

This brings us to the end of this lesson. We are going to break here because from this point we depart Sinai and the journey begins. Though we did not work through the verses specifically, we covered the better parts of chapters 1-10, including:

- Chapter 1: The census and calling of the leaders, the numbers and the names
- Chapter 2: The layout of the camp according to the armies
- Chapters 3 and 4: The census, family divisions and duties of the Levites
- Chapters 5 and 6: The laws of isolating unclean people, confession and restitution, the laws concerning the unfaithful wife, the law of the Nazirite vow, and the priestly blessing
- Chapters 7 and 8 were mentioned in the discussion of other chapters
- Chapters 9 and 10: The significance of the second Passover, the glory in the cloud and the silver trumpets.

We are now at the end of the month. We have all celebrated the Passover and identified with that Passover lamb. God has lifted our head, mentally setting us on the first step in our spiritual journey toward glorification. We have been given our new identity rooted in our relationship with Him. We have been established as individuals with responsibilities and accountabilities and given the freedom of choice, including the choice to abstain.

He has given us a purpose. We are His army, His priests, and His servants.

We have been given a place in the camp, each with our own role, authority level and physical boundaries. This is the environment in which we will relate to God in the days to come.

In the next lesson, our journey begins.

LESSON THREE

Taberah

CHAPTERS 10:11–11:3

Our journey begins. We are leaving Sinai, heading for Kadesh in the Wilderness of Paran. This leg of the journey should take 11 days (Deut. 1:2). Our first official campsite will be Kibroth Hatta'avah, a three-day's journey from Sinai, but before we get there, we will experience our first failing at a place called Taberah.

I am going to divide this lesson into two parts. First, we will walk through our departure from Sinai (10:11-36). In verses 29-32, there is a conversation between Moses and his brother-in-law, Hobab, which we will examine in the next lesson. Second, we will role-play as the children of Israel to examine our failing at Taberah recorded in Numbers 11:1-3, and then take the lesson into a New Testament application.

Departing Sinai (Numbers 10:11-36)

Imagine the controlled chaos of 600,000-plus people being set into motion. This is our highly-orchestrated moment of departure. There is a lot of detailed information and an important picture in this passage, but it is all a bit scattered. The passage is easier to study when the information is organized into a timeline. Refer to the diagram below as we walk through this.

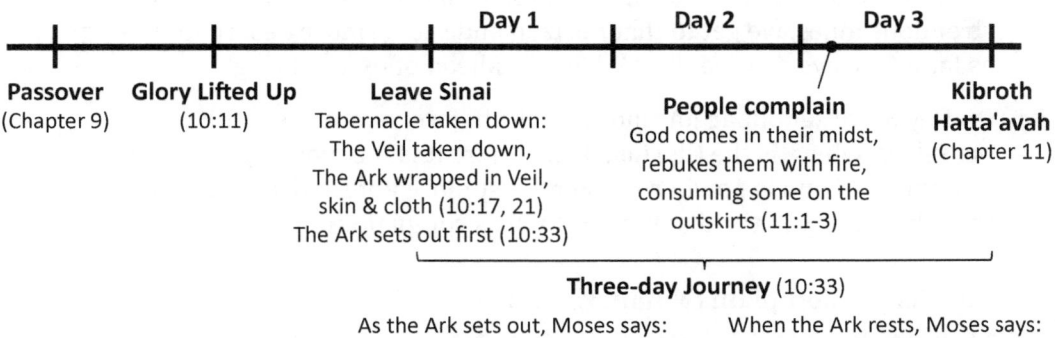

Starting Point: Passover

We have just celebrated a second Passover on the 14th day of the second month (chapter 9). Having completed the second Passover, we set out on the 20th day of the second month.

Glory Lifting Up, Leaving Sinai

In rapid order we see the glory lifted up (v11) and the Tabernacle dismantled (v17). The Veil is taken down. The Ark of the Covenant is wrapped in the Veil, skins, and cloth. The Ark of the Covenant, carried by the Kohathites, sets out ahead of camp (v33). Then the armies march out in their order (v14-28).

Three-day Journey

The text tells us this will be a three-day journey to Kibroth Hatta'avah, but we don't know this as we begin walking. All we know is that we are following the Ark on our way to the Glorious Land, wherever it leads us.

As the Ark sets out, Moses says *"Rise up, O Lord!..."* (v35) When the Ark comes to rest at Kibroth Hatta'avah, Moses is going to say *"Return, O Lord!..."* (v36). Let's play this out in real time.

On Day 1, we start walking out of the Wilderness of Sinai. As the Ark sets out, Moses says in a mighty voice: *"Rise up, O LORD! Let Your enemies be scattered, and let those who hate You flee before You."* Hurray! Here we go! The Glorious Land is just over that set of hills on the horizon. At the end of the day, after an arduous day of hiking, we get to that horizon and on the other side we see ... more desert stretching as far as the eye can see. Here we stay for the night.

On Day 2, we set out again. Hurray ... here we go ... again. The Glorious Land is just over that set of sand dunes. At the end of the day and another strenuous miles, we get to that horizon and see ... more desert stretching as far as the eye can see. The Ark is still ahead of us, out of sight.

On Day 3, we set out again, another hike before us, and we think to ourselves, where is the Glorious Land? Here it is the morning of the third day and the Land is nowhere in sight. Just more hot sand and mountains stretching away in the distance. But who's complaining?

The People Complain (Numbers 11:1-3)

The text doesn't say exactly at what point we start complaining, but if the Old Testament picture follows its parallel in the New Testament, I am going to speculate that it is started on the third day. At this point, the reality of the walk begins to set in. This is what it is going to be like, this trudging through rock and sand, and what makes it even harder is not knowing how far we have to keep going. All we are doing is following the Ark and trusting that it is leading us the way we should go. The complaining begins.

God hears the complaining. He probably said to Himself, "What is wrong with you? It's only been three days!" He sees we are already losing faith, and it makes Him angry. He comes among us and His rebuking fire burns us, consuming some in the outskirts of the camp (v1). Then we appeal to Moses, he intercedes for us, and the fire is extinguished (v2). For a memorial, Moses gives this place the name, Taberah, which means burning in the sense of being consumed (v3). The journey continues. On the third day, we make camp at Kibroth Hatta'avah.

Picture of Christ

Before we get to the spiritual lesson that comes out of this incident at Taberah, I want to take a look at this timeline that we have just built, because there is a picture of Christ in it. Look at the elements on that timeline. How do they translate into the New Testament picture?

Crucifixion to Grave

Jesus' celebration of Passover with His disciples intiates the parallel sequence. Then the elements of His death are marked. The Glory being lifted up is Christ lifted up on the cross.

Leaving Sinai is a composite picture of Christ's burial. In the New Testament, a tabernacle is used as a metaphor for the earthly human body,

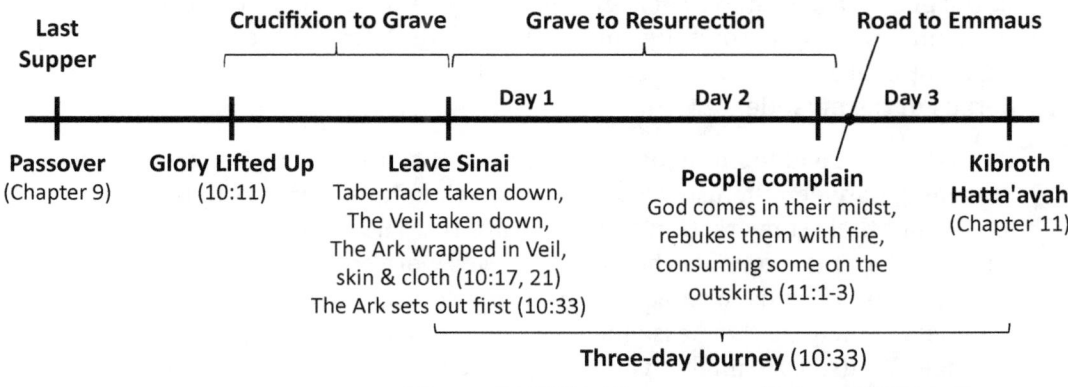

which in this case is Christ's body being taken down from the cross in death. With it the Veil is also taken down, or in the case of Christ's death, torn down from top to bottom.

Then there is the preparation of the Ark of the Covenant for a journey, a picture of Christ as He is laid in the tomb. The shadow imagery of the Ark with its mercy seat overshadowed by cherubim was echoed in the picture of the two angels sitting at either end of the slab on which Jesus' body had lain, as seen by the women when they entered His empty tomb. His body, laid in that place, fulfilled the blood sacrifice required to atone for our sins.

Now take that imagery of the Ark and wrap it in the Veil. The Veil is symbolic of His flesh, and also the way by which we may now enter the presence of God, as described in Hebrews 10:19-20.

All that imagery is then wrapped in an animal skin (a common skin) and cloth coverings, representing His human flesh and grave shroud.

So, from Passover to leaving Sinai on our timeline, we have a detailed picture of Jesus' death and burial. Then comes the three-day journey to Kibroth Hatta'avah, which takes us from Jesus' burial to resurrection.

Grave to Resurrection

As the Ark sets out, Moses says, *"Rise up, O LORD! Let Your enemies be scattered, and let those who hate You flee before You."* That sets an expectation of God imminently bringing His people into the Glorious Land that was just over the horizon. When we walked that path ourselves, we saw that disillusionment set in pretty quickly. Jesus' disciples had the same expectation of the Christ returning immediately to set up the Kingdom, and their disillusionment had set in by the morning of that third day.

In the gospel account, we see a group of followers walking on a desert road, murmuring sorrowfully among themselves because the Kingdom hasn't appeared as they thought it would. Luke 24:13-27 gives us the details of the episode.

On that dusty road to Emmaus, we see two of His disciples walking and reasoning between themselves mournfully, when Jesus appears to them and asks about their conversation. Verse 16 says His true identity, His glory, is still veiled in this moment. The disciples' eyes were restrained. He rebukes them and then begins to explain about Himself from "Moses and the Prophets." I imagine this passage in Numbers might have been one of the passages He used. He might even have pointed to the complaining children of Israel and said "Look! That's you! That's how you are behaving right now."

Jesus' rebuke isn't nearly as ferocious as God's response to the children of Israel. He grants them grace and opens their eyes. Yet it is important to note that this journey into a wilderness of doubt and disbelief is a shared experience for God's people—the children of Israel in the wilderness, the disciples on the road to Emmaus, and we ourselves in our own spiritual journey. Many of us begin this journey with unrealistic expectations of the timeline, the Kingdom and what the Christian walk is going to be like. It doesn't take long for reality to set in.

The first steps of this journey are going to challenge our expectations, and we can either keep walking in faith or we can balk and complain.

Taberah (Numbers 11:1-4)

We are only two weeks away from the Promised Land. We are somewhere on the road on this three-day journey to Kibroth Hatta'avah. We are facing a barren wilderness and having a crisis of faith. It is May–June, temperature in the 100's, no shade, no food, no water, hot sand—but we only have to endure it a short while. So who's complaining?

The word "complained" in verse 1 is the Hebrew word, *anan*, meaning to murmur with sorrow. It is the picture of a people sunk in self-pity, an excessive, self-absorbed unhappiness over one's own troubles. It begins softly in murmuring, a persistent grumping and grousing, moaning and sighing, always under the breath, but just audible enough for the people around to hear. It is the kind of complaining that drives leaders up the wall because it's not outright rebellion or confrontation at first but just a slow drip-drip of resistance.

When the first difficulties arise, some of us will sink into self-pity.

Self-pity can be a pitfall in the journey. It is one thing to cry out to the Lord in these moments and ask Him to lift us up. That is a way of reacting to adversity that gives glory to God. It is another thing to seek our lifting up from others, and that takes glory away from God.

Be aware of who we turn to when we need lifting up.

The Character of Self-Pity

At heart, self-pity is self-focused and self-promoting. It casts us in the identity of a victim and demands others lift us up. It seeks out those who feed it, like fire seeking air. Self-pity always seeks an audience and an opportunity to complain. Once the complainer finds a sympathetic audience, the complaint strengthens, gets louder, and begins to spread.

Self-pity is socially contagious. Once it establishes a foothold, it is spread by the tongue. What is spoken by one gets heard by another and repeated. Spoken, heard, repeated. Moving from tongue to tongue, it makes its way through all the people.

It should not surprise us that the first stumbling in our sanctification journey has to do with the unrestrained tongue. Here at Taberah, the Lord is going brand us with the understanding that the tongue is a fire.

James understands this Old Testament picture.

> *"For we all stumble in many things. If anyone does not stumble in word, he is a perfect man, able also to bridle the whole body. Indeed, we put bits in horses' mouths that they may obey us, and we turn their whole body. Look also at ships: although they are so large and are driven by fierce winds, they are turned by a very small rudder wherever the pilot desires. Even so the tongue is a little member and boasts great things. See how great a forest a little fire kindles! And the tongue is a fire, a world of iniquity. The tongue is so set among our members that it defiles the whole body, and sets on fire the course of nature; and it is set on fire by hell." James 3:2-6*

The tongue is such a little thing, and yet has the ability to alter our path from the direction the Lord wants us to go. We are already getting off track in our journey, thanks to these tongues of ours. It is the instrument that causes spiritual defilement. Notice that the burning takes place in the outskirts of camp, right in that no-man's land between the clean and unclean people.

How does the Lord deal with our tongues? How does He stop the fire from spreading? Here is Old Testament justice—an eye for an eye. He fights fire with fire. He sets a backfire. A backfire is a firefighting technique where a controlled fire is intentionally started to create a dead zone to stop the advance of a wildfire. The Lord creates a physical dead zone between those outside the camp and those inside the camp.

When we get to Kibroth Hatta'avah, we will see that God's preventative action didn't stop the complaining. The complaining will begin again. Why didn't God's judgment stop the complaining?

Our problem wasn't with our tongue but with our heart.

> *"A good man out of the good treasure of his heart brings forth good; and an evil man out of the evil treasure of his heart brings forth evil. For out of the abundance of the heart his mouth speaks."* Luke 6:45

The tongue was punished at Taberah, but the heart problem wasn't resolved. So often we focus on trying to keep our tongue in check, when we haven't really gotten to the root reason why we say the things we do. This is why when James speaks about taming the tongue, he immediately moves to the issue of the heart.

> *"Who is wise and understanding among you? Let him show by good conduct that his works are done in the meekness of wisdom. But if you have bitter envy and self-seeking in your hearts, do not boast and lie against the truth. This wisdom does not descend from above, but is earthly, sensual, demonic. For where envy and self-seeking exist, confusion and every evil thing are there."* James 3:13-16

Our tongue is not our problem. Our heart is. Our tongue simply reveals what our heart is feeling and our mind is thinking. The Lord uses the tongue as His tool for making our inward corruption evident on the outside. Our tongue tells us what we need to work on in our personal relationship with the Lord. Deal with the heart, and the tongue will become much less of an issue.

What are some other destructive ways we use our tongue? I think of gossip, criticism, and angry outbursts, to start with. When we indulge in these, we let our tongue run amok because of the satisfaction, attention, or status we get from it. All these things boil down to self-glorification. We take glory in being the first to hear news and share it, especially if it's a catty little bit that makes us look better than others. Gossip gives us a rush of power and status among our peers. Criticism can be a way of tearing someone down to lift ourselves up, if it's not done with the right heart. Angry outbursts get us noticed. They are our way of exerting dominance and control in a situation. All these bring glory to us but take glory away from God.

What passes our lips is going to be the main instigator of every trouble in the camp and our relationships with others throughout this whole journey. It isn't until the end of the journey that we begin to learn what to ask for and how to ask. When our words begin to bring glory to God, then the Lord begins to give us little victories. But even after a victory, we are still prone to fall back into that old behavior pattern. This episode at Taberah is just a blip on the journey, and blends into the next incident at Kibroth Hatta'avah. It is going to reveal a heart issue behind the complaining tongue.

Camp Check

Don't forget to note where we are physically in the camp. Where did the burning take place? In the outskirts of the camp. Who is in the outskirts of the camp and what is their spiritual status? Outside the camp is reserved for the mixed multitude—the Gentiles, the defiled, and unclean. The complaint starts outside the camp and spreads into the camp.

How did that boundary get crossed? There is no physical boundary here. It's just a line in the sand that has to be kept in the mind and heart and by restraint of personal relationships. The defilement has crossed a boundary by means of the tongue. We can violate boundaries with our tongue. Be aware of that.

In the next lesson, mixing with this multitude creates the first point of friction in the camp. How we mix with the world and the amount of influence we allow it to exert on us becomes the first point of conflict in our spiritual relationship with God and a major battle line in the journey. On to Kibroth Hatta'avah.

LESSON FOUR

Kibroth Hatta'avah

CHAPTER 11:4–34

The lesson at Taberah blends right into the events that take place at Kibroth Hatta'avah. For this lesson we will be covering Numbers 11:4-34, which is a long passage. To make this more manageable, I am going to break it down in these sections:

- **Mixing with the Multitude** (11:4-9). This is the opening passage where we are engaged with the mixed multitude. As we begin to separate from the world, we are challenged with breaking away from the old ways of thinking and dealing with life. It is a mental challenge we are facing, and some strategies the Enemy is using against us here to get us off the journey. We are going to talk about leaving behind old ways of coping with difficulties and letting go of the old identity and values system.
- **Leadership Meeting** (11:10-23). This passage records the leadership meeting between God and Moses over what to do with the congregation. Moses has a two-part complaint that he lays before the Lord, first with bearing the responsibility of so many people in general, and second, with struggling to meet unrealistic expectations. We will take some lessons from leadership on how to deal with these same issues in our spiritual journey.
- **God Deals with His Children** (11:24-34). God answers Moses' complaints first, by the appointing of the seventy elders, and the second, by sending quail. Standing in the congregation's shoes, we are going to learn a hard lesson in self-control and the value of abstinence.

After we go through the text, I am going to return to a few application points:

- The practice of self-control and abstinence
- The lesson from leadership in dealing with unrealistic expectations

Mixing with the Multitude (Numbers 11:4-9)

Before we get into the dynamics of what is going on in this account, we need to identify who these "mixed multitude" are in verse 4. We can get a basic back-story on them from Exodus 12:35-38.

When we came out of Egypt, it was in the wake of God's glory. He brought us out with power, and He brought us out rich with Egypt's gold, silver, finery, and livestock. Having witnessed the shock and awe of this display, a mixed multitude decides to follow us out of Egypt and into the wilderness.

Anything of a mixed nature in the Old Testament has the taint of uncleanness about it. The Hebrew word for mixed multitude is *aspesuf*, a contemptuous term meaning the rabble. Let's sketch a character profile of the kind of people we are dealing with.

They are people who:

- Still live in the periphery of our current lives. They cling to us from our old life.
- Have seen the mighty work God has done in our life and are drawn to it because of its "shock and awe" quality. It is a thrilling novelty.
- Pursue the wealth and luxuries. They keep themselves in our lives because they think they will have some benefit from us.
- Live for extremes and excesses. Moderation is not part of their thinking.
- Live for the moment and immediate gratification. Self-control is not part of their thinking.
- Are not interested in a relationship with God. They have little heart for sticking around once the excitement dies down and the real work of building a relationship with God begins.

These are people who want to go back to Egypt and take us with them. They don't go out of our lives without causing some trouble. They are not interested in having a relationship with God, but they want to keep the relationship with us, which makes them the perfect tool for the unseen Enemy to use in getting us off track.

They are the ones who have yielded to intense craving, and yet somehow, we have become their voice. We are the ones who have championed their cause as if it was our own. I want to discuss the dynamics of what is happening because there is a two-fold mental challenge working against us in this moment. First, there is our separation from Egypt which involves leaving behind some old behavior patterns and ways of thinking. In the midst of this internal challenge when we are weakened, the Enemy brings some external pressure to bear on us. The second challenge is to recognize and combat the Enemy's strategies at work on us through the mixed multitude.

Let's examine the internal mental challenge of separating from Egypt first.

Leaving Behind Old Ways of Coping

When I read this passage, I couldn't help wondering, why this cry over food? How is it that we forget Egypt so quickly? In Egypt we were beaten and abused daily for being unable to meet unrealistic expectations, worked to death, never able to please our masters, never able to rest, never able to break away from that dysfunctional life. So how is it that we have these memories of Egypt like a rosy glow in the distance? Why is it that we only remember the food?

I think food means something more to us in this case. Food is a comfort. It is our go-to pleasure whenever life gets difficult. Food is our escape, and we want to escape this wilderness we are in, just like we wanted escape from Egypt. I think it represents a coping strategy.

Let's step into the shoes of the children of Israel and play this out.

Life in Egypt was brutal for us. We grew up in that abusive, dysfunctional setting as slaves, and daily life was really a matter of coping. Early on, we began to pursue the feel-good things that help us forget the horror of daily life. Maybe it was food for us in Egypt. Compared to the horror around us, this was a good thing. It made an unbearable situation bearable. It was what we used to forget Egypt.

We have food on this journey. We have manna. Numbers 11:7-9 reminds us that it's good food. Not a single person has died on this journey for lack of food, so this is not about having our needs neglected. It is about our comfort level.

Life in the wilderness is a different kind of uncomfortable for us and we are looking for our feel-good coping tool. We are looking for that old-life pleasurable crutch that is now being denied to us.

Maybe for us it isn't food. Personal "appetites" can run in any number of directions. Some of us may filled in that blank with "golf," "shopping" or "brownies." Maybe it is something relatively harmless like these, or maybe it is something much more destructive like addictions to cigarettes, alcohol, or drugs that we use to take the edge off life. Maybe it's brief physical or emotional relationships that give us a fleeting sense of love and validation. It is whatever we turn to when we need to switch off from the difficulties in life.

Modern Day Scenario

It's a little hard to identify with slaves in Egypt in our modern context, so I am going to give you a more relevant scenario that parallels this coming out of Egypt moment. This is loosely based on the experience of a young man who was a foster child in my neighborhood. I will call him Gene. The conversation with his counselor is what I imagined from the scraps of information Gene and Maggie shared with me, and I have embellished it with some paraphrasing from James 3:13-16.

> Gene came from an abusive, dysfunctional home. His parents were alcoholics and drug addicts. He suffered abuse and neglect, and early on his parents taught him that smoking and taking drugs were ways to cope with life. These were good things to him.
>
> Then when he was fifteen, the powers-that-be decided to take Gene out of this environment before it killed him. So they sent a social services worker to Gene's Egypt to bring him out.
>
> "Moses" took Gene out of that situation, and the coming out was bad. Gene's parents didn't want to let him go. There was a monstrous confrontation that, in Gene's drug-dulled mind, dissolved into a dark haze of angry words, police sirens, noise, confusion, and fear. But in the end Gene left with Moses. Later he found out his dad had gone to prison, and his mom was in rehab.
>
> Moses brought Gene to the foster home of "Maggie," a Christian lady in my neighborhood. It was a temporary place completely different than the world he knew. He was uncomfortable. After the noise and confusion he was used to dealing with, this place was a wilderness. It was too quiet, too empty. He was given a new living arrangement, new rules, and new highly structured routine. His basic needs were met as best as Maggie could manage, but Gene was still plagued by feelings of emptiness and loneliness. He felt out of place. He felt powerless. He knew he didn't belong here, and he knew he wasn't going to be there long. At eighteen he would be out of the foster care limbo but into another life on his own. He didn't know what to expect of the future.
>
> Life became a new kind of difficult for Gene, and when life got difficult, he automatically wanted to return to his old coping mechanisms— cigarettes and drugs. They were his crutches to take the edge off the unbearableness of life. But in this foster home, his crutches were denied him. He was in rehab for the drugs, and Maggie wouldn't let him smoke. He started thinking about those things that he thought were good in the old life, and his cravings began to grow. Every time he talked

with his mom or dad on the phone, those cravings came back with a vengeance. Bitterness and lust for the old life began to consume him, and depression took over. He was convinced he couldn't live without those coping crutches. It became his driving ambition to get the good feelings back.

There was a social services counselor, "James," assigned to Gene at this time. In their meetings, all Gene could talk about were those "good things" he used to have in Egypt and how he was determined to go back home. This life was just not working out for him.

James listened to Gene, but then he got up in his face a little. He told him his thinking was wrong. He wasn't being wise about this. Those things that Gene thought were good, those earthly, sensual, feel-good things, were really evil in his life. They were the demons that lied to him and told him life in Egypt was good.

Gene didn't want to hear this. He was tired of this wilderness, and he wanted what he wanted. Gene told James life in Egypt had been tough, but he had been coping just fine. The good life is all about the cigarettes, alcohol, and drugs. This foster home is nothing. It's too quiet. He can't sleep without the drugs. He can't find peace.

James came back at Gene with equal strength. Quit boasting about what you think you know. You don't know. Your parents have screwed with your thinking. Quit lying to yourself about the truth. The truth is you were beaten, abused, neglected. You needed the drugs back then to help you cope and forget. You think that was the good life? That's not the good life. That life was killing you. The good life is where you can live without fear. Where you can rest and be at peace without the drugs. Where you can breathe without the smoke. Where you can be healthy and whole, in body and mind and spirit. That is the real glorious life.

Moses brought you to this wilderness to heal you and make you whole, to teach you how to walk without the crutches. Why do you envy people still on those crutches? While you are here in this temporary place, learn how to walk without crutches. That is all you have to do. Let go of the crutches. Just walk. It's going to be tough for a while, but the place you are going to is so good. You just have to learn to walk.

I am going to leave Gene's story here for a moment. It illustrates how difficult it can be to leave our coping mechanisms behind when we enter this new life, and how easily we can forget the reality of the old life when we are focused on getting our crutches back.

Separating from the World

When we left Egypt, we left with the world's way of thinking and the world's definition of the good life. Now we are being asked to wrap our minds around this new way of thinking and new definition of glorious living. We had some coping strategies to deal with life when it got difficult in Egypt but those escapes are now being denied us. We are not going to live by the old way of coping anymore. We are being called to walk without the crutches.

As we separate from that old life, the old crowd often trails after us, trying to draw us back. That memory is kept alive by people from our old life that have remained on the periphery of our new life and are still in a position to influence us. For Gene, it was the conversations with his mom and dad that called to him and spurred his cravings and depression. It would be easier if there were some physical barrier to completely cut us off from that life, but there isn't. It's just a line in the sand and a boundary that the tongue crosses easily, as we have seen. The voices behind us call to us.

Coping mechanisms so carefully nurtured in Egypt come with us into this wilderness. They are habits now. Whenever life gets difficult, they become our go-to happy memories that make us forget our struggle.

This early challenge is going to involve learning how to come out from the world, out of the world's way of thinking and mixed-up priorities, and how to walk without crutches. The whole point of this journey is to make a formal break between the life we once lived in Egypt and the life we are going to experience in the Promised Land. The Lord is making a distinction between those two realities by bringing us through this momentary wilderness passage. He brings us to this empty place on purpose to show us something about ourselves. What we are using to try to fill the emptiness of this place reveals a lot about where our heart and mind are and how well we have grasped our identity in God and aligned ourselves with His vision and values.

Many of us are not going to survive this test. This will be the end of our progress in our relationship with God.

Five Tactics the Mixed Multitude Use to Get Us off the Path

In the midst of this internal struggle, the Enemy is going to use the mixed multitude to exert some external pressures on us to get us off the path. Five strategies play out in the dialogue of Numbers 11:4-6. The mixed multitude is going to:

1) Get us to identify with them as victims to undermine our identity with God
2) Get us focused on issues that mask the real problem

3) Present us a skewed comparison
4) Focus us on our freedom of choice and asserting our right of choice
5) Create a demand for their options

1) Identify with Them as Victims

All of us have been eating manna for a while now. It is the mixed multitude that have yielded first to the craving for more. They have cast themselves as victims, and we have sympathized with them because we understand their craving. We have it, too. Then we take up their complaint as if it were our own. In taking up their cause, we are now identifying with them instead of God. So we have lost some of our identity by scorning what the Lord has given us.

What is happening here is an intentional effort by the Enemy to uproot our identity with God.

There is a difference between being a victim and having a victim identity. Many people in this world are victimized in various ways. Some of them turn that victimization into a perpetual personal identity. We see this in groups like the LGBT movement and the Feminist movement. They class themselves in groups of people who are entitled to special treatment and consideration solely on the merit of being victims. This kind of identification with a victimized population takes away our individuality and returns us to a faceless, nameless group identity—completely opposite of what the Lord intended. They are no longer a people but a social cause. They have rooted themselves in that identity, and as a result, they can never stop being victims without losing their identity.

The victim identity is self-pity taken to an extreme. Beware of identifying with social causes based on a victim identity.

When you become a child of God and are rooted in an identity with Him, past victimization should no longer define who you are. We were all slaves—victims—in Egypt, but now the Lord has given us each a new identity as free men in Himself. He sees each person individually, judges each offense individually, and holds individuals responsible for their actions. Just because one authority is abusive and oppressive doesn't mean that all authorities are that way. Just because some men have victimized women does not mean that all men are evil and should be put under a woman's foot. That kind of polarized, absolutist thinking upsets the balance God intended in our relationships and makes us forget our own capacity for sin.

Lift your head! The world makes us out as victims for pursuing a relationship with God, but the validation and eternal reward we get from God will outstrip any validation the world will can offer. Worldly people think they can achieve validation by the number of people they have on their side. Yet no matter how many people join their cause, no matter how many laws get passed, even if the whole world is on their side, they will never feel satisfied or justified. To maintain their identity, they have to perpetuate their victimization.

That is what happens when we try to lift ourselves up instead of letting God lift us. If our validation comes from our own effort, then our life will become a continual fight to maintain our personal value, and we will end up sacrificing our peace and joy and rest. We will lose any taste we might have had of God's glorious living. You don't need numbers of people to lift you up.

Let God lift you up.

Don't get sucked into a victim mentality and a victim identity. We are not defined by our past injustices or present circumstances. These are temporary conditions.

When we walk this journey, we are going to be mixing with people who embrace and promote the victim identity. They may truly be victims, or they may be people who have sympathized with victims and joined their cause. As believers, we may understand and sympathize with their hurt, but we must stop short of joining them in that identity because it undermines our own identity in the Lord. Minister to victims, but work with victims as individuals in their specific circumstance. Help them, encourage them, seek justice for them if it is possible, but do not take on the victim identity. Seek to bring them *out* of it.

2) Focused on Issues That Mask the Real Problem

The rabble left Egypt for the promise of something even better in the Promised Land, but now find themselves entering a second year on a diet of manna and water. The shock and awe has worn off. This isn't the easy life they thought it would be. Because the promise wasn't realized immediately and there was no immediate gratification, they have become discontented and focused on the issue of the food.

The food isn't really the issue. The rabble have food the same as us, and it is good food. They have eaten the same manna with us, they have drunk from the same rock as us, the Lord has provided for them in the same way He provided for us. It is not that their needs aren't being met. It is not that they have been asked to go without food altogether, or indefinitely. They were just being asked to restrain their cravings for a period of time. If you are engaged in building a relationship with God, food should be a minor issue.

The food is the surface issue that masks the real problem. The *real* problem is that they don't want to have a relationship with our God. Their roots are in Egypt. Food is just an issue to rally around and start the retreat. That is the second part of the strategy of the mixed multitude. They get us embroiled in issues. Where the Lord lifted our heads and challenged us to see His greater vision, the multitude has us looking back down and focused on the weeds. They convince us that these external issues *are* the problems, when the real problem is their heart rebellion against God. If you are not focused on God's vision, mission, and the big picture, the rabble will have you sunk in a sea of issues.

Issues are real obstacles in the journey that we have to deal with. There really isn't any way of getting around them. They intrude into the camp, and we have to push back to maintain that boundary. We have to address the issues as they come to us.

The key to dealing with issues is to address them in a way that glorifies God. To do that, we have to be rooted in our identity with God, aligned with His position, and in control of our tongue. Be aware of words, but also the tone of voice or attitude that we argue with (easier said than done). Our tongues can cross those boundaries and defile us really quickly.

3) Present Us a Skewed Comparison

The rabble's next strategy is to offer us a skewed vision of our situation. They try to sway us by making comparisons between what God is offering at the moment (because these people only live for the moment) and what Egypt had to offer. They prey on our present difficulty and make it seem like this is going to be our reality for the rest of our lives. They convince us that we cannot live like this a moment longer. We are missing out on glorious living! Very subtly they begin to paint a twisted picture of Egypt and redefine God's definition of glorious living.

Eating and drinking are part of the world's definition of glorious living, not God's (Rom. 14:17). By getting us worked up over superficial concerns like eating and drinking, the world has robbed us of righteousness, peace and joy. Righteousness, peace, joy and eternal well-being—in whatever circumstances—are God's definition of glorious living. When we let the world skew our definition of glorious living, they rob us of the glory God has planned for us. They get us puffed up with this victim identity and convince us to take glory for ourselves by demanding our rights.

4) Focus on Freedom of Choice

The mixed multitude tries to convince us that a relationship with God takes away our freedom of choice. In their mind, freedom of choice is all about what we have and what we deserve. Having meat and melons, power and riches, are the world's idea of glorious living.

God is giving us manna. We've had manna day in and day out for over a year now, and we still have a couple more weeks to go. In Egypt we had variety. We had choices. We are individuals now. Isn't it every individual's right to have choices and to make their own decisions? This is a very tempting argument because it capitalizes on our sense of individuality and self-determinism. Let's poke some holes in that argument.

If freedom is defined by getting to pick what we eat, then yes, in that very limited sense, we had freedom and individuality in Egypt. But the obvious, overwhelming reality is that we were *slaves* in Egypt. We may have had a variety of food choices, but we didn't have a choice over how we lived, where we lived, what we did for work, how much we worked, how we were treated, or how we worshiped.

So what if we have freedom to choose what we eat? What does it matter when the rest of our lives is utter bondage?

So what if we eat manna for two more weeks? What does it matter if we are going to sit down to table abounding in every delightful thing for the rest of our lives?

Lift your head! God has given us the choice to live as slaves or free men. He has given us the option of settling for what we can get for a moment or reaping 100 times the benefit for the rest of our lives into eternity. All we have to do is walk. All we have to do is endure a brief period of abstinence. He is not asking us to go without. He is providing for us all the way. So what does it matter if, for fourteen months out of eternity, we have to live with these less-than-ideal conditions and limited choices?

Abstinence is a Choice

There is just as much freedom in choosing what *not* to have or abstaining from something for a period of time, as there is in choosing what *to* have. You can choose to pursue meat and melons and cucumbers and such things. You have the freedom to do that. You also have the freedom to choose to put those aside for a period of time to get the magnificent reward God has prepared for you down the road, a reward that will include all those things and so much more.

Remember the promise:

> *"But seek first the kingdom of God and His righteousness, and all these things shall be added to you." Matthew 6:33*

Making the choice to go without something for a period of time reveals a heart desire to be nearer to God. Choosing to submit our will to God's will reveals a desire to be like God. These are the lofty choices God asks us to make, and practicing abstinence is one of the choices that sets us apart from the world. It is one of the ways we maintain that boundary by drawing a line in the sand.

Remember Camp Rule #4, about the Nazirite vow? I think this is part of the reason this law is introduced here in Numbers, to counteract this twisted argument over choices. The Nazirite vow tells you that you have a choice to abstain from something that represents worldly pleasures and separate ourselves from those things to draw closer to God. Performing a Nazirite vow is a voluntary practice of self-control.

The principle and practice of abstinence is very much a part of New Testament doctrine. While on this journey we are to abstain from the lusts of the flesh (1 Pet. 2:11). We are to abstain from things polluted by idols, sexual immorality, and every form of evil (Acts 15:20; 1 Thessalonians 4:3, 5:22). We are even called to abstain from anything that causes a brother to stumble, be offended, or be made weak—even the things we know or believe to be good (Rom. 14:14-21).

Abstinence for a period of time is endurable. Abstinence for a lifetime can be a battle. For the children of Israel this journey was only supposed to last for fourteen months, but ended up lasting a lifetime. We as believers today are on the spiritual version of this journey, and it will last for the rest of our lifetime, but only if you think of a lifetime as a physical life ending in physical death. If you understand that a lifetime encompasses all of eternity, then this physical life that we live is a merely a breath.

5) Create Demands for Their Options

If we are not careful, we will be swayed by this skewed comparison between God and the world. If we do not keep our heads up, we will become focused on glorious living as the world defines it instead of the truly glorious living the Lord has planned for us. The mixed multitudes are going to try to push their options and convince us that we are giving up our freedom of choice to become slaves to this God of ours. And many of us are going to be convinced.

These are the options they are setting up for us: manna vs. meat-fish-cucumbers-melons-leeks-onions-and-garlic.

For every one thing the Lord has given us, the world makes it seem like there are seven better options. Those outside the camp live in a world of numbers where more is better. It is a skewed value system, and it is part of the skewed argument. But in reality, food is food, and food is not where our focus should be.

We live in a world that is very adept at creating demands for things. They have a way of redirecting our attention away from the necessary, need-to-have things, and get us focused on unnecessary want-to-have things. Marketing strategists have made an art of it. If you listen to them or watch their advertising long enough, they will convince you the unnecessary nice-to-have things in life are really need-to-have things. The want-to-haves become need-to-haves. Then the need-to-haves become right-to-haves. Next thing you know, we are way down the path to entitlement. Entitlement is driven by an over-inflated sense of self. It is self-glorification over a superficial issue.

The rabble are feeding our ego and puffing us up, while at the same time sucking us back into that world of numbers, peer pressure, and group conformity. So much for individuality. If we accept their argument, it will completely undermine our identity with God and rupture our relationship with Him. It's a very effective, but hellish strategy.

Final Thoughts on Enemy Tactics

These five main tactics manifest themselves in the conflict between those outside the camp and those inside the camp. The Enemy's goal is to uproot our identity with God and defile the camp body. If we are going to withstand this attack in a way that brings glory to God, we need to be thoroughly immersed in Him, in mind and heart, and in control of our tongues.

This challenge at Kibroth Hatta'avah is going to be a failure for us. It is going to give us a taste of the consequences that play out in the worst case scenario.

Next we are going to see Moses' reaction and the leadership meeting he has with God over what to do.

The Leadership Meeting (Numbers 11:10-15)

As we move on into Numbers 11:10-23, I want to step out of the shoes of the congregation and into Moses' shoes. For this section we are going to look at what is going on in camp from leadership's perspective. But first let's begin with what we know about Moses so far.

Moses is God's chosen leader of the children of Israel for this journey. He is God's representative to the people, the go-between. He is also the go-to man for hearing complaints, interceding, judging, giving direction, and coordinating camp life for 600,000+ people.

There is a lot of responsibility in this position, but also a lot of personal glory. Moses has been lifted up to a very high degree. Over a period of time, Moses has come to be seen as the great problem solver for the nation . . . but when his solutions don't meet expectations, he gets the blame. In reality the people have lifted Moses up to a position of authority and responsibility that the Lord never intended he should have to shoulder. This is one way we take glory away from God: by exalting others unduly.

Moses' Crutches

At the start of this study I talked about leaving old coping behaviors—those crutches—behind on this journey. It is worth noting that Moses has some crutches of his own. Crutches aren't just the feel-good things that comfort us. They can also be the people in our lives on whom we rely for advice and comfort. Moses' crutches were his Midianite mentors he left behind at Sinai.

Moses has had a long-running relationship with the Midianites. When he fled Egypt, he came to live with a Midianite priest Jethro (aka Reuel in Numbers 10:29) and eventually married his daughter Zipporah. When the congregation camped at Sinai, Jethro brought Zipporah and Moses' sons to the camp. While there, Jethro gave Moses some advice on organizing an administrative structure by appointing the leaders of 1,000's, 100's, 50's, and 10's to help Moses judge the people (Exo. 18:13-26).

Jethro's solution to managing the burden of responsibility reflects the world's way of thinking, that is, "by the numbers" and more is better. The world's solution is to create a gigantic bureaucracy to make the burden of responsibility manageable.

In the chart at the right, I crunched the numbers for what an administrative structure like this would entail for a mere 600,000-plus people. Once you add the (unnumbered) women and children there must have been far more than double that number. But a congregation of 600,000+ would require a minimum of 78,600 lawyers (because all of these men would have to be trained in the Law).

There is the world for you. Nothing much has changed today.

Moses got this advice from his Midianite father-in-law, and it helped him at the time (although it doesn't seem to be helping him at Kibroth Hatta'avah). So when the camp prepared to leave Sinai, it was Moses' desire to bring his Midianite mentors with him. I want to back track just a moment to Numbers 10:29-32 and look at this conversation Moses had with his brother-in-law, Hobab.

Moses tries to convince his brother-in-law, Hobab, to come with the camp, even promised him a share of all the good things in the Land if Hobab would be Moses' eyes on this journey. Interesting how quickly Moses turns to Hobab for direction on where to camp in the wilderness when Moses should be depending on the Lord's leading. If Moses had been allowed to depend on this mentor for the journey, how quickly we all would have wandered off the path! It is not clear whether Moses succeeded in convincing Hobab to come, but it is clear that the guidance Moses expected from him was never realized.

Rulers of 1,000s	600
Rulers of 100s	6,000
Rulers of 50s	12,000
Rulers of 10s	60,000
Total	**78,600**

This is a warning to us. When we get into trouble in life, our human mentors can become our go-to people for helping us solve problems instead of God helping us. It is a little scary to let go of that tangible human resource and trust in God. And yet God can solve situations in ways that no human mentor can. Be careful of becoming overly dependent on people in this way. They can have good intentions in counseling us, but they can also get us off the path.

When this difficulty arises at Kibroth Hatta'avah and Moses is once again struggling with the overburden of responsibility, his frustration level is going to be very high because he is learning how to cope without his crutches. I think this is why the tone of his conversation with God is a little stressed.

Moses' Complaints

In this moment, God is angry with our continued complaining. In the Hebrew, the phrase describes God flaring His nostrils and sucking in His breath. Moses is "displeased," which is also a tame translation. In the Hebrew the phrase means it was "evil to his eye." He sees their behavior for what it is: immature children behaving badly over something that should not be an issue. Moses identifies with God. Moses is trying to stay aligned with the will of the Lord at this point. He has the Spirit of the Lord in him, and yet, despite a strong relationship with the Lord and an indwelling Spirit, he still struggles with the frustration and difficulties of being the group problem-solver.

Even if we are aligned with God as best as we can be in this life, and even with the power of the Spirit helping us along the journey, we are still going to have to deal with expectations of people who are not aligned with God. This is another journey-long battle we have to deal with.

In the course of the leadership meeting, Moses lays a two-part complaint before the Lord. First is his struggle with bearing the responsibility of so many people in general.

I chuckle a little when I read this. When children are behaving badly, I can imagine one frustrated parent turning to the other and saying, "Did I ask for these children? These aren't my children. These must be your children. You deal with them."

Moses points out that he has been given a level of responsibility that he cannot bear alone. He lays the children of Israel at the Lord's feet because they are God's children, not Moses'. God is the one leading this endeavor. He is the one who made the promise to bring them into the Land. He, Moses, is not God and he wants out of that expectation.

Moses gets pretty sarcastic with God here. I don't know if I would have used this tone of voice with the LORD. But I think God grants him some grace because first, he does this in a private conversation with God and not in front of everyone. Secondly, he gives God glory in acknowledging this is God's responsibility. He gives God His rightful place in this instance. It is okay to wrestle with the Lord in private, so long as you do not forget who He is and who you are.

The second part of his complaint is his struggle to meet unrealistic expectations, specifically the cry for meat. The children of Israel have shown up on Moses' doorstep with this expectation over their physical craving for meat. The people have placed a humanly impossible demand on Moses, *and Moses has let them*. Instead of pointing them back to God, he has shouldered this role as being the camp problem-solver and go-to man, but it is more than he can handle.

Notice the emotions Moses is displaying in this moment. Anger. Frustration. Self-pity. He has succumbed to an attack of self-pity which he voices to God with complaining, resentment, and depression, to the point of wanting to die. All classic signs of misplaced glory. When glory that should belong to God is misplaced on someone else, it robs them of God's glorious living. That is what the children of Israel have done to Moses. Sadly, when faced with complaining, demanding, self-absorbed people, we ourselves often react with our own self-absorbed complaining and demanding.

This isn't the first time Moses has struggled with the children of Israel crying for meat. This same cry happened way back in Exodus 16:7-8, and I want to compare Moses' response then and his response now in Numbers 11:13-14.

> *"'And in the morning you shall see the glory of the LORD; for He hears your complaints against the LORD. But what are we, that you complain against us?' Also Moses said, 'This shall be seen when the LORD gives you meat to eat in the evening, and in the morning bread to the full; for the LORD hears your complaints which you make against Him. And what are we? Your complaints are not against us but against the LORD.'"* Exodus 16:7-8

> *"Where am I to get meat to give to all these people? For they weep all over me, saying, 'Give us meat, that we may eat.' I am not able to bear all these people alone, because the burden is too heavy for me. . . ."* Numbers 11:13-14a

Look at the difference in attitude. In Exodus, Moses makes no pretense of effort to solve the problem of meat for Israel. He points them to the Lord and says, in essence, "The Lord Himself will take care of you. This isn't our responsibility, and complaining to us isn't going to get you anything." That was the more correct response I think.

Here in Numbers, Moses has assumed that mantle of being the camp problem solver. Somehow, over the course of this journey, he has begun to lose perspective in his leadership role, and it has gotten him off his walk. This happens to the best of leaders.

When we get to the end of this lesson, I am going to revisit this example from leadership in dealing with unrealistic expectations and take it deeper into application for the spiritual journey.

Appointing the Seventy Elders (Numbers 11:16-34)

God lets Moses rant, listens and then responds to both parts of the complaint. He begins by addressing Moses' struggle to bear the responsibility of so many people by appointing the seventy elders. Then He takes the struggle of providing meat for all the people off of Moses and personally deals with their craving by sending quail. Let's talk about the seventy elders first.

The Seventy Elders

Remember, the world's solution to managing people is to create a gigantic bureaucracy with people well-versed in processes, laws, and ordinances. The inherent problem with this is that the quality and effectiveness of this solution really rests on the character of the men you pick for those positions. In spite of having 78,600 judges to help him, Moses is still struggling in this moment.

God's solution is much simpler. Appoint seventy Spirit-filled elders.

The solution is not in the numbers or in the knowledge of the laws and ordinances. The solution is in the Spirit. These men will be of a different nature altogether. I want us to take careful note of who these men are, where they are in camp, and what they are doing.

They are leaders within the tribes. That means their realm is in the main body of the camp, outside the ring of Levite tents that guard the Tabernacle compound. As a rule, the Levites are the only ones allowed to approach the Tabernacle. Not only do the elders approach the Tabernacle, but in verse 24 it says that Moses placed them around the Tabernacle.

These men are being called to cross a major boundary. They are stepping into the domain of the Levites. Just as the Levites were given to Aaron and the priesthood as helpers, these elders are being given to Moses. They are being called alongside the Levites in service. Any time you cross a boundary, it represents a change in status for better or worse. In this case, the elders are entering a more glorified status.

Moses positions them around the Tabernacle, then the Lord places the Spirit on them, and they begin to prophesy. Some translations say "and they never did so again" while others say "they did not cease." There is ambiguity in the Hebrew word, *yacaph*, which means to continue on in a particular state, either in a course of action or after a course of action is completed (to continue doing or not doing something). It is not clear in this case if they continued prophesying or continued on not prophesying. We know that in the spiritual journey parallel, there are select people given the gift of prophecy, and it is not just a once-and-done thing but a spiritual gift. I think if the Old Testament picture and New Testament understanding are meshed, perhaps the most consistent interpretation is one of not ceasing in prophesying.

Eldad and Medad

In verse 26, it is noted that two of the seventy have not come up to the Tabernacle. These two are the only ones out of the seventy that are named. In the book of Numbers there is a very consistent practice of recording of names of leadership, yet here the seventy elders remain unnamed except for these two. That distinction tells us something pivotal is happening.

Eldad and Medad are still in the camp. They are not where they ought to be, and they are doing something that just isn't done in camp. They are prophesying.

It is highly unusual for any of us to be called by Moses to the Tabernacle, and it is astounding to have anyone from the tribes be visited with the Spirit and prophesy. That is something reserved for highest realms of leadership. Yet in spite of the unprecedented nature of what is happening, we get a sense of an orderliness, restraint, and correctness in this act of commissioning of these elders.

Imagine being in the camp at this moment, watching the commissioning of elders, when suddenly someone next to you begins prophesying out of the blue.

This causes a stir in the camp and a very interesting reaction in Joshua.

Joshua's Reaction

This is the first time Joshua makes his appearance in the book of Numbers, but we know a little about him just from this verse. He is Moses' assistant, one of his choice men. Joshua is leadership in training under Moses and a junior member of that leadership circle. He hears of Eldad and Medad prophesying in camp and tells Moses, "Forbid them!" In the Hebrew that phrase means to shut up or restrain. Shut them up!

There is a parallel picture in Mark 9:38-40, where John, a disciple of Jesus, a choice man of His elite inner circle of leadership, has a reaction one day to seeing a lone man who is not a part of the approved group casting out demons in Jesus' name. John's response is to forbid the man to do such things.

John and Joshua have a problem with what these men are doing, because these men aren't where they are supposed to be. They are acting like disciples but aren't associating with the rest of the authorized group. They aren't acting under the supervision of the correct authority (so it seems), but acting independently, presumptuously, and without restraint.

Joshua and John want these men to be put in their place. You see, it all comes down to a sense of people in their places—of not crossing boundaries and not presuming to take authority or glory that doesn't belong to them.

This scenario brought some questions to my mind about the views we take of ministry even today. We can take the same stance as Joshua and John in creating boundaries for ministry that the Lord never intended. Does ministry only happen within church walls? Is ministry reserved only for those of the inner circle of a leadership team? Do you have to be part of a particular congregation or denomination to be approved for ministry?

I have seen many mature, well-meaning Christians over the years put up just such boundaries. Perhaps a better question is why we hold these views. Let's get past what Joshua's tongue is saying to where his heart is.

What heart attitude is spurring this response in Joshua?

Moses' response drives right to that point by asking Joshua if he is zealous for Moses' sake (v29). The word, zealous, is interchangeable with the word, jealous, in the Hebrew. Are you jealous for my sake? Moses' question is meant to prompt a bit of self-assessment in Joshua. Who am I to you? Do Eldad and Medad represent a threat to me?

Sometimes, it suits God's purpose to put people like Eldad and Medad in places they shouldn't be just to act as catalysts and cause a reaction in the people around them. That reaction is going to bring to the surface certain heart attitudes or ways of thinking that God wants corrected. These two out-of-place men have revealed the fact that Joshua has a wrong perspective of Moses. Moses holds a very high place in Joshua's estimation—too high. So high that Joshua sees the Holy Spirit at work in these men and yet thinks Moses has the authority and ability to override the work of the Holy Spirit of God. He sees Eldad and Medad are rivals to Moses, and that is why Joshua is jealous. In reality, Joshua has lifted Moses up as a rival to God.

Joshua has identified himself and aligned himself as a disciple of Moses, and begun to see his own place relative to Moses, not God. He has rooted his identity in Moses instead of God. God wanted us rooted in His identity so that our glory is tied to His glory, and a measure of His glory extends to us now. The same dynamic happens when we root ourselves in human leadership as Joshua did. The glory of that leadership becomes a reflection on our glory as disciples. So the threat that Eldad and Medad represent to Moses becomes a threat to Joshua as well.

Moses' Response

Joshua's words reveal a wrong heart attitude, and Moses needs to bring his perspective back into balance. There are a number of ways Moses could have responded to Joshua in this moment. The words he chooses are disciplinary but not critical of Joshua personally. Instead he turns Joshua's focus outward and upward (v29).

Whose people are they? The Lord's people.

Who is the one giving the Spirit? The Lord Himself.

What is the goal of this journey? For *all* God's people to be glorified.

Moses' response is a good model for us. There is no self-glorification in it. There is no criticism that tears down Joshua or harshly puts him in his place. It is a positive, gracious discipline that restores God to His place and His glory in Joshua's understanding.

Going back to our parallel picture with John and Jesus (Mark 9:40-41), we see Jesus' response is similar. What this man is doing doesn't take any honor or glory away from Jesus. It does not diminish or demean Him in any way. It does not matter that this man is not one of "the group." His ministry of casting out demons is aligned with God's will and is glorifying to God.

If we go out into this world and minister in a way that brings glory to God and aligns with His purpose, then our ministry is approved.

Where We Root Ourselves

Joshua has fallen into one of the pitfalls in the journey. He has rooted his identity in the wrong place. We should take a warning from this and be careful where we root our identity. Be rooted in a spiritual God and not in physical people, places or things because the physical things on this journey will come and go and continually change.

Don't root yourself in a physical place like a Tabernacle court or church building. Don't think that ministry only happens within church walls. Don't build unnecessary boundaries. God is at work in many ways and many places.

Don't root yourself in a human leader. Don't lift human leaders up as rivals to God's leadership. Human leaders, even strong ones like Moses, are just as susceptible to failure as we are. God uses all people, but He alone is sovereign.

Don't root yourself in a group identity such as a church denomination or ministry team. Churches rise and fall. Changes in leadership can take the congregation in a wrong direction. Congregations can split over doctrinal differences or because sin has corrupted them. Ministry teams may change their mission, vision, or values along the way. If we are rooted in a particular denomination or group, we may find ourselves being led down a path we shouldn't go. The Holy Spirit lives and works in every member of the Universal Church.

If we root ourselves in these physical things, we will lose our identity at some point on this journey.

Also, do not group people into categories of approved or unapproved workers based on their group affiliations. God works through individuals, and sometimes He purposely puts them in places we think they shouldn't be or has them do things that go against the norm.

Foreshadowing of the Day of Pentecost

Eldad and Medad never did go up to the Tabernacle to join the rest of the elders. Notice that Moses and the elders leave the Tabernacle and go out to the camp (v30). They join Eldad and Medad. In this there is a foreshadowing of the Day of Pentecost.

Note where we are on the physical timeline. We are somewhere at the end of the second month, perhaps the beginning of the third month. There is a feast of Israel in the third month called Shavuot that marks the giving of the Law at Sinai. At this point on the journey we are nearing our first anniversary of that event.

This feast is also the day of the giving of the Spirit in Acts 2, the day known as the Day of Pentecost. Here in the Numbers journey, with the anniversary of Shavuot imminent, Moses delivers these prophetic words:

> "...Oh, that all the LORD's people were prophets and that the LORD would put His Spirit upon them!" Numbers 11:29b

His statement is in the context of a group of men being called to the Tabernacle, having the Spirit of God put upon them and then being sent out from the Tabernacle to the greater population. What is being played out in the calling of the seventy elders is a picture of the Day of Pentecost and the beginning of the Church.

In the later fulfillment, we have disciples who are not of the priesthood being called, not by blood but by the Spirit, to serve not in a physical Temple but to minister to the greater body of people out in the world. The elders, and later the disciples, are a parallel of the priesthood.

God Deals with His People's Cravings (Numbers 11:18-20)

Having addressed Moses' need for help with congregational care, God now turns to deal with His people and their cravings. In the leadership meeting, God tells Moses He will handle this personally. All Moses has to do is deliver this message:

> "Then you shall say to the people, 'Consecrate yourselves for tomorrow, and you shall eat meat; for you have wept in the hearing of the LORD, saying, "Who will give us meat to eat? For it was well with us in Egypt." Therefore the LORD will give you meat, and you shall eat. You shall eat, not one day, nor two days, nor five days, nor ten days, nor twenty days, but for a whole month, until it comes out of your nostrils and becomes loathsome to you, because you have despised the LORD who is among you, and have wept before Him, saying, "Why did we ever come up out of Egypt?" ' " Numbers 11:18-20

All Moses has to do is deliver the message, and yet he argues. Even though the Lord has taken the responsibility off Moses, Moses is still in there trying to act as go-between and do something. When you go to God for help with people's unrealistic expectations, you should be prepared to step out of the picture and let God have the glory of dealing with the problem His way.

Let's look at God's message to the people piece by piece.

"Consecrate yourselves for tomorrow and you shall eat meat..." A sensitive conscience should recognize a note of warning in this. Consecrating ourselves is supposed to be an act of setting ourselves apart and making ourselves holy and clean so that we may receive a blessing. Set apart from what?

We should have been separating ourselves from the rabble outside the camp, but instead we have become one with them in this grievance over meat. So when the Lord tells us now, "consecrate yourselves," what else can we do? Some kind of outward cleaning like washing our bodies and clothes? Refrain from relations with a spouse for a night? Seriously, if we haven't performed the spiritual act of consecrating ourselves, what else can we do? We are anything but consecrated in this moment, yet we still expect the blessing.

Look at the blessing God proposes.

"You shall eat, not one day, nor two days, nor five days, nor ten days, nor twenty days, but for a whole month, until it comes out of your nostrils and becomes loathsome to you..." We will eat meat the way we ate manna—until we are sick of it. The manna was never really the problem. The problem is that we have been sucked into the rabble's argument and are now identified with Egypt again. We have despised the Lord and what He has given us (although we are more than ready to take the meat He is going to provide).

Tomorrow we will have meat. We have one night to think about it. There is still time to come to our senses and change how we act tomorrow. Fair warning.

Remember the first time we cried for meat? When we first came out of Egypt, we cried for meat and the Lord gave us quail and manna then, without any judgment attached to it. He is going to give us quail and manna again, but those who take the quail this time will suffer judgment for it.

Let's revisit Exodus 16:1-18 before we go through Numbers 11:31-34 and note the differences.

Exodus 16:1-18

In Exodus 16, we are newly started on this journey. We are taking our first steps of faith but haven't much of a history with God's faithfulness to go on yet. We have run out of provisions that we brought from Egypt, and there is little to be found in the Wilderness of Sin. So we cry for food and the Lord gives us food: quail in the evening and bread in the morning (Exo. 16:12-13).

Pay particular notice to where the quail are in relationship to the camp. The verses say the quail came up, that is, ascended, and covered the camp. They were inside the camp (Exo. 16:16, 18).

Every man gathered according to his need, which was one homer. We gathered in the morning and evening, sufficient for the day, and an extra portion on the day before the Sabbath.

Now, let's contrast this with what happens in Numbers.

Numbers 11:31-34

We have just passed the anniversary of when the Lord first began to give us manna, which happened on the fifteenth day of the second month, one year ago (Exo. 16:1). We have a history now of walking with the Lord for over a year and should have matured in our understanding of His faithfulness to us, yet our complaint is the same. We have wept before the Lord, crying for meat.

Numbers 11:21 tells us a wind went out from the Lord and brought quail from the sea. The sea to which we are closest is the finger of the Red Sea called the Gulf of Aqaba. That is east of us. That means the wind from the Lord is blowing from the east. In the Old Testament, the east wind is often a harbinger of judgment. In the dream Joseph interpreted for Pharaoh, the withered heads of grain signifying famine had been blighted by the east wind. The east wind also brought the locust plague on Egypt. It is our first warning sign.

Unlike the last time when the quail ascended, this time the quail come raining down. There is an echo of the plagues of Egypt and Noah's flood in the epic amounts of quail that fall—two cubits (three feet) deep, a day's journey on either side of the camp. This is a second warning sign.

Notice that they fall near the camp, not inside the camp like they did last time. What is the Lord telling us about the direction we are heading spiritually in pursuit of our cravings? We are heading outside the camp—into a place of defilement and death. This is a third warning sign.

We go out of camp and begin to gather for two days and a night. Each gathered at least gathered *ten* homers (v32). Then we brought them back and spread them out all over inside the camp. What have we just done? We've defiled ourselves and now the camp.

Verse 33 says while the meat was between our teeth, before it had even been chewed, the Lord strikes us with a plague. Some will look at this verse and ask if the Lord gave us the quail, why is He punishing us for taking it? If we are going to understand the Lord's response here, we need to look at James 4:1-4.

We already touched on James 3 in the last lesson at Taberah in regards to the tongue and complaining. The lesson in James is going to extend into this episode at Kibroth Hatta'avah. Consider this passage in the light of what is going on in camp at this moment.

> *"Where do wars and fights come from among you? Do they not come from your desires for pleasure that war in your members? You lust and do not have. You murder and covet and cannot obtain. You fight and war. Yet you do not have because you do not ask.*
>
> *"You ask and do not receive, because you ask amiss, that you may spend it on your pleasures. Adulterers and adulteresses! Do you not know that friendship with the world is enmity with God? Whoever therefore wants to be a friend of the world makes himself an enemy of God." James 4:1-4*

Some translations render verse 3 "you ask with wrong motives." The New King James Version renders it "you ask amiss." What does it mean to ask "amiss"?

The Greek behind the phrase "wrong motives" or "amiss" is an atypical use of the word *kakōs*, which is used most often throughout the New Testament to refer to people being sick, and it is often a sickness born of spiritual evil (Mark 1:34; Matthew 4:24, 8:16, 9:12, 14:35, 15:22, 21:41). In James 4:3, the cause of our contentions is a sickness within us that communicates itself in what we ask for and how we ask it.

Here in Numbers 11, our old cravings are a sickness within us, and it is a sickness that has communicated itself through our words—our mouths. Given free rein to pursue our lusts, we have shown ourselves to be friends with the rabble of this world and enemies to God. God very pointedly returns the sickness whence it came—into our mouths, while it is still on our tongues. He makes our hidden inner sickness outwardly apparent in the form of plague.

As a consequence of acting on our cravings, death has entered the camp body. Those who gave in to cravings have died, and so this place is given the name Kibroth Hatta'avah, the Graves of Craving.

Those who gave in to craving died, but they are not the only ones affected. Those who have the job of cleaning up their dead bodies become defiled in the process. Remember Camp Rule #1: if you are defiled by death, you get put outside of camp. So now a number of people have to be put out of camp and wait until a priest comes and cleanses them. We are going to be in need of continual washing throughout this journey because of repeated defilement, and not always on account of our own sin.

When a wealth of worldy goods is laid before us for the taking, a wise man considers what it will mean to his relationship with the Lord before indulging in them. Proverbs 23 reminds us to be careful when we sit down to eat in the presence of a king, and if you are person given to appetite, put a knife to your throat and do not desire his delicacies. Daniel and his friends remembered this and refrained from eating at Nebuchanezzar's table because they understood what it would mean to their relationship with God. Depending on the circumstances, it may be wiser to go to the opposite extreme and abstain entirely rather than let our appetites run away with us.

Conclusion to the Modern Day Scenario

Earlier in this lesson I gave you a modern-day coming-out-of-Egypt story about a boy named Gene who struggled to let go of the cravings from his old life when he came to live in Maggie's foster home. I want to share with you how that story turned out, because it goes hand-in-hand with what has played out here in Numbers.

> Gene's cravings continued to grow until he could not restrain them anymore. All he needed was opportunity and access. One day when he was at Wal-Mart with Maggie, he shoplifted a large quantity of drugs off the shelves and took them to school to share them with friends there. At school the next day, Gene took those drugs and overdosed. It nearly killed him.

> Gene disappeared from the neighborhood for a year. I thought he had been moved to another foster home and thought nothing of it. Only later when he came back to Maggie's house did I hear the whole story. He had spent some time "outside of camp." He had been in the hospital for a while, then in juvenile detention and rehab for a year. It was only by Maggie's grace that he was allowed to come back into her house at all when he finally got out.

> Those drugs were to Gene what the quail were to the children of Israel. They were his crutch and his craving, and when the opportunity presented itself, he gorged himself on them. They would have killed him, had it not been for God's grace. Gene's life began to turn around after that. He came out of his depression and began to live life differently. Maggie and I even got him to church a couple times. A year later, Gene graduated high school and left Maggie's place to go to college. I haven't heard from him since, but I remember this episode in his story like it was yesterday.

Now, a couple points for reflection and application.

The Practice of Self-Control and Abstinence

The mixed multitude lives life to extremes. You can become a slave to extreme living. Extreme living can lead us into addictions of which we cannot break ourselves. Extreme living can bind us in a way that we become very inflexible and that inflexibility can be a hindrance to the work the Lord gives us to do. Here are some examples:

- We can be an excessive savers (misers) with our earthly wealth, which prevents us from giving to those in need.
- We can be an excessive spender and get ourselves in debt, which likewise prevents us from giving and limits our options for ministry.
- We can pursue something we need in life like food, drink, or medicine, to the point of obsession and addiction.
- We can have extreme character traits. Moses was exceedingly humble, which was not a bad thing at all, but because he shied away from speaking out, his brother Aaron had to assume the role in his stead. We can be exceedingly shy or exceedingly aggressive. Both extremes can be a hindrance and bondage, and need moderating if we are going to have good balance in our life and relationships.

The Corinthian church was plagued by extremes which caused strife in the congregation. Some congregants felt that only vegetables should be eaten while others said there were no boundaries whatsoever to what food was allowed, even food given to idols. Paul called the Corinthian church to moderation and sensitivity to conscience in their relationship to God. We are all called to this kind of self-examination and to identify extremes in our life that need balancing.

If we have identified something in ourselves that is an unhealthy extreme, how do we moderate that in our life? Sometimes simply going to an opposite extreme can help re-establish balance in our lives. A period of abstinence may be needed to break a behavior. Permanent abstinence may be needed in dealing with addictions.

Sometimes going to an opposite extreme can help break you out of that rut. Common examples of going to alternate extremes are:

- If we are overeaters, we go on a diet.

- If we are shopaholics, we cut up the credit cards.
- If we are penny-pinchers to the extreme, maybe we force ourselves to give to a charity.
- If we are extremely shy, we enroll in a public speaking class.

Countering an extreme with an extreme can be helpful in bringing us back into balance, but it can also backfire on us.

Why Abstinence Fails

Abstinence fails when we treat it as a punishment instead of an agent for change or a way of separating ourselves to God's purpose. What happens so often is that we yo-yo back and forth between extremes. We over-indulge and then punish ourselves with complete abstinence. Abstinence may restrain the habit for a period of time, but the minute the abstinence is broken, the behavior comes back with a vengeance.

Severe abstinence—especially from things that are good or necessary—can produce severe craving beyond what you can control. We see this in the command concerning husbands and wives abstaining from relationship only for a period of time so that they should not be tempted to defile themselves with sexual immorality (1 Cor. 7:5).

Abstinence must be kept in balance. Separating ourselves from worldly things can be taken to unhealthy extremes. It can make us overly focused on self to the exclusion of others. Roman Catholicism tried this idea of separating oneself from worldly pleasures by calling people to be celibate monks and nuns, housing them in monasteries and cloisters, and yet sin was often rampant in these places.

Abstinence that is only for outward show and not inward heart change is useless. If not done with the right motive, it becomes a means of self-glorification.

In the practice of self-control, abstinence represents one extreme that we can exercise of our free will. But what happens when God sends you to extremes?

When God Sends You to Extremes

Sometimes God sends us to extremes in life. This journey that we are on, in itself, is a study in extremes. We left bountiful Egypt for a barren wilderness. We have left slavery under a foreign master to be free men under God. We have left the fruitfulness we had by our own works for the promise of fruitfulness that the Lord will give us, if we will only endure a brief period of what seems to us a fruitless wandering. God responds to our craving by giving us a glut of food to make our lack of self-control that much more evident. God is taking us from extreme to extreme for a purpose.

Experiencing different extremes can bring this journey into perspective.

When we have been given prosperity in life, only to have a change of fortune and find ourselves in need, that experience gives us perspective on life. If we have come through a life-threatening illness, that experience changes us. If, by the blessing of the Lord, we are restored to health and prosperity, we tend to live our life with different priorities.

The point is to learn how to be content in the place where He has put us, and how to live for God's glory regardless of which extreme we are in, as Paul tells us,

> *"Not that I speak in regard to need, for I have learned in whatever state I am, to be content: I know how to be abased, and I know how to abound. Everywhere and in all things I have learned both to be full and to be hungry, both to abound and to suffer need. I can do all things through Christ who strengthens me." Philippians 4:11-13*

Lessons from Leadership: Meeting Other People's Expectations

Meeting other people's expectations isn't limited to those in a leadership role like Moses. It affects all of us to a greater or lesser degree. We are bombarded daily with other people's expectations. Husbands, parents, children, bosses, co-workers, mentors, friends, and the church body in general—all people have expectations of us.

The most demanding expectations come from people who depend on us for basic needs like being fed and clothed, taken to the doctor or school or church, or even being loved. There are expectations over how we manage our relationships.

These can include:

- How much time we are expected to spend on various relationships
- How much attention we are expected to give to various pursuits in our lives
- How much influence or authority parents or bosses expect to have over the direction of our lives, and how we balance that with the expectations of our husband or wife.

Some are big expectations that people place on us like:

- How we live our lives and our lifestyle choices
- How we conduct our business
- What world-view we embrace
- How we fit into social conventions

Then there is the greatest set of expectations, and that is what the Lord expects of us, which is pretty much the responsibility to keep all the other expectations in their correct place and priority according to what He has given us to do.

Not all expectations are bad or out of alignment with God's expectations of us. We are expected to care for ourselves, our children, our spouses, our home, maybe even our aging parents, and to plan for their future care. But . . .

Expectations can be unrealistic. They can demand more resources than we are able to give physically, mentally, or emotionally. They can demand more time of us than there are hours in a day, and more money than we can hope to see in a lifetime.

Expectations can be out of place. A relationship can exceed its natural boundaries of authority or influence. People may lift you up beyond the role God meant for you, like the children of Israel—even Joshua—did to Moses. People may idolize leadership the way Joshua did Moses. A relationship can assume a greater priority than it should, and create conflict.

Authorities may be competing in our lives. When we have competing authorities (parents vs husband, boss vs family), meeting their expectations can cause conflict. The expectations of a husband can conflict with the expectations of children. The husband is the greater authority, but the child is the dependent. The expectations of a job can overrule family expectations, but the job is needed to support the family. Parents can try to retain a level of authority and direction over their children even after those children have married and started their own lives. Society in general has come to expect a certain "correctness" and alignment with a world-view that often conflicts with God's expectation of us and His world-view. All these expectations war with our own personal expectation of the kind of person we should be and the life that we should live.

Trying to meet unrealistic or wrongly-placed expectations robs us of glorious living. We get twisted around into thinking that if we can just meet these expectations, we will have rest and joy and peace and well-being, and that is one of the most insidious lies that Satan uses through this fallen world to derail us from the journey.

As we see with Moses, insisting on managing these things on our own can keep us from giving glory to God and giving God His proper place in our lives.

The Enemy's Strategy

The Enemy's strategy is two-fold in this dynamic.

First, he tries to warp our own expectations of ourselves. He gets us to embrace the unrealistic expectations and be the problem-solver or person with all the answers. In consequence, we get swamped by our own weakness and overwhelmed by the burden of responsibility. We react with distress, anger, resentment, complaining, self-pity, and depression.

Next, he gets us embroiled in conflicts by misplaced expectations. Our sense of priorities and boundaries get screwed up, and we lose perspective of our own place in these relationships. We accept blame for things that we never had control over. We allow others more authority over us than they should have, to lift us up or put us down.

We know when these things are happening. We recognize when an expectation is beyond our ability to meet. We know when relationship boundaries have been exceeded and are out of balance. We know when people have lifted us up to a level of responsibility that we were never supposed to have, or when they put us down wrongly.

When we find ourselves acting out with distress, anger, resentment, complaining, self-pity, and depression, we should recognize these as signs that relationships are out of balance, and an assessment of the situation is needed. Sometimes a godly counselor or a mentor can help identify where the problem is coming from so that you can deal with it.

What We Need to Do

When we see our life is out of balance, that those boundaries need to be re-established and expectations reined in, there are a couple things we need to do.

When dealing with unrealistic expectations, we need to take those to God. We need to confess to Him our own weakness and inability to meet these needs. When we go to Him with those requests we are giving Him glory and acknowledging His preeminence in our lives. That is a good thing.

We may need to have a conversation with the people who are making the demands. We may redirect these people back to God as the only one who can meet their needs, and then we step out of the mix and let God have the glory of working in their lives. That is what Moses did in Exodus but what he failed to do the second time around in Numbers. We saw the difference it made in his life. Identify the source of the expectations, point them to God, and then step down. Determine in our hearts to be at peace with His handling of the situation, even when it is not the result we were hoping for.

When dealing with expectations that are out of place, re-establishing boundaries can be tough because it often causes explosive conflict. People often react to the word "no" in anger or crying or some form of extreme emotion, especially if we are dealing with a self-centered person who is not aligned with God or filled with the Spirit, but bent on serving their own lusts. A person who has assumed an inappropriate authority or priority in our lives will fight before relinquishing it. They may use guilt. They may use threats. A boss may fire us. There is a lot of backlash when we set out to correct the balance of our life. Be prepared for their reaction.

Be firm in our understanding of God's expectations of us and our place in His camp. Ask Him for His help and intervention and trust in Him to help us through this battle. He may come up with a solution we would never have imagined.

Why We Don't Deal with the Issue

Let's face it, the whole point of trying to meet expectations is to avoid the conflict. It is easier to give in than confront. But that is a lie we tell ourselves, isn't it? We avoid the confrontation with someone else by internalizing it, but the conflict raging inside us eventually brings us to the point of breaking.

The dread of confrontation makes re-establishing boundaries very hard to do, but there is a second reason. We don't want to give up the glory of being lifted up by others. There is a lot of glory in being known as the go-to person, the intercessor, the person in demand, and great problem solver. It's a humbling thing to step down from that position and admit you don't have the answers or know the right path to take. If our identity has become rooted in that role and its status, it is going to be very hard to give it up. It is our own ego that often keeps us in the conflict and in that tyranny of blurred priorities and unrealistic expectations. We become slaves to ego.

Our own ego sets us up in rivalry to God and robs us of the joy and peace and well-being we could otherwise be experiencing by giving that glory back to God.

We have been talking about how expectations can be out of place and can cause conflict. We have seen how people who are out of place can act as catalysts to reveal attitudes that God wants corrected. In the next lesson, we are going to see how this dynamic plays out in a family conflict between Miriam, Aaron and Moses.

LESSON FIVE

Hazeroth

CHAPTER 12

So far we have been through two places that were given names that reflect the nature of our particular failing there. Taberah was the "burning" where the Lord burned among us for our complaining. Kibroth Hatta'avah was the "graves of craving" where we buried those who gave into cravings. Hazeroth also is a particularly appropriate name for the conflict that plays out here, so let's look at this name for a moment.

The Hebrew word, Hazeroth (Chatseroth), is the feminine plural form of the word *chatser* which means court or enclosure—something with a fence of sorts around it. It is possible that Hazeroth was a small village or settlement that the children of Israel came to, although no mention is made of who its inhabitants were.

Chatser is used most often in the Old Testament when describing the courtyard of the Tabernacle or the Temple, particularly the place where trumpets are blown for worship and praise of the Lord.

Here at this place, trouble is going to break out within the inner court, among the leadership of that inner court, and that trouble will come from a decidedly feminine quarter. It will center around one woman who has decided to lift herself up and blow her own horn in a place where she should have been humbling herself and giving glory to God.

Miriam

Here in Numbers 12 we see a family squabble in the inner court among Miriam, Aaron and Moses. The key figure in this incident is Miriam. What do we know about Miriam?

She is Moses' older sister (Exo. 2:4). After his mother hid Moses in that basket and set him among the rushes, Miriam stood and kept watch over him to see what would happen to him. When Pharaoh's daughter finds Moses in the basket, Miriam is on hand offering to find him a nurse and facilitating his temporary restoration to his mother. She is the older sister, ever on guard, ever watchful, quick to assess the situation, ready to take initiative and even some risks for this little brother of hers. She has perhaps assumed a certain amount of authority and responsibility over Moses' life, as big sisters tend to.

She is a prophetess endowed with a gift of song. She is distinguished in particular for "Miriam's song" (Exo. 15:20-21), leading the women with timbrels as they danced and sang this song of glory to God after the defeat of Egypt's armies. How appropriate that such a woman be found in the courts of the Lord, singing and giving praise to Him!

Where is Miriam's physical place in the camp? There is no mention of Miriam ever marrying in the Scripture, so we will assume she is unmarried.[1] As an unmarried woman, she has remained in the household of her older brother, Aaron. That means she sits at the table with the priesthood, eating of the priestly portions of the sacrifices, grain, and drink offerings. Her place in the camp is one of great status but only by blood association with the High Priest, because she is not under a marriage covenant. If she should marry another Levite outside the priesthood, she would still be in the family, but she would lose some status. If she should marry outside the Levite tribe, she would lose her exalted place altogether. Miriam is a woman who is very conscious of her place, as we will see.

Miriam is mentioned in Exodus a couple of times, but nothing more is said of her until here in the book of Numbers. She has an intimate family relationship with Aaron and Moses, and yet always out of the limelight of her famous brothers. She had an early hand in directing Moses' life, but that is no longer her role and now she has withdrawn into the periphery of his life.

In Exodus she is dancing and drawing women to join her in singing praise to God for His glorious works. Here in Numbers she is trashing Moses and his wife, and she has gotten Aaron to join her.

What has happened? How is it that out of the same mouth comes both blessing and cursing, worship and backbiting? It happened to Miriam, and it happens to us, too.

Miriam's issue with Moses (Numbers 12:1-3)

Numbers 12 opens with Miriam's grievance over Moses marrying an

---

[1] Jewish tradition (Babylonian Talmud, Sotah 12a) that she was married to Caleb but there is no support for that within the Scriptural text. There is no mention of husband or children or a lineage that springs from her line.

Ethiopian woman, and then segues almost immediately into an attack on Moses himself for having assumed a place and authority in the family that he shouldn't. I think her issue with Moses' wife and Moses himself are two instances of the same basic grievance about people knowing their place.

I don't know if this wife of Moses was Zipporah or not. Zipporah was a Midianite, and the Midianites lived along the eastern side of the Red Sea whereas the Ethiopians or Cushites live on the western side of the Red Sea in Africa, south of Egypt. Moses may have taken another wife, in addition to Zipporah or after she died. If so, this is the only place she is ever mentioned, and she remains unnamed. Instead the text focuses on the fact that she is an Ethiopian.

Ethiopians are Gentiles. Where in the camp are Gentiles supposed to stay? Outside the camp.

Where in the camp is this Ethiopian woman as a result of her marriage covenant with Moses? She is inside the camp, and not just inside the camp but inside the Levite family circle.

There is no ban for the Hebrew people against intermarrying with other nations, with the exception of nations that dwell in the land of Canaan.[2] There is no ban for a Levite against marrying a foreigner. In God's eyes, there is nothing wrong with this. Foreign wives are given the same provision as the Levite himself because they fall under the canopy of the marriage covenant. That means they sit at the Levite family table and partake of the food provided for the Levites, which are the tithe offerings described in Numbers 18.

So this Ethiopian woman has attained a very exalted status for a Gentile woman, and this rankles Miriam and Aaron. In their eyes, Gentiles have no place in the camp of Israel, and most certainly not within the inner court where only Levites were allowed to enter. Moses should have kept this Ethiopian woman in her place outside the camp; because he married her, she now sits at the family table. Moses has given her a preeminence even above the other Israelites and made her equal with Miriam. This woman is out of her place.

The Issue Hiding the Real Problem

In reality, Moses' marriage is just a surface issue. Miriam's real problem is

---

2   Deuteronomy 21:10-14 allows for the marrying women who have been taken captive in war, but Deuteronomy 7:3 sets a ban on intermarriage with the specific nations that the Lord is driving out of the Land.

with Moses having overstepped his place (as Miriam sees it) which we will read in the next verse. The Ethiopian woman is just Miriam's opportunity to launch her actual grievance with Moses.

We all do this from time to time. Little irritations can happen on a daily basis, but if we are already angry over something, then the little irritation gets added to the greater anger and causes it to bubble over.

It's like finding that red sock in a tub of white laundry. On any normal day, it is irritating to open the washer and find that a stray red sock has turned a tub of white laundry an odd shade of pink. It just makes more work because you have to rewash everything. But on this day, if the person who put that tub on to wash was your spouse, and if you are already harboring grievances against him or her over other issues of carelessness, then that red sock in the wash becomes an opening for starting World War III.

This out-of-place Ethiopian woman is the red sock in Miriam's white laundry. She is Miriam's excuse and opening for starting the conflict with Moses.

Remember, sin in our life seeks an opening. Given the opportunity, the Enemy is going to use that opening to get you off track in this journey.

It isn't just about Moses' wife, although she is an easy target. For Miriam it is really about bringing Moses down a peg and putting him in his place, and she enlists Aaron's support in this. They are, after all, the highest leadership within the Levites, so naturally they would be the ones to bring the grievance into the open. Of anyone, they would be the ones with enough natural right and authority over Moses as his older siblings to set him straight.

This becomes an act of putting someone in their place. How do we put someone in their place? Most often we use our tongue.

- We undermine their standing among their peers, or speak of them in a way that puts them in a bad light.

- We devalue them. We make them seem common, replaceable, or expendable.

- We harp on what we consider to be their bad choices in life, like a poor choice of spouse.

The Skewed Comparison

Miriam the prophetess and Aaron the priest looked at Moses and said, "God may speak through Moses, but God speaks through us as well." If God speaks through us as well, then what makes Moses any different from us? Carry that thought a little farther and we could say "We are equal to Moses in this respect, so why not in every other respect?"

That is a skewed comparison, isn't it? They make it seem like the only reason for Moses being lifted up is because God speaks through him.

Miriam and Aaron see that the Lord has given Moses more honor than themselves, yet they have not perceived the reason why. There is a presumption of equality based on gifts alone and not on the character of the man himself.

Sometimes, it is not the most gifted person or the person with the most important connections who is right for the job. Sometimes, the main reason that God chooses a person for a particular role or ministry is based on who they are in their character and their understanding of Him.

God picked Moses for his humility (v3). When we read this parenthetical verse, it may seem like an out-of-place comment in the narrative, but it brings into focus this issue of being chosen for one's character as opposed to one's works.

In the world's eyes, humility is a weakness, especially in leadership. Humility is unworthy of the truly great and powerful. If honor is given to you, then take that honor and wear it on your sleeve for all the world to see. Glory in your own honor, and do not dirty yourself with what is defiled or common. Guard your associations, and if you are a prominent Levite, definitely do not stoop to marry an Ethiopian Gentile. That's how the world sees humility. That's how Miriam and Aaron see Moses.

In God's eyes, humility is a strength and a very valuable trait in any person. Humility puts others first, and seeks to give glory to others instead of taking it for oneself. Humility allows God to reveal His glory and be the glorious one among His people.

God glories in being the one to lift a person up. It is a way He reckons His glory. But He can't lift up a person up who is exalting himself. Any honor God would have given Aaron and Miriam at this point could have been credited to their own efforts in putting Moses down and would have devalued God.

God is sovereign. He does not share His glory.

The irony is that, humble man as he was, Moses would have probably shown Miriam and Aaron a great deal of honor and preference without their having to trash him like they did. And perhaps that was part of the problem. It wasn't honor from Moses that they wanted. They wanted to be honored by the same person who honored Moses—God. In this world, it matters who gets the glory, but also who gives the glory. A person can get a landslide of praise in life from colleagues, friends, or family, but if they were looking for praise from one particular person and do not get it, then they count all the rest as nothing.

Miriam and Aaron are so lacking in their understand of the Lord that they fail to see 1) why God chose Moses in the first place, 2) the depth of loyalty the Lord feels toward this faithful, humble man, and 3) the particular delight God takes in lifting up those who are downtrodden for His sake. The whole point of this journey was to learn about God, and in this they have failed.

When you offer criticism of people, never forget that the Lord is listening. Never underestimate the consequences of tearing down someone whom the Lord stands behind, and never forget this proverb:

> *"Do not exalt yourself in the presence of the king, and do not stand in the place of the great; for it is better that he say to you, 'Come up here,' than that you should be put lower in the presence of the prince, whom your eyes have seen." Proverbs 25:6-7*

God is the king, and Moses is the prince. Aaron and Miriam have exalted themselves above God's prince, and God is going to put them in their place. It is going to be a place lower than Moses, and He is going to do it right in front of Moses.

God's Judgment (Numbers 12:4-10)

No sooner do these words come out of Miriam and Aaron's mouths than they are summoned by the Lord. All three of them: Moses, Aaron and Miriam. Then, of the three, Aaron and Miriam are called forward for some face-to-face with God (v4). What an honor, to be called forward by name by God Himself! This is just the honor they felt they deserved.

Miriam and Aaron have counted themselves as equal to Moses, so God says, "Okay, I speak face-to-face with Moses, so let's see how well you like face-to-face interaction with Me." And in verses 6-8 He masterfully dismantles their argument.

"If there is a prophet among you . . ." Remember there are now 70 Spirit-filled elders who have prophesied throughout the camp. Miriam and Aaron aren't so special in that respect as they make themselves out to be.

"I, the LORD, make Myself known to him in a vision. I speak to him in a dream . . ." I, God, am the one who initiates the relationship and gives the gift for My own purpose. The gift is not by your own power or merit. You are nothing

apart from Me. Just because you are a prophet doesn't mean you see clearly or understand at all. You speak words which you yourself do not understand, whose meaning is hidden from you. You think you see clearly, but in fact you are like one who sleeps.

It is interesting that Miriam was a prophetess, and yet she did not see the prophetic picture in a Gentile being given a place at the priestly table.

"Not so with My servant Moses; He is faithful in all My house." God is making a comparison of His own here. Moses is faithful, in comparison to Miriam and Aaron. He is implying that what they have done is an act of unfaithfulness to God. But they are also being unfaithful to their brother—which, according to Camp Rule #2, is counted as unfaithfulness to God. Miriam and Aaron think Moses' place is attained by works, when that place is really attained by faithfulness apart from works.

"I speak with him face to face, even plainly and not in dark sayings; and he sees the form of the LORD." Moses, by comparison, sees Me correctly. Moses is faithful to Me, he understands My character, therefore he as been honored with a closer relationship with Me, closer even than the exalted status the two of you hold among the priesthood.

"Why then were you not afraid to speak against My servant Moses?" God responds to their bid for glory in a very pointed way. Instead of breaking out against them, God turns His back on them and departs. He shuns them in a very public way, and it's not quite the reaction they were expecting and most certainly not the acknowledgment they were hoping for.

Remember Camp Rule #3, the passage about the Aaronic blessing (chapter 6)? When God lifts you up, He turns His face toward you. When He is displeased, He turns His face away, which is His rejection. The priesthood were meant to be the ones who delivered that message of God's love to the people in that Aaronic blessing. How can you be a conduit of God's love when the Lord has turned His face from you? You cannot deliver the blessing without loving the people God has blessed. Miriam and Aaron have failed to love their brother and for Aaron in particular, it has hindered his ministry.

Between Aaron and Miriam, it appears the Lord has singled Miriam out as being the instigator. In the wake of His departure, Miriam has become leprous. Her tongue has revealed the corruption in her, which has become contagious and spread to Aaron. The Lord has made that sickness visible on the outside. Most pointedly, He has afflicted her with a specific sickness that affects her place in the camp.

Where did this conflict begin? With Miriam's criticism of Moses bringing an outsider into the family. The Ethiopian woman should have kept in her place outside the camp.

So where is God sending Miriam as a punishment? Outside the camp.

The Lord's judgment on Miriam is absolutely on point. Miriam set herself up as the judge of other people's place, and the Lord is now going to challenge Miriam's understanding of her own place. Her place is now outside the camp. As punishment, God has done to Miriam what she desired in her heart to do to another. And she is not just to be sent outside the camp temporarily, but permanently. Leprosy isn't something you recover from. She is now one of the living dead.

Responses to Conviction or Lack of It (Numbers 12:11-14)

Aaron's Response

Remember Camp Rule #2. Sin against a brother is equal to unfaithfulness to God. First go make up with your brother. Confess your sin. Seek forgiveness. Intercede for each other. Aaron's response follows Camp Rule #2 by the book.

The sin was against Moses, and the sin was a lack of respect. Aaron begins by addressing Moses as "my lord," the Hebrew word *adon*, meaning master of servants. Aaron humbles himself as a servant to Moses, and then he asks Moses not to lay this sin on them (meaning the penalty for this sin). He doesn't ask God to forgive them, but asks *Moses*, as if Moses' forgiveness is necessary to lift the Lord's judgment and take away the curse of death on Miriam. Interesting that he attributes that level of power to Moses.

Do we ever consider the spiritual power of forgiveness when it comes to healing a person and reconciling a person's relationship to God?

Moses' Response

Moses, humble man that he is, godly man that he is, has understood this nature of God. He himself had a bout of leprosy back in Exodus 4 when he balked at what the Lord had asked him to do (Exo. 4:6-7). He knows that the Lord can afflict with leprosy, but He can also restore a leper. He does not hesitate to speak on behalf of his sister. "Please heal her!"

How many of us would be that forgiving after receiving this kind of unfair criticism or personal attack on ourselves or a spouse?

Miriam's Response

We have heard from Aaron. We have heard from Moses. We hear nothing from Miriam. There is no confession, no acknowledgment of Moses, and no humbling of self. There is still rebellion in Miriam's heart. It runs very deep, and the Lord knows it.

God's Response

God does not deny Moses' request, but neither does He let Miriam off the hook.

Miriam is exiled for a period of time, and her exile is a very public shaming. She is put out of the camp and away from the family table. Everyone in the camp watches as she makes her way out of the camp to take her place with the lepers. They are going to want to know all the gory details of how she came to have leprosy, and she will undoubtedly suffer the lash of some wagging tongues. On top of all that, God deliberately delays the journey until Miriam is brought in again (v15). Everyone is forced to wait another week in this hot, miserable wilderness for her release.

Her sin has impacted the entire camp, and I am sure she felt the full weight of it. Usually when you have puffed yourself up to this extent, a judgment like this can really take the wind out of you.

Outside the Camp

I wonder if spending some time outside the camp spurred Miriam to reflect on what was needed for her own sanctification. For one week she was cut off from family, and the only sight she might have gotten of them was when the priests brought the sin sacrifices outside the camp to be burned and to cleanse people. For seven days, she was confronted over and over by the dirty and distasteful side of the sin sacrifice, the reproach of it, and the rawness of it.

Miriam counted her own glory in being associated with the High Priest and being allowed to sit at the table in cleanness and holiness, and partake of the sacrifices. She identified with the glorification and benefits that came as a result of the sacrificial system, but she did not appreciate the reproach and cost associated with that sin sacrifice. She did not identify with its death in being burned outside of camp.

Somewhere along the road, she evidently forgot that her sanctification and her place at that table only came as a result of a sin sacrifice that had to be facilitated outside the camp to make her clean. Not from her gifts or works. Not by her blood ties to the priesthood through Aaron.

Day after day the priests would come to release others to return to the camp, but Miriam had to wait until her days of exile were fulfilled. It would be that by the end of that week, Miriam ached for that sin sacrifice to be offered on her own behalf, to atone for her uncleanness. Part of the Lord's lesson was to teach Miriam to give up the glory and suffer reproach before she could come back to the table.

Camp Rule #1: we all end up outside the camp at some point.

Nothing else is said of Miriam in the journey until her death in Numbers 20. She returns to camp, and goes through the rest of the journey with us, all forty years of wandering, only to die in that wilderness. She is not going to enter into the Land or that reward of glorious living.

Leprosy in the Old Testament

Leprosy is not the dread disease today as it was back in Old Testament times. The Lord has given us the knowledge of medications to deal with it now. But in Old Testament times when the Lord dealt with His people in a very hands-on way, leprosy was understood to be one of the tools God used to deal with a particular kind of sin in a person. This kind of sin tends to be very deep-rooted and pervasive, almost to the point of being a character flaw. Its source is difficult to detect and diagnose.

Leprosy as a punishment was a sign that we had a corruption inside us (or even within our house, that is, our extended family) that we needed to deal with. It was a corruption inside us that would otherwise go unchecked and lead to our death. He would, in essence, make our inner corruption evident with an outward manifestation of corruption. The death that was taking over in our heart would also overrun our flesh. It was a living death and 100% fatal without intervention.

Leprosy in the Old Testament is punishment meted out for overstepping our place or presuming an authority that we have not been given. In addition to this example of Miriam, there is King Uzziah who enters the Temple and offers incense like a priest and is struck with leprosy (2 Chr. 26:19). There is Elijah's servant Gehazi who tried to take payment for the healing the Lord gave to Naaman the Syrian and was struck with Naaman's leprosy as a consequence (2 Kin. 5:27). Leprosy is also a punishment visited on the house of Joab for his murdering Abner out of personal vengeance (2 Sam. 3:28-29). Joab's motives and actions were misplaced and overstepped his authority, and as a result, David curses his house with leprosy.

The Leprosy of the Old Man

I did some research on leprosy which I have summarized here.

Leprosy is a disfiguring, infectious disease that primarily affects the skin and the nerves. It may also strike the eyes and the nose. The main symptom is pale-colored skin sores and nerve damage. Nerve damage can lead to loss of feeling in the arms and legs and muscle weakness. This nerve damage eventually leads to a dangerous loss of sensation, such that a person with leprosy may not feel pain when the extremities are cut, burned, or otherwise injured.

The results of leprosy are blindness, weakness, disfigurement and loss of a sense of pain to the point that you could mortally wound yourself and not know it. Leprosy is hard to detect and may be thoroughly entrenched before the symptoms come to the surface.

Add to these the spiritual elements of uncleanness and being sent out of camp to join the realm of Gentiles, the unclean, and those defiled by death, and what we have is a picture of our "old man" nature that Paul describes in Ephesians 4.

> *"This I say, therefore, and testify in the Lord, that you should no longer walk as the rest of the Gentiles walk, in the futility of their mind, having their understanding darkened, being alienated from the life of God, because of the ignorance that is in them, because of the blindness of their heart; who, being past feeling, have given themselves over to lewdness, to work all uncleanness with greediness."*

> *"But you have not so learned Christ, if indeed you have heard Him and have been taught by Him, as the truth is in Jesus: that you put off, concerning your former conduct, the old man which grows corrupt according to the deceitful lusts, and be renewed in the spirit of your mind, and that you put on the new man which was created according to God, in true righteousness and holiness." Ephesians 4:17-24*

This is the journey of sanctification, and it begins with putting off the old man and putting on the new. The old man is worldly and is described as being spiritually leprous:

- Like the rest of the Gentiles, alienated from God (outside the camp, in that place of uncleanness and death)

- Blind of heart

- Past feeling. The old man is desensitized to his own condition to the point where his conscience doesn't trouble him about the sin in his life, if he feels it at all.

I always thought putting off the old-man nature was something that happened at the start of the journey, when I first became a believer. I left that leprous old man outside the camp when I was cleansed and allowed to enter the camp. To a certain extent that is true. There is an initial step to putting off the old man and putting on the new man which is part of becoming a new creation, and yet Paul says there has to be a renewing of the mind, which is an ongoing thing.

The old man is not so easily put off because of the blindness we suffer at times over sins that were part of our old life. We can still be insensitive to old behaviors and attitudes that we should have left outside the camp. Our old man can be so deeply rooted that we don't even realize it is there. We may need a catalyst to bring our old man to the surface so we can deal with it.

Miriam was no newcomer to this journey. She was a prophetess and a worship leader. She had an exalted place in the inner circle of leadership. Even so, there was an old-man nature lurking in her that hadn't been rooted out. God used an out-of-place Ethiopian woman to get that nature to manifest itself in Miriam.

Some of the character faults that were part of Miriam's old man seemed to have included pride, a deep issue with submission to authority, and a sense of entitlement. Has God convicted any of us with those things? Those are not things to which any of us would readily confess because they reveal a blindness in us, a weakness, and insensitivity. But they are a leprosy in us.

God gave that Ethiopian woman a place at the family table in part to challenge Miriam's idea of who is clean and who isn't, who is an outsider and who isn't. Miriam was a prophetess, yet she had closed her eyes to the possibility that a Gentile might be counted among God's priestly family based on a covenant relationship and be allowed to partake of the offerings, the same as a Levite.

Miriam had to step into those Gentile shoes and see herself in the place of that Ethiopian woman before she could judge her rightly. We all came from outside the camp. Regardless of who we are physically, we all have the same spiritual old man to put off.

Our old man can be buried pretty deep. Sometimes we only see symptoms of the old man at work. Recognizing those symptoms can help us know when our old man needs rooting out.

Symptoms of the Old Man

Symptom #1: Criticism that devalues or tears down another's place in the body.

Not all criticism is bad. The motive behind the criticism can make a difference.

Miriam's criticism of Moses and his wife devalued them and their place in the camp. Criticism that devalues or tears down is the old man at work.

God's purpose can only be carried out by a camp body that is knit together in harmony and working in unity toward God's goal. God has placed each of us within the body to build one another up, to edify, and strengthen the whole. It is not enough to identify with God. To keep unity in the body, we have to identify with one another as well, and understand how we are knit together. Building unity includes acknowledging the value of each person in the place God has given them in the body. It is vital that we learn to see the value in each other.

One of our goals in the body should be to keep the unity of the Spirit in the bond of peace. Paul teaches this extensively in Ephesians 4.

> *". . . walk worthy of the calling with which you were called, with all lowliness and gentleness, with long-suffering, bearing with one another in love, endeavoring to keep the unity of the Spirit in the bond of peace. There is one body and one Spirit, just as you were called in one hope of your calling; one Lord, one faith, one baptism; one God and Father of all, who is above all, and through all, and in you all." Ephesians 4:1b-6*

> *"And He Himself gave some to be apostles, some prophets, some evangelists, and some pastors and teachers, for the equipping of the saints for the work of ministry, for the edifying of the body of Christ, till we all come to the unity of the faith and of the knowledge of the Son of God, to a perfect man, to the measure of the stature of the fullness of Christ . . ." Ephesians 4:11-13*

Apostles, prophets, evangelists, pastors, and teachers—those are all title roles in the body, but not all roles in the body come with titles. The role that Moses' wife played in Miriam's life didn't have a title. She wasn't an apostle, or prophet, or evangelist, or pastor. Not once in this scenario did she even engage Miriam directly. She was simply the wife who came to dinner. But she was a radical catalyst for the Lord's work in Miriam's life. God put her there simply to be there.

Sometimes God puts us in people's lives just to be there, to be the salt and light. We don't always have to do something. Sometimes we draw fire just because of who we are and not for anything we have done. That is God using us to challenge the old-man nature in others.

You may not be a title role in God's camp, but are you a catalyst in someone's life? You can't always put a title on the part people are playing. Our new man value system should not focus on titles.

Our criticism can reveal our old-man value system still at work. Our old-man identity will often be anchored in our sense of rank. The old man glories in titles and positions of prominence, and covets them because the old man values social status. Leadership positions become an ambition and a measure of personal worth. That is where the glory is for him. Miriam certainly puffed herself up and scorned the housewife.

We communicate our value system through our criticism. Lesser roles are criticized, devalued, or ignored. We may not realize that our old-man value system is still with us until that criticism rolls off our tongue. Our tongue reveals our heart, as Ephesians 4 goes on to tell us.

> *"Therefore, putting away lying, 'Let each one of you speak truth with his neighbor,' for we are members of one another. Be angry, and do not sin: do not let the sun go down on your wrath, nor give place to the devil . . . Let no corrupt word proceed out of your mouth, but what is good for necessary edification, that it may impart grace to the hearers. And do not grieve the Holy Spirit of God, by whom you were sealed for the day of redemption. Let all bitterness, wrath, anger, clamor, and evil speaking be put away from you, with all malice. And be kind to one another, tenderhearted, forgiving one another, even as God in Christ forgave you." Ephesians 4:25-27, 29-32*

These instructions could easily have been applied to Miriam and Aaron as they are to us.

Ephesians 5 develops these concepts of walking in love, in light and in wisdom more fully, ending with an admonition for us.

> *"Speaking to one another in psalms and hymns and spiritual songs, singing and making melody in your heart to the Lord, giving thanks always for all things to God the Father in the name of our Lord Jesus Christ, submitting to one another in the fear of God." Ephesians 5:19-21*

Miriam, who once sang and danced before the Lord and gave glory to Him, had become a gossiping, back-biting, and malicious force within the body because of her pride in her position. She felt entitled to make her own judgment calls about other leaders and their relationships. She incited disunity in the family and in the camp body. Her old-man nature asserted itself with a vengeance, so much so that she had to be physically put out of the camp body for a while.

Symptom #2: Disunity in leadership that disrupts the camp

Sometimes the only symptom we see of a leprous old man at work is the disunity evident in the camp. The old man doesn't work well with the rest of the body, because the old man isn't interested in growing in unity with others and God. If the old man is not dealt with, it will cause disunity in the body and impede spiritual growth and progress.

We don't always see what goes on inside the *hazeroth*—within the enclosures, behind closed doors of leadership meetings, within homes. But if the old man isn't dealt with internally by the people within the body, the repercussions quickly become systemic, and public.

Disunity in the body also happens when cliques develop in the congregation. These are man-made *hazeroth* that divide the body along superficial lines and can cause splits and divisions among believers. Cliquishness is an old-man tendency.

The People's Response to Miriam Exiting Camp

I imagine it must have been a shock for everyone in camp to see a leprous Miriam emerge from the Tabernacle enclosure and make her way outside the camp. Imagine the public shame of it. People will want to know what has happened.

How do we react when we see someone being put out of a congregation because of sin? Do the tongues start wagging? If you are the one who has been attacked for no reason, like Moses' wife, do you rejoice to see Miriam put out of camp?

> *"Do not rejoice when your enemy falls, and do not let your heart be glad when he stumbles; lest the LORD see it, and it displease Him, and He turn away His wrath from him." Proverbs 24:17-18*

Your reaction in this moment is going to affect your relationship with this person if, by God's grace, they are restored to the fellowship.

It is a tribute to God's grace that He waited for Miriam's return. Even though He hid His face from her in that moment, the cloud did not lift itself from the Tabernacle to continue the journey without her. God made everyone wait for her return.

Not all cases are given the grace that Miriam receives nor should they. There are some leaders who must be put out of the congregation for the health of the congregation because they are a leprosy among us.

False Leaders

Paul warns us of the great apostasy of these false leaders who *"speak lies in hypocrisy, having their own conscience seared with a hot iron"* (1 Tim. 4:2).

A seared conscience—a conscience that no longer feels pain—and a hypocritical, self-righteous attitude are forms of spiritual leprosy.

Apostate leaders are rooted in the physical things and physical relationships of this journey. They have an old-man value system that covets worldly pleasures, titles, and positions of prominence. They skew the truth of Scripture to fit their own value system, so that the truth becomes a lie.

They focus on physical requirements instead of the spiritual relationship, particularly placing the Law above a relationship with God. They teach that our physical relationships, such as who we marry or what we eat, are what define and rule our spiritual relationship. Funny how Miriam's complaint began with the woman Moses had married. The apostate leaders of whom Paul speaks pick up similar issues of forbidding to marry and not being allowed to eat certain foods. Both positions stem from the idea that the spiritual relationship depends on the keeping physical separation or cleanness.

Ultimately God decides which people are clean and unclean and who will sit at His table, just as He decides what food is clean and unclean.

Apostate leaders must be put out of the camp. If allowed free rein, they will lead the people in the wrong direction and will defile the camp. Apostate leaders must be removed from the congregational leadership to prevent the corruption of the church body.

A Prophetic Picture

There is a future picture in this chapter that the author of the book of Hebrews picks up on. The elements of the picture are:

- A Gentile who has come into the family circle and becomes a partaker of the food from the altar as a result of a covenant relationship.

- A Levite without a covenant relationship, who previously had a right to eat of the altar but now has had that right taken away.

The covenant relationship is the key that allows the Gentile woman to cross those boundaries. Without that covenant relationship, she would have remained outside the camp. She is the picture of Gentile believers who would be brought into God's family in the future as a result of the New Covenant, and those from the Old Covenant would have problems with them.

Under the Mosaic Covenant, those who had the right to eat of the physical altar, like Miriam, had that right only by blood relationship to that physical High Priest and not by covenant. But under the New Covenant, those who could partake from the spiritual altar would be allowed only by reason of the covenant relationship with our spiritual High Priest, Christ.

The fulfilled picture is detailed in Hebrews 13:9-15. I encourage you to consider that New Testament understanding in light of this Old Testament picture.

For Self-Reflection

In our day-to-day life, do we forget that our place at the Lord's glorious table was purchased at a cost? We wouldn't be there without the sin sacrifice being burned outside the camp.

How good are we at identifying the signs of our old-man nature asserting itself in our lives? Are there symptoms we are not recognizing?

How do we react when the Lord reveals a blind spot or insensitivity in our thinking?

How do we react when the Lord puts one of us "outside the camp" for sin in our lives? Do we glory in that person being put down? Remember we all began outside the camp on account of our sinful nature, and that old-man nature can still crop up in life once we are inside the camp. This is why we need the constant cleansing and renewing in Christ.

Be careful when you seek to put someone in their place. Put yourself in their shoes and consider your own place before passing judgment.

"Therefore let him who stands take heed lest he fall." 1 Corinthians 10:12

In the next lesson we will come to Kadesh in the Wilderness of Paran. It should have taken 11 days to get from Sinai to Kadesh, but progress has been slower than expected. We have lost a week while a member's old man was being put out of camp, but now we are on our way again.

LESSON SIX

Kadesh

CHAPTERS 13–14

We have moved on from Hazeroth and are camped now at Kadesh in the Wilderness of Paran. The Wilderness of Paran is meant to be the last stop on our journey of sanctification before we enter the Glorious Land. When we enter the Land we are going to be engaged in years of battles and kingdom building. Before that begins, God brings us to this place of quietness and rest while the twelve spies scope out the Land.

This episode at Kadesh is a major turning point in the journey, so I am going to break this into two lessons. Here in Lesson 6 we will walk through Numbers 13, 14, and half of chapter 15. This will include an examination of the narrative and a discussion on the issues of decision-making, fear, and mob mentality.

In the next lesson, we will go back over these same events and discuss their consequence and implications for the future of the physical and spiritual journeys.

As we get into our narrative, let's begin with an exploration of the names of the places to which we have come.

Paran

The Hebrew word, *Paran*, comes from the root word, *pa'ar*, meaning to glorify, beautify, or adorn. There is nothing glorious about the physical appearance of this wilderness. It is a hot, barren wasteland. The glory or the beauty of this place isn't going to be in its physical aspect but in what we experience here in our relationship with God.

We know God will be with us in the Glorious Land, but we can easily forget that He is also in the desolate places. When we come to desolate places in our lives, remember that God is there with us. The circumstances we find ourselves in may be anything but glorious, but our experience of God in the midst of desolation can be glorious and beautiful. It is in these desolate places that God's glory can shine the most, if we let it.

In our place of desolation, we can choose to give glory to God and allow Him to glorify and beautify us or we can take glory for ourselves by trying to overcome our circumstances by our own power. The word, *pa'ar*, can be applied to God being glorified or us being glorified as His people, but it can also mean to glorify oneself. It can describe someone who vaunts themselves in pride and arrogance and boasts in the face of God, like Pharaoh did before Moses. Whether we choose to make God or ourselves the object of glorification will make for a radically different experience and outcome in this wilderness. Our choice will either carry us into the glorious Promised Land with a blessing, or carry us back to the wilderness with a curse.

Kadesh

We have crossed through the Wilderness of Paran and come to Kadesh. Kadesh is located on the border of the Wilderness of Paran where it meets the Wilderness of Zin. In Numbers 13, Kadesh is associated with the Wilderness of Paran. In Numbers 20, it is associated with the Wilderness of Zin. It is, however, the same Kadesh. It is a mere 50 miles from the southern border of the Promised Land. Driving this stretch would take us about an hour. With 600,000-plus people walking with children and livestock, it will probably take a couple days. We are that close.

Kadesh is a curious word in the Hebrew. It is a single word that can describe two completely opposite natures. The only way you know which nature is being presented is by the vowels that are added to the Hebrew consonants. You can either spell it *kadash* with an "a", or *kadesh* with an "e" (also spelled *kedesh*). The original Hebrew did not include the vowels, which were added later to help with pronunciation. So in the original Hebrew, the word is spelled KDSh. We would have to read the context of the passage to understand which nature is being presented.

Kadash (with an "a") means to be consecrated or sanctified; to be pure and clean, holy and separate to God. This describes a holy priesthood serving and worshiping a holy God.

Kadesh (with an "e") is an unholy, profane form of service and worship to an idol. It takes the picture of a holy priesthood and twists it into the picture of a counterfeit priesthood. It is a term that describes male cult prostitutes.

The word, KDSh, is like one coin with two sides, each side opposite in nature and facing in a different direction. There is a Jekyll-and-Hyde nature about it. One side represents all that is holy and clean; the other, what is unholy and unclean. What really makes the difference between them is who gets the glory, God or His rival.

We have come to Kadesh with an "e" which is a bit foreboding. The lesson of Kadesh is going to focus on the decisions we make that reveal the nature within us—that flip of the coin that will either come up Jekyll or Hyde. That choice is going to reveal which side we are really on, and which direction we are going to take in this journey.

The Mission (Numbers 13:1-33)

The Spies

Numbers 13:1-16 tells us about the spies sent into the Land. Twelve men are selected—one representative from each tribe—to make an initial foray into the Promised Land and bring back a report. They are leaders in their tribe, but not the same ones who are leaders of the armies.

The Objective

Numbers 12:17-25 gives us the mission objective. The spies are to travel the length of the Land and report what they witness. They begin by passing through the Wilderness of Zin in the South and travel north as far as Rehob near the entrance of Hamath, the northernmost point of the Land of Israel, bordering Syria today. They are tasked with assessing the Land, whether it is good or bad, rich or poor. They are to note the terrain and bring back a sample of the fruit. They are to assess the people of the Land, whether they are strong or weak, few or many, and whether their cities are camps or fortresses.

We should note the time of year. It is the beginning of the grape harvest in the Land (v20), which means we are in the fourth month of Tammuz (June/July). The spies will return 40 days later (v25) which puts us in the fifth month of Av.

The First Report

Numbers 13:26-29 records the initial report that the spies brought back. The Land flows with milk and honey (v27). The people are strong and their cities are large and fortified (v28). The Anakim giants live there (v28). The Amalekites dwell in the southern desert; Hittites, Jebusites and Amorites dwell in the mountains; Canaanites dwell by the sea and Jordan River (v29).

The report is short, concise, but fairly thorough. The Land sounds good, but that mention of giants sends a ripple of fear through our congregation.

One of the spies, Caleb, stands up to quiet and reassure the people, and encourages them to move forward with confidence (v30). Caleb is on board with God's mission. This is the confidence we should all have in the Lord, even when facing giants. He sees the opportunity and richness of the Land. He feels assured of victory in the Lord.

He remembers God's promise:

> "... I will bring you into the land which I swore to give to Abraham, Isaac, and Jacob; and I will give it to you as a heritage: I am the LORD." Exodus 6:8

He knows God's power and His plan:

> "I will send My fear before you, I will cause confusion among all the people to whom you come, and will make all your enemies turn their backs to you. And I will send hornets before you, which shall drive out the Hivite, the Canaanite, and the Hittite from before you. I will not drive them out from before you in one year, lest the land become desolate and the beasts of the field become too numerous for you. Little by little I will drive them out from before you, until you have increased, and you inherit the land." Exodus 23:27-30

True to his name, which means "dog" in the sense of being aggressive or forceful, Caleb doesn't hesitate at the thought of engaging the enemy but urges an immediate push forward to enter into the Land. His aggressive confidence is met immediately with opposition.

The Skewed Report

Ten of the twelve spies do not want to enter the Land, and they try to dissuade the people from entering the Land also. They take the initial report and skew it to stir the people up against Caleb and Moses.

The first telling of the report was based on facts. The second iteration of the report skews the facts into a lot of emotional hyperbole. They've focused on the negative with the intent of stirring up the people. Look at how the rhetoric spins up:

- "The land flows with milk and honey" (v27) becomes
  "The land devours its inhabitants" (v32).

- "The people are strong and cities large" (v28) becomes
  "all the people they saw were men of great stature" (v32).

- "We saw the descendants of Anak there" (v28) is embellished with
  "We were as mere insects in our own sight, and so we were in their sight" (v33).

These men have already made a decision that we should not enter the Land. They've forgotten God's promise, His power and His plan. Their decision is based on their own assessment of themselves and their abilities. They imagine that the people of the Land see them in the way that they judge themselves, as mere insects. But the Lord has promised that He would make these people afraid of us.

If we let go of that promise, the fear that should have taken the enemy is going to take us instead. If we fail to give glory to God in our decision, the fate that would have been visited on our enemies will fall on us instead. That is going to be the consequence of making a wrong decision at this crossroad.

One Man against Ten

The rest of us in camp have to make a decision between these conflicting reports. Which side do we believe, Caleb or the ten? (Joshua, the twelfth man, doesn't voice his opinion in this moment, so the argument stands as one against ten.)

All have seen the Land and had the same experience in the Land. All these men are leaders among the people, so their judgment carries weight.

One man is aggressively confident and ready to charge into battle. Ten are afraid. When we see fear or faltering in leadership, does that affect our decisions?

One man has given a good report. Ten have given a bad report.

One man is exceedingly confident and optimistic that we should enter the Land immediately. Ten are equally confident that we should not enter the Land at all.

How do we decide between the two reports? Do we decide based on:

- Popular opinion? Ten out of twelve spies agree we should not enter the Land. If we judge by numbers then we would side with the majority.

- Facts? How much is fact and how much is exaggeration?

- The reaction we have to the emotionally-charged rhetoric?

- Our assessment of the one man's character vs. the other ten?

- This one report? Is this the only thing we base our decision on? What about the Lord's promise? What about His power and plan?

- Fear of opposition? If we stand with Caleb, we'll have to contend with his opposition. Does this influence our decision-making?

I think about how we make decisions for our own nation's future; we face the same quandaries over how to make decisions. All of the factors listed above are part of our own experience, and it is amazing how many of our decisions are influenced by fear. We are no different from the children of Israel in this moment.

The People's Decision (Numbers 14:1-4)

We have listened to the bad report of the ten expert witnesses and made a decision based on the popular opinion—by the numbers. We are swayed by the skewed report with its emotional spin, and perhaps a negative reaction to the aggressive confidence of the one man. Most of all, we're swayed by the fear we see in our leadership and the imagined threat of giants. Perhaps a few of us are swayed by the fear of facing the opposition of the ten.

Numbers 14:1-3 reveals our miserable state. Because of fear, we have no peace or rest. We're weeping and crying in our tents through that night. We are complaining against Moses and Aaron and against the Lord for bringing us to the Land to die by the sword. *"If only we had died in the land of Egypt!" "If only we had died in this wilderness!"*

These men may have brought us a taste of the fruit of that glorious Land, but they have robbed us of glorious living. Fear robs us of God's power and love, and it robs us of a sound mind. From this point we proceed to make a series of costly decisions and actions, the first being to select a new leader. We want to throw off the yoke of the Lord's kingship over us and choose for ourselves a new leader who will take us in the direction we think we should go—back to Egypt.

Remember the Enemy's strategy:

- Get us to identify ourselves as victims. These men have told us that our death is assured if we continue on this path. Our innocent women and children will fall prey to the inhabitants of the Land.

- Get us focused on issues that mask the real problem. They have gotten our focus off the big picture of what God has planned and onto this smaller issue of fighting giants that becomes the rallying point for rebellion.

- Twist the facts and present us with a skewed comparison to make us afraid.

- Focus on our freedom of choice and our options. They've brought us to the point of choosing a new leader and heading back to Egypt.

- In addition to all that, they've intimidated us with their numbers. The opposition stands ten against one. There are a lot more of the opposition, they are loud and negative, and they capitalize on fear.

Is this happening in our world today? You bet. We live in a world of people who have failed to acknowledge the glory of God, despised the good gifts He has prepared for us, and set their hearts on keeping us from glorifying God and His gifts. They are many. They are loud. They paint us as mad-dog Christians if we stand up to them. They spin an argument against us with a lot of twisted facts and emotion. They are quick to engage the rest of the world's sympathy for those they feel have been made victims of our beliefs. All this causes fear to work on us.

We have a decision to make. Are we going to side with Caleb or the other ten?

There is nothing wrong with being cautious in making decisions. There is nothing wrong with considering both sides of the issue. There is nothing wrong with acknowledging the pitfalls and difficulties. But the one thing we cannot fail to do in this moment is lose sight of the power and glory of God and His promise. These things should be the deciding factors.

Lift your head! Look to the glory of God and the hope of His promise! Look to the long game. Consider the two sides, not according to the number of people who support one side or the other but how they are aligned with God and understand His goals and His plan. In this case, the Lord has told us to go into the Land and take it. The direction is very clear. There should be no hesitation.

Beware of leaders who push their agenda by riling people up instead of calming them down. Beware of leaders who persuade by playing only to emotion and try to sway you with underhanded tactics like character assassination.

Above all, beware of letting yourself get sucked into the fear.

The Fear

Fear is a powerful thing. We have come so far on this journey as to be on the doorstep to the Glorious Land and that glorious life of rest, peace, joy and oneness with God. We have experienced tangible evidence that the Lord is real and He is with us. He has provided for us. He has protected us. He has given us freedom and a sense of individual worth. We have tasted the fruit of the Land. We have come so far with so much proof, and still, there is one thing that derails us from entering the Land—fear.

What are some of the fears we face in life? I made a list for myself that included fear of loss, pain, persecution and death. I fear for what is going on today in our own country and in our world. I fear for what will happen to our children who are growing up in this changing world.

Fear is one of the greatest agents that the Enemy uses against us to get us off the journey, and he often focuses his worst attack on our leadership, knowing that is one of the easiest ways to mislead an entire congregation. Strike the shepherd and the sheep will scatter.

Fear is also one of the greatest agents God uses to test our faith. Fear reveals whether or not we understand both the power of God and the love of God.

> *"For God has not given us a spirit of fear, but of power and of love and of a sound mind." 2 Timothy 1:7*

The Power of God

There is only one thing to fear in this life, and that is God Himself. Nothing happens to us apart from His allowing it or even His orchestrating it. Fear of God—that understanding of His absolute power over our lives—is a good and godly thing. Fear shows that we understand who He is and who we are, and places us in a correct relationship with Him. We should not fear to follow Him into the Land if that is where He is leading us. We should only fear not entering it.

We give power to the things we fear in life. Fear is a way of giving power to someone or something. When we transfer our fear of God to a fear of someone or something else, we make that person or thing a rival to God in its power over us. Fear of this world is the ultimate form of unfaithfulness to God, and becomes a form of spiritual bondage. It robs us of the power of God in our lives and the glorious life of joy and peace and rest the Lord wants for us.

The Love of God

> *"Love has been perfected among us in this: that we may have boldness in the day of judgment; because as He is, so are we in this world. There is no fear in love; but perfect love casts out fear, because fear involves torment. But he who fears has not been made perfect in love." 1 John 4:17-18*

His power is tempered by His love, so that we do not fear to stand before Him in judgment, knowing His great love for us. The fear of the power God has over our lives is balanced by our understanding of His great love for us. 1 John speaks about having that oneness with God, abiding in Him to the point where His character is so perfected in us and our understanding of it so clear that we overcome fear of this world. Perfect love casts out fear because fear involves torment. If you are still living in fear of torment, you have not fully understood God's love or achieved that abiding oneness with Him. Fear is a test of how far we have grown in oneness with God.

Fear robs us of a sound mind. Fearful people often make bad decisions. Fear drives us in the opposite direction that the Lord would have us go.

Caleb conquered fear by clinging to the promise. Do we know the promise?

> *"Let not your heart be troubled; you believe in God, believe also in Me. In My Father's house are many mansions; if it were not so, I would have told you. I go to prepare a place for you. And if I go and prepare a place for you, I will come again and receive you to Myself; that where I am, there you may be also. And where I go you know, and the way you know." John 14:1-4*

Caleb knew the plan. Do we know God's plan?

Yes, the Book of Revelation tells us much of what will happen in the end times. When the Lord comes again to establish His Kingdom, it is going to be a lot like what happened to Egypt, particularly in terms of plagues and disasters. But are we going to suffer those things? No. We teach that the believers living at that time will be raptured before the days of Tribulation. These are called the days of His wrath and we are not destined to experience that wrath (Rom. 2:5-9, 5:9).

Does that mean that we will not see the groundwork being laid for these tremendous events? Are we just going to be raptured out of a perfect utopia and then all hell will break loose on earth? No.

There will be wars and rumors of wars. There be widespread conflict on the earth in which an insanity will take over and people will begin killing each other. There will be persecution of believers worldwide. These things have already begun.

There will be a reapportioning of world powers in preparation for a world leader to take the stage. The climate is going to change in those days as the wrath of God falls on the earth as described in Revelation 8. The groundwork is already being laid such that when that happens, this wicked world will give credit to man for it and not to God. These things have already begun.

Are we supposed to be afraid of these things? There will be trials. There will be sickness and hunger and scarcity for a time. The enemies that rise before us will seem like giants, and the swirl of world events will make us feel powerless.

Lift your head! Focus on the power of the Lord and the love He has for us. He will not leave us or forsake us. Remember His promises. We are not destined for His wrath. Remember the battle plan. We've come this far. Keep the glorious Land in view and do not fear to follow Him. To succumb to fear at this point will be the pivotal act of unfaithfulness to God.

Joshua's Response (Numbers 14:5-9)

So far we have heard from eleven men. One is for entering the land; ten are opposed. Now there is a twelfth man, Joshua, who stands up with Caleb when the people begin agitating for a new leader. Both Caleb and Joshua tear their clothes in mourning for this great failure of the children of Israel.

Numbers 14:5-9 gives us Joshua's argument. He defends the glory of the Land and lifts up the Lord to a place of glory. Let's walk through his dialog in phrases.

> *"If the Lord delights in us..."* It is the Lord's decision that we enter the Land, according to His judgment, not ours.

> *"...then He will bring us into the land..."* It is the Lord's leadership and power that will accomplish this. He is our salvation, our redeemer and deliverer. He will bring our enemies to desolation and lift us up.

> *"...and will give it to us..."* This Land is the Lord's gift to us. Our fortune lies in His hands.

> *"Only do not rebel against the Lord, nor fear the people of the land for they are our bread..."* Do not withdraw from the Lord or the Land. We will be the ones devouring its inhabitants. That's a direct shot at the ten men who said the Land devours its inhabitants. Joshua sets that skewed comparison right.

> *"...their protection has departed from them and the Lord is with us."* The Lord is our protection. When He rises up in His majesty, He is greater than any opposition that comes against Him.

What a resounding argument for the glory of the Lord!

Does it do any good?

The People's Response (Numbers 14:10)

The people's response to Joshua is to stone the opposition and go back to Egypt. A once holy, orderly army as now flipped and become something of an opposite nature—an unholy, unruly mob. The fact that the people have now succumbed to a mob mentality shows a new level of failing.

Mob Mentality

Throughout the book of Numbers we have seen an emphasis on the importance God places on individuals and not just faceless masses. He has been trying to break us out of that group identity, because there is danger for us when we let a group of people make decisions for us.

I found an article titled "Examining the Mob Mentality"[1], an interview with Dr. Tamara Avant, psychology program director at South University–Savannah, that explains the psychology behind mob mentality. Mob mentality involves the loss of individual identity and its replacement with a social identity. The outworking of mob mentality is characterized by the loss of self-awareness, loss of restraint and inhibitions, diffusion of responsibility and accountability because of perceived anonymity, and a pressure to conform to the group behavior.

Mob mentality stands in stark contrast to the individual autonomy God has given us.

- As individuals, each person has individual identity, but mobs create a sense of anonymity and reduce self-awareness.

- As individuals, each person has individual responsibility and accountability. Mob mentality diffuses that.

- As individuals, each person acts on individual choice. Mob mentality demands conformity to group thinking.

- As individuals, each person is expected to exercise self-control. Mob mentality promotes a lack of inhibition and disregard of social norms.

- As individuals, each person has the power to think rationally for himself, but mobs encourage you to quit thinking and act on emotion alone.

---

1 Donely, Megan. "Examining The Mob Mentality" *South Source*. South University–Savannah, Issue 1, 14 January 2011. http://source.southuniversity.edu/examining-the-mob-mentality-31395.aspx.

We have seen mob mentality increasingly at work in our own country today with appalling results.

Mob behavior runs against everything the Lord has been trying to instill in His children. The people's mob-like behavior in the narrative is manifested in a very base and destructive form of behavior, incited by a group of divisive men who 1) rejected God and 2) rejected authority.

There is a path leading to destruction that begins with ungodly and unrighteous men who suppress the truth in unrighteousness. Paul warns us of such people in Romans 1:

> "... although they knew God, they did not glorify Him as God, nor were thankful, but became futile in their thoughts, and their foolish hearts were darkened. Professing to be wise, they became fools, and changed the glory of the incorruptible God into an image made like corruptible man..." Romans 1:21-23

Paul goes on to talk about the physical and spiritual debasement that follows this rejection of God that brings such people to this end:

> "And even as they did not like to retain God in their knowledge, God gave them over to a debased mind, to do those things which are not fitting; being filled with all unrighteousness, sexual immorality, wickedness, covetousness, maliciousness; full of envy, murder, strife, deceit, evil-mindedness; they are whisperers, backbiters, haters of God, violent, proud, boasters, inventors of evil things, ..." Romans 1:28-30

Much of what Paul describes here can apply to the character of the ten spies whose report turned the people against God and the Land. There is a punishment that awaits these men, and it will fall on us also if we allow ourselves to be swayed into following their example. Therefore, Paul warns us:

> "Reject a divisive man after the first and second admonition, knowing that such a person is warped and sinning, being self-condemned." Titus 3:10-11

We see two "admonitions" given to the divisive men here in the Numbers narrative. First Caleb, then Joshua, pushed back against the arguments of the ten. Instead of siding with Joshua and Caleb in glorifying the Lord, we join the ten spies and give ourselves over to murder, strife, and evil-mindedness.

The Lord has lifted our head. When asked to make a judgment call, we must be discerning of the arguments being presented to us and the character of the people making the arguments. Consider what course of action gives glory to the Lord and is aligned with His purpose. Don't get sucked into group-driven decisions and mob behavior and stay far away from people given to this kind of behavior. There is no glory to be had, for God or for ourselves, in violence and lack of restraint.

Here in Numbers 14, we have given ourselves over to this mob behavior and rational thinking is clearly gone. The mob is telling us life was good in Egypt. Go back to Egypt.

Back to Egypt

Can we go back to Egypt, really? What was Egypt's condition when we left?

Egypt was crippled by plagues on account of the children of Israel. Their fresh water was polluted. They'd been overrun by vermin, and then had to deal with the clean-up when all those vermin died. They lost their livestock to disease (more clean-up). They lost their crops to locust and hail. This last year when we have been receiving manna from God, Egypt was in famine condition. Their food supply was lost. To cap it all they lost their firstborn males of both humans and animals. If you are responsible for the death of someone's child, do you really think that person is going to welcome you back with open arms?

They sent us away with their wealth. We plundered them. They lost all their army in the Red Sea in their effort to pursue us. Their defense is gone. Their gods were put to shame by the glory of the God of Israel.

God brought us out of Egypt with mighty works and great judgments. He put all His power and glory on display for us, and Egypt was crippled in the encounter. This isn't distant history; we have just passed the one year anniversary of all that destruction. Even if we went back to Egypt at this point, it would be to a much different Egypt.

We cost Egypt too much for them to let us back into their land, even as slaves. If we returned now, we would be killed the minute we got there, out of vengeance for Egypt's loss, for their dead, and for their gods. This time God would not be there to protect us.

We cannot go back to Egypt. We will die if we go back to Egypt. We have refused to go forward into the Land, and we cannot go back to Egypt. We are at a stalemate here at Kadesh, and the Lord is going to break that stalemate in a moment. But before we get to the Lord's response in Numbers 14:11-38, I want to pause and revisit the names of the spies in light of the decision we have made to side with the ten who gave the bad report.

Names of the Spies (Numbers 13:4-15)

Just like the names of the leaders listed in chapter 1, the meanings of the spies' names also reflect the glory of God—if God is the one getting the glory. The names have very opposite meanings when the glory is being claimed by the man. I want to walk through the meanings of these names and discuss the implications of giving glory to God or man in each case, and what God's response will be if glory is taken away from Him in this moment. What we find in most of these cases is that the action the Lord planned to visit on our enemies will instead be visited on us.

Shammua, son of Zaccur, from the tribe of Reuben

In the Hebrew, Shammua means "renown" from the root meaning to bring desolation in an appalling way. It implies the desire to make a name for oneself by visiting shocking defeat on your enemies. His father's name, Zaccur, means "to be mindful" in the sense of being remembered or brought to mind and carries a similar connotation as the son's name.

God, in His glory, made a name for Himself when He brought us out of Egypt. He visited appalling desolation on Pharaoh and the Egyptians when they set themselves up as His enemies. His name will be glorified before the nations again when He brings us into the Promised Land. As His army, we are meant to be glorified with Him in that kingdom. Our glorification is tied to His glorification. Remember Joshua's speech? Joshua said, *". . . then He will bring us into the land . . ."* It is the Lord's leadership and power that will accomplish this. He will bring our enemies to desolation and lift us up. We can side with God and go down in history for having brought appalling desolation upon our enemies and taken their kingdom.

If we try doing this by our own power without God, the consequences will flip on us. We will go down in history having made a name for ourselves as faithless followers and for suffering the most appalling defeat in the face of our enemies. The desolation we will bring will be upon ourselves. A sovereign God can make that happen, particularly if His glory is being challenged. This spy was one who gave a bad report of the Land. He stood in the face of God and said God was wrong about the Land, and we took his side over God's.

Shapat, son of Hori, from the tribe of Simeon

In the Hebrew, Shapat means "judged," from the root word meaning to judge, govern, vindicate, or punish. His father's name, Hori, means "cave dweller." Hori has a rather negative character associated with it, speaking of man having base instincts or the nature of a wild animal (like one who dwells in holes in the ground). Put the character of these two names together, and we have a man who judges himself to be inferior, an insect in his own eyes and in the eyes of others (Num. 13:33). This spy judged the Land according to his own estimation of himself and his limits, apart from God.

Joshua said, *"... nor fear the people of the land for they are our bread..."* We will devour them. We may be grasshoppers in size to those giants, but who can withstand a plague of grasshoppers when they invade the land and devour its grain? Egypt couldn't. Grasshoppers have strength when directed by the Lord.

Joshua said: *"If the Lord delights in us..."* What counts is the Lord's estimation of us, not our own. He has lifted us up from our baseness to be His own special people. Entering the Land is the Lord's decision, according to His judgment, and will be by His strength, not ours. It would be glorifying to God if we trusted Him and relied on His judgment in this moment.

We can side with Caleb and Joshua who have judged the Land according to the Lord's judgment and aligned themselves with His glory, or we can side with the ten spies, throw off God's kingship and appoint ourselves new leaders to take us back to Egypt. Which side do we choose?

It's almost funny how we think the giants are impossible to overcome, but the Lord can be dismissed so easily. We have flipped that relationship upside down to our own hurt. When we decide that we are better judges than God in which way we should go or how we should be ruled, we will find ourselves on the receiving end of the Lord's judgment and the decision will go against us. Because we rely on man's worldly wisdom, we will not enter the Land.

Caleb, son of Jephunneh, of the tribe of Judah

As previously mentioned, Caleb means "dog" in the sense of forcefulness or aggressiveness. This is a true likeness of Caleb's personality in his willingness to enter the Land and engage the Lord's enemies aggressively and wholeheartedly. Aggression and forcefulness are not bad things when you are a soldier in the Lord's army. A soldier should be determined, single-minded in his loyalty to his commander, and willing to throw himself into the mission to attain the reward.

The name Caleb has the same Jekyll-and-Hyde character as the word Kadesh. The original Hebrew is comprised only of the CLB consonants, with the vowels "a" or "e" added later.

Caleb with an "a" is the fiercely loyal dog who strains at the leash, eager for the master to set him loose for his task and purpose.

Celeb with an "e" is the flip-side. Its character is that of a feral dog who wanders wild without a master, one that is rabid, fierce, brutal, unclean and shameless. Like kadesh, the *celeb* dog is often used in Scripture as a figurative name for male cult prostitutes who are aggressive and predatory in their nature.

His father's name, Jephunneh, means "he will be facing" or "for whom a way is prepared." The Lord has prepared the way in leading His people to the Land and in how He plans to take the Land from His enemies. When the Lord has prepared the way, then victory is guaranteed. His people should have Caleb's aggressive confidence in entering the Land.

Caleb holds true to his name. He doesn't flip. The other ten spies refuse to believe the Lord will prepare the way and bring them safely into the Land. Moreover, they bring out the *celeb* nature in the people, turning them into an unruly, unholy maddened mob.

Igal, son of Joseph, of the tribe of Issachar

In the Hebrew, Igal means "he redeems" from the root, *ga'al*, meaning kinsman redeemer or avenger of blood. I want to focus on the redeemer role for the moment, but we will discuss the avenger of blood aspect more in Lesson 12 where the issue of taking vengeance for a brother's murder comes up.

God showed Himself in His glory as our redeemer when He brought us out of Egypt. He avenged us on those Egyptian masters and bought our redemption with the death of their firstborn sons. We can give glory to God for our redemption, or we can take glory from God by denying His power to redeem us and devaluing the price that was paid for us.

These spies have come back from the Land and brought with them the fruit of it. We have tasted that fruit, of the goodness and gift to come and we have devalued its worth as well.

We have declared our desire to return to Egypt, making the death of the firstborn and our redemption of no value. We have scorned the fruit of the Land, devaluing God's gift. We have flipped and it is going to be a permanent reality for us. Once we cross this line, there is no option for us to flip back again.

> *"For it is impossible for those who were once enlightened, and have tasted the heavenly gift, and have become partakers of the Holy Spirit, and have tasted the good word of God and the powers of the age to come, if they fall away, to renew them again to repentance, since they crucify again for themselves the Son of God, and put Him to an open shame."* Hebrews 6:4-6

If the price of the firstborn son was insufficient to redeem us from Egypt, what will redeem us a second time if we go back and are made slaves again? What other fruit can be given us if we scorn the fruit of the Land? When we take glory from God in this way, we put Him to open shame and He must answer us for the sake of His glory. We will not go into the Land, but neither will we return to Egypt. He is going to exile us to this wilderness for the rest of our lives.

I am going to talk more about this passage from Hebrews in the next lesson.

Hoshea, son of Nun, of the tribe of Ephraim (named changed to Joshua)

In the Hebrew, Hoshea means "my salvation." Moses changed it to Joshua meaning "Jehovah is salvation." Given the role Joshua is destined to play in bringing the children of Israel into the Land, I think Moses makes a deliberate change in his name to remind Joshua that he himself does not bring about salvation for anyone. The Lord is the one who brings salvation and prosperity, and He alone is to be credited with that glory. Joshua is one of two men who keeps his vision clear at this moment.

Nun means "prosperity" from the root "to increase or continue." It carries the sense of something that increases in perpetuity, as in Psalm 72:17, *"His name shall endure forever; His name shall continue as long as the sun. And men shall be blessed in Him; all nations shall call Him blessed."*

Joshua, son of Nun translates into "Jehovah is salvation, He shall increase in perpetuity." What a glorious prophetic vision of a future Savior, of which Joshua is a type.

The rest of us are going to look to our own salvation, and as a result Joshua will lead our children into the Land instead of us. Little do we know that Joshua is destined to take Moses' place. We have picked the wrong men to rally around.

Palti, son of Raphu, of the tribe of Benjamin

In the Hebrew, Palti means "my deliverance," in the sense of escaping from something or slipping away. Raphu means "healed" or made healthful.

We could give glory to God for His deliverance from Egypt and for being our healer. Our identification with God as our deliverer is a direct reflection of our trust in Him, but now we seek escape, not from Egypt but from this wilderness to which God has brought us. We have convinced ourselves that we must bring about our own deliverance from this place.

Yet we will not escape the Lord. What will escape us is the blessing we would have known in the Land. As we will see shortly, our health will also begin to decline as a consequence of our unfaithfulness. Like the unfaithful wife, the generation that made the decision not to enter the Land will begin to waste away and become fruitless until it dies in this wilderness.

Gaddiel, son of Sodi, of the tribe of Zebulun

Gaddiel means "God is my fortune," sharing the same root as Gaddi, but with an emphasis on where the source of fortune lies—in God. This spy would have done well if he had remembered that. His father's name, Sodi, means "acquaintance" in the sense of being one of the council or assembly.

These spies should have been acquainted with God and givers of good, godly counsel to the people in this matter of entering the Land. Instead they took counsel among themselves against the Lord and His judgment. When we allow ourselves to be swayed by them, instead of pressing onward to the good fortune that awaits us, we decide to try our luck at making our own fortune back in Egypt.

Gaddi, son of Susi, of the tribe of Manasseh

In the Hebrew, Gaddi means "my fortune." His father's name, Susi, means "my horse" or horseman.

Many kings have rested the security of their kingdoms on the strength and swiftness of their horses and chariots. Egypt trusted in horses and chariots and they fell before the Lord's power. We should be careful what we put our trust in.

If we trust in the Lord, we will be lifted up. Fortune, fortune, double portion, waits for the man who enters the Land. Seek first the kingdom of God and His righteousness and all these things shall be added to you. Joshua said, ". . . the Lord will give it to us . . ." Our fortune lies in His hands.

Not so for this spy. He judged his strength by the power of his own resources, which was found lacking, and decided his fortune lay elsewhere. He convinced the rest of us as well.

Ammiel the son of Gemalli, of the tribe of Dan

In the Hebrew, Ammiel means "kinsman of God" or "people of God."

Can a people who have tried to throw off the rule of a sovereign God still call themselves kinsmen of God? The claim to be a kinsman of God is going to resurface again in Korah's Rebellion in which the people accuse Moses of killing "the people of God" who are none other than the rebels themselves.

People who rebel against God are enemies of God, not kinsman.

It is the walk of faith that makes us kinsmen of God and brings us into the Land.

Paul takes this understanding even further in Romans 4, where he speaks of the heirs of the kingdom being of the faith of Abraham and not the circumcision of Abraham. It does not matter if a man is counted as one of the circumcision in his flesh. If he does not walk by faith in God, he will not be heir to the promise.

True sons of Abraham would have followed their ancestor's example, as Paul describes:

> *"He did not waver at the promise of God through unbelief, but was strengthened in faith, giving glory to God, and being fully convinced that what He had promised He was also able to perform." Romans 4:20-21*

If we think our claim to this blessing is rooted in our physical kinship with Israel or even our works by the keeping of the Law, and not our faith in God, we will lose the inheritance, and our lives, in this wilderness. This generation of the circumcised did not enter the Land, but their children—who they failed to circumcise—would enter the Land. The unfaithful, though circumcised, fell short; the faithful, though uncircumcised, attained the promise. (Jos. 5:3-7, Rom. 4:9-13)

In regards to the father's name, Gemalli means "camel driver," as one who possesses camels or is carried on a camel. In truth, I cannot find a significance to the father's name as I have with the others. Perhaps camels, like horses, are a resource by which strength or fortune are assessed. There may be other cultural connotations I am not aware of.

Sethur, the son of Michael, of the tribe of Asher
Nahbi, the son of Vophsi, of the tribe of Naphtali

In the Hebrew, Sethur and Nahbi both mean "hidden." Sethur means "hidden" in the sense of being concealed, and Nahbi "hidden" in the sense of being withdrawn. Michael means "who is like God." Vophsi means "rich." Many things are hidden in the Lord, and it is like God to hide the richness of Himself from His enemies and reveal it to those who seek Him.

The ability to hide or conceal oneself is an asset for a spy being sent on this particular mission. The nature of concealing can be used toward God's mission, but it can also be twisted into an act of deception that works against God's agenda.

This event at Kadesh has revealed double agents in our midst. These men went out on this mission on God's behalf, but when they returned, they concealed the glory of the Land with a bad report based on a skewed comparison. They devalued the Land in the eyes of the people to the point that the people withdrew from the Land. In doing that, they have denied the glory of God and robbed the people of glorious living.

Joshua warns, *"Do not rebel against the Lord . . ."* Do not withdraw from Him. Withdraw from God, and He will withdraw from us and take our fruitfulness with Him. Conceal the glory of the Land when we know the truth, and the way to the glorious Land will be concealed from us. Seek to throw the veil over the people's eyes, and we will fall into calamity out of which we will not be able to see our way.

Geuel, son of Machi, from the tribe of Gad

In the Hebrew, Geuel means "majesty of God" in the sense of rising up and being exalted in triumph. This word for majesty is used in both the song of Moses and the song of Miriam referring to the Lord rising up like mighty waters and triumphing gloriously over His enemies. He has promised to do the same when He brings us into the Land.

Machi means "to decrease." Our glory is tied to God's glory. When we glorify the Lord, we are lifted up as His people. When the majesty of God is caused to decrease, our own glory decreases despite every attempt on our part to take it. This is exactly what happens in this place.

Summary

When God hand-picks men for tasks and calls them by name, it is worth studying the meanings of those names because they are often relevant to the narrative. Each one of the names reflects ways that we can either give glory to God or take glory from God in the decisions that we make, and the repercussions of those decisions. The fate that should have befallen our enemies most often ends up falling on us when we are unfaithful.

Now for God's response.

God's Judgment on the Rebels (Numbers 14:11-38)

We are picking up again now in Numbers 14:11 and working through the end of the chapter.

We have another leadership meeting between Moses, Aaron, and God. For the sake of His glory, God cannot take us into the Land, He cannot let us go back to Egypt, and He cannot kill us outright as He desires to do. As Moses points out, the nations will hear about it.

How God deals with us in this moment is going to reinforce His glory as sovereign God to His people and to unbelieving nations. He is going to grant the rebellious generation their wish. They are not going to die in Egypt, but they will die after a lifetime walking in this wilderness. He is going to walk them to death.

I Will Give My Kingdom to Little Children

All who were 20 years old or older at the time of the first census will die except for Caleb and Joshua (v29-30). That leaves all the children 19 years and younger to inherit the Land. God tells us, "I will take the kingdom and give to the little children. The children will know the blessing and rest that their parents rejected." In this we have a shadow picture of the spiritual kingdom that Jesus speaks of:

> *"Let the little children come to Me, and do not forbid them; for of such is the kingdom of God. Assuredly, I say to you, whoever does not receive the kingdom of God as a little child will by no means enter it." Luke 18:16-17*

Only those who believe with the simple faith of a child will enter the Land. The first generation could not enter in because of unbelief.

The whole congregation wept at the thought that the children would be victims of the people of the land. Instead, their children are going to grow up suffering from their parents' own infidelity (v31-33) and then inherit the blessing the previous generation forfeited. They did not merit this punishment, but God will use the experience for His purpose in their lives. In the end, the children who continue in faith will receive a blessing that their parents do not.

The entire camp will wander the wilderness 40 years, one year for every day of spying the Land (v34). Those who believed the lie that the glorious Land would devour them will be consumed by the wilderness instead. From this point the years will be marked by the number of deaths. The congregation had complained, saying, *"If only we had died in the land of Egypt! Or if only we had died in this wilderness!"* Now we all will become intimately acquainted with death.

How many funerals does the average person attends in a lifetime? I asked my class this question, and the highest number they came up with was 50, counting family, friends, family of friends, etc.

In the next forty years, Joshua and Caleb will witness 625,550 kinsmen die. They will be the only ones out of that entire generation to enter the Land.

They are also the last men standing out of that group of spies. The Lord delivers immediate judgment on the spies who brought the bad report, and they die by plague (v36-37). Imagine being Caleb and Joshua, watching the men who had just spent 40 days with you—men who had opposed you and incited the people to stone you—drop like flies around you. There is vindication in it, but what a horrible consequence to see visited on a person, even an enemy. It was probably like experiencing a tornado rip through a community and being the only two houses left untouched in the middle of all that devastation.

Defeat at Hormah (Numbers 14:39-45)

Numbers 14:39-45 ends the chapter with our defeat at Hormah. We are supposed to be the Lord's army destined to take the Promised Land from the nations, but now that we are not entering the Land, we are an army without a purpose. We mourn over the Lord's judgment and decide to take matters into our own hands. We rise the next morning and make a vain attempt to lift ourselves up by heading to the top of the mountain (v40). We are going to try to take the Land ourselves. We admit that we have sinned, but there is nothing repentant about it. It's more of a response along the lines of "Our bad, we'll be good now, so let's go take the Land!" This is not repentance. In fact Moses points out we have added sin upon sin first by refusing to enter the Land with God, and now trying to enter the Land without Him (v41-43).

Moses tells us we are transgressing the Lord's command if we go up the hill. He warns us that the defeat we will suffer if we press on will not be because the Lord walked away from us but because we walked away from Him (v40-41). There is never a question of God's faithfulness to His people on this journey. The unfaithfulness is always on our part. We are the ones physically walking away from Him in this moment.

We presumed to go up the mountain, meaning we have swelled up in arrogance, lifted ourselves up and heedlessly headed into the face of the enemy on our own. We have overstepped ourselves. The protocol for this journey is that so long as the Lord's glory remains in the Tabernacle, we don't move, and we most certainly don't push out ahead of the Ark of the Covenant. The camp has stayed put, which means we are heading outside the camp. Death waits outside the camp.

We come back down that hill on the run, chased by the sword. The Amalekites and Canaanites drive us all the way back to a place called Hormah. Hormah, in Hebrew, means utter destruction. That is what we have come to. We are the Lord's army, but we are 0-1 in battles.

More Laws (Numbers 15:1-21)

In the aftermath of the Lord's judgment and our defeat, we are given some more laws. The first half of chapter 15 contains instructions for when we do finally enter the Land. The second half of the chapter (Num. 15:22-41) goes on to teach us how to judge presumptuous sin from unintentional sin, and then we get our first practice in judging in the case of a man guilty of work on the Sabbath. Chapter 15 ends with the command to wear the tassels. I want to briefly cover the first half of chapter 15 here, and the rest in the next lesson.

When We Enter the Land

Numbers 15:1-21 contains two commands that are instructions for when we come into the Land. Whom are these instructions for? They are certainly not for the faithless generation that refused to enter the Land. It must have been salt rubbed in their wounds to hear these words of the Lord and know they would never have reason to practice them.

The first command (v2) says when you have come into the Land, you will offer a grain and drink offering with your sacrifices. Bread and wine are elements missing in this journey. When we come into the Land we were meant to enter into a greater experience of communion with the Lord.

The second command (v18) is like the first. When we enter the Land, we will give back to God the first fruits of the grain of the land. This offering would be incorporated into the feasts of Israel: the Feast of First Fruits (barley harvest) and the Feast of Weeks (wheat harvest). When we enter into the Land, the Sabbath year (a year of rest for the Land), also comes into effect as part of the harvest.

Entering the Land was meant to take us to a new level of experience with the Lord which is characterized by fruitfulness. Unlike the manna which we are given only a day at a time and cannot store up, the fruitfulness of the Land is going to be given as a renewable source to harvest, store up, and begin cultivating in our own lives. It is a qualitatively different experience from the simple provision of the Sabbath Day manna that we have in the wilderness. Fruitfulness is something that the wilderness doesn't offer.

Fruitfulness is something denied to the unfaithful wife.

Camp Rule #3: Unfaithfulness results in unfruitfulness.

—⊙⃕—

Our refusal to enter the Land was a major turning point in our physical journey and in the spiritual one as well. Before I go on to Korah's Rebellion in chapter 16, I want to delve into the deeper implications of what has happened here at Kadesh. We will walk through the greater consequences of our decision in the next lesson.

LESSON SEVEN

Wilderness of Paran: Consequences

We are going to pause in the journey to discuss the physical and spiritual consequences of not entering the Land. There are some sweeping consequences that we should keep in mind, and so this lesson is the "big picture." I want to talk about what it means to enter the Land or not enter the Land, both physically and spiritually.

Physical Consequences of Not Entering the Land

Our collective refusal to enter the Land has changed the group dynamics in the camp. The Lord has now divided us into three different categories:

- Those who are assured of entering the Land, namely Caleb and Joshua.
- Those who are assured of never entering the Land, namely the rest of the first generation.
- Those for whom it has yet to be determined whether they will enter the Land or not, who are the second generation, the children. This wilderness wandering is going to be their time of testing.

This separation of people into three groups as a part of judgment is a pattern that carries into both Christian and Jewish eschatology.

In Christian eschatology, it echoes of the moment of separation associated with the Rapture. There is a separating of those who have held to the faith and are gathered up to Christ from those who have fallen away and given themselves over to the lie. Following that, there is a second generation of believers who come to faith during the Tribulation for whom the Tribulation will be a time of testing to see whether they will be found faithful in the end. The three-fold division within the Numbers camp parallels the End Times Rapture to a certain extent.

This three-fold separation is also echoed in Jewish teachings: 1) in their teaching regarding the Feast of Trumpets and the Day of Atonement, which then project into 2) their prophetic eschatology. Both festivals fall in the seventh month of Tishrei, beginning with the Feast of Trumpets on the first of the month (the New Moon) and the Day of Atonement on the tenth of the month.

The Jewish Talmud teaches that the Feast of Trumpets signals a moment of judgment to separate the people of Israel into three categories:

> "Three books are opened on New Year's Day [Rosh HaShanah, aka, Feast of Trumpets]: one for the utterly wicked, one for the wholly good, and one for the average class of people. The wholly righteous are at once inscribed, and life is decreed for them; the entirely wicked are at once inscribed, and destruction destined for them; the average class are held in the balance from New Year's Day till the Day of Atonement; if they prove themselves worthy they are inscribed for life, if not they are inscribed for destruction.
>
> ... There are three divisions of mankind at the Resurrection: the wholly righteous, the utterly wicked, and the average class. The wholly righteous are at once inscribed, and life is decreed for them; the utterly wicked are at once inscribed, and destined for Gehenna, as we read [Dan. xii. 2]: 'And many of them that sleep in the dust shall awake, some to everlasting life, and some to shame and everlasting contempt.' The third class, the men between the former two, descend to Gehenna, but they weep and come up again, in accordance with the passage [Zech. xiii. 9]: 'And I will bring the third part through the fire, and I will refine them as silver is refined, and will try them as gold is tried; and he shall call on My name, and I will answer him.' Concerning this last class of men Hannah says [I Sam. ii. 6]: 'The Lord causeth to die and maketh alive, He bringeth down to the grave and bringeth up again.'"[1]

There is a similarity between the three divisions of people judged at the Feast of Trumpets and the three divisions into which the camp has now been split: those found righteous (Caleb and Joshua), those found unrighteous (the rest of the unfaithful first generation of Israel), and the third class of those who must undergo refining to see if they will be faithful (the second generation).

The Jewish Talmud is drawn strictly from the Old Testament pictures of Resurrection but the understanding falls short for its lack of understanding of Messiah. Even so, both Christian and Jewish eschatology follow the pattern of three-fold separation pictured here in the events at Kadesh. There is a prophetic picture in this.

---

1 Talmud Tractate Rosh Hashana: Chapter 1. [online] Available at: https://www.jewishvirtuallibrary.org/tractate-rosh-hashana-chapter-1 [Accessed 23 Jun. 2018].

Experiencing God in Our Desolation

At the start of the previous lesson, we talked briefly about experiencing God in the desolation of Wilderness of Paran. But that was when our stop at Kadesh was only temporary. Now this wilderness—this desolation—has become our permanent situation. We are going to wander for the next 39 years in the Wilderness of Paran until an entire generation passes away.

Remember we talked about that name, Paran, and how it comes from that root word, *pa'ar*, meaning to be glorified or beautified. The glory and beauty of this wilderness is not in its physical aspect but in the experience that we have with God here.

God will be glorified here, either by the praise of His people whom He lifts up or else by putting down those who have made themselves His enemy. Those who have set themselves against God are going to know the desolation of this wilderness as they begin to suffer the consequences of His judgment. It is a testament to the fierceness of God's power—but also the fierceness of His love—that He does not abandon us in this place. God does not put us away in this moment. God is with us even in our desolate places, even when we are under His rebuke.

We ourselves as believers today who have suffered a time of rebuke for disobedience and walking away from the Lord understand the desolation of being in that place. In this place God's power shines, but so does His love for us. The lesson of this wilderness from now on will be learning how to experience God and glorious living even in the midst of our desolation.

Becoming Others-Focused

As a result of this new living situation, we are going to experience a change of focus. We all began with one focus in this journey. We were the Lord's army, and our mission was to take the Land. But in the course of the journey, we have become completely self-focused and self-serving. It has always been about us—what we want to do, where we want to go—and our self-focus derailed us from the mission.

The Lord isn't going to disband us just because we failed that mission, but He *is* going to refocus us. The first generation is going to learn, almost overnight, what it means to be others-focused. For those of us from the unfaithful first generation, this journey is no longer going to be about us. We are never going to enter the Land, and we are never going to go back to Egypt. We have come as far as we are ever going to get in this journey and here we will finish out our lives.

Our only hope for entering the Land is in our children. This time of wilderness wandering is going to test the parents' faithfulness to God in preparing our children to enter the Land.

- We will have to instill in our children an understanding of the Law. We will have to teach them to value a relationship with the Lord that we ourselves did not value.
- We will have to instill in those children the hope of a blessing that we ourselves have lost, and the desire to press on toward that goal of entering the Land when we ourselves abandoned it.
- Having failed in our own faithfulness, we will now have to teach our children to be faithful to the Lord. We are going to have to wrestle with the fact that we ourselves are the worst examples of faithfulness to God and probably least qualified to teach our children.

Think of how difficult it is to demand self-control out of our children when we failed at abstinence in our own life. Think of how difficult it is to face our children when they are rebelling and saying to us "but you did it!" Our own sense of shame convicts us of our guilt in those moments, because many of us have a history of bad decisions from our past before we became Christians, or maybe even after we became Christians. That guilt can derail us from the mission the Lord has given us as parents.

Lift your head! Yes, we did those things. We made the mistakes, and we are suffering the consequences. Our own suffering bears witness of why the path we chose was wrong. Let it be a warning to our children. Turn it into a lesson for them of God's power and love and forgiveness.

These are the physical consequences that affect everyone in the group.

Spiritual Consequences of Not Entering the Land

This defining moment in Numbers is picked up in multiple New Testament teachings. The writer of Hebrews in particular uses this moment of failure in the Numbers' journey as an admonition to us when he discusses what it means to not enter the Lord's rest. He is going to explain the spiritual consequences of not achieving the final goal.

We are going to be looking at Hebrews 3:7–4:11 when discussing what it means to enter the Land in a spiritual journey. Before we begin our comparison, I want to outline the Hebrews passage to get a feel for the flow.

- Hebrews 3:7-19 opens with a quote of Psalm 95 talking about how we hardened our hearts in the days of the rebellion, which is the 40-year wilderness journey as explained further on in verses 16 and 17. We know that, as a punishment for our disobedience and unbelief in the journey, some of us did not enter the Land. In David's psalm, there is the additional punishment of not entering in the Lord's rest. The reasons for not entering the Lord's rest include:
    - ❖ Unbelief in departing from the Lord (v12, 19)
    - ❖ Being hardened through the deceitfulness of sin (v13)
    - ❖ Disobedience (v18)
- Hebrews 4:1-3 continues with a discussion of how a promise remains of entering the Lord's rest.
- Hebrews 4:4-11 contain a definition of the Lord's rest. It is the Sabbath rest. It is a rest that remains to us even today. Nestled in these verses is the statement that even Joshua did not give them rest when he brought them into the Land. In most translations, it names Joshua there, but in a few like the King James Version, it names Jesus. Joshua is understood to be a type of Jesus, but the reference to Joshua bringing them into the Land is in keeping with the rest of the passage.

That is the basic outline of the Hebrews passage. Now let's pick out some of the points and discuss their implications.

Hebrews 3:12-19 speaks of not entering the Lord's rest because of unbelief or lack of faith.

- 3:12 contains a warning against departing from God because of an evil heart of unbelief. The act of departing from the Lord implies that a person can be a believer and then depart from the Lord in unbelief. This point can then be carried into the argument that departing from the Lord means losing one's salvation on this journey as a result of disobedience and unbelief.
- 3:18-19 pairs disobedience and unbelief, disobedience being the outward manifestation of the inward heart of unbelief.
- 4:1 sets out the possibility of some coming part-way in belief but falling short of entering His rest.
- 4:2 sets up a comparison between those who believe the gospel and

- profit by it as opposed to those (pointing back to the example of Israel) who did not believe the gospel and did not profit from it.
- 4:3 says we who believe do enter that rest, which seems a little at odds with 3:12 which says some who believed don't enter the rest. Do you enter into the rest truly, or is there a possibility of slipping into unbelief, departing from the Lord and losing one's salvation?
- 4:6 says some enter His rest, while others won't because of disobedience.

So we have a number of statements as to who enters the Lord's rest and who doesn't. There is some ambiguity in these passages as to whether salvation can be lost over the course of a lifetime.

The Psalm speaks about not entering into the Lord's rest. The writer of Hebrews speaks of those who died in the wilderness. By assumption, these things become equated with one another in his passage and then attached to this idea of losing one's salvation:

Not entering the Land = not entering into the rest = losing one's salvation

This assumption seems plausible, but deeper investigation of the text reveals some inconsistencies in this equation. We can already see the first part isn't true from Hebrews 4:8-9 where it says that if Joshua had given them rest when he brought them into the Land, then David would not have spoken afterwards of another rest remaining for God's people (Heb. 4:8-9). So we see entering into the Lord's rest does *not* equate in Hebrews to entering the Land. These are two separate events. Even though Joshua and the second generation entered the Land, they did not enter the rest either. So that part of the equation is incorrect.

Not entering the Land ≠ not entering into the rest

Even so, entering the Land is somehow connected with that greater goal of entering into that rest. Otherwise, the writer of Hebrews would not have used that comparison.

Today, I want to sort out this picture so that we can come to an understanding of exactly what it means for us, spiritually, to enter the Land, how that relates to the greater goal of entering into the rest and also how salvation fits into all this.

Anytime a New Testament writer introduces Old Testament imagery, he expects us to bring the full context of those pictures into what he is saying. In this passage of Hebrews, the writer points us to two Old Testament pictures: our failing to enter the Land and the Sabbath.

What the writer of Hebrews is asking us to do is mesh the context of the journey with the understanding of the Sabbath—look at how one fits with the other—and then overlay that picture onto what he is teaching here. We have been studying the wilderness journey, so let's bring the Sabbath into that context.

The Sabbath Growth Chart: Three Levels of Physical Sabbath Experience

At the beginning of this class, I explained that there is a Sabbath theme that runs through this journey. We talked about God's definition of glorious living, and I explained that the Sabbath was a picture of that glorious living in its rest, peace, and provision from God. We talked about how this entire journey is something of a Sabbath for us, a formal break between the work that we did as slaves and the work we will do in the Land.

The first thing we have to remember is that when we talk about the Sabbath, we are not just talking about the Sabbath Day. There are three levels of Sabbath, and each is experientially different from the other.

Sabbath day (Exodus 16:23-29)

- On the Sabbath day, we are given one day of rest from work, and provision for that day so we aren't relying on our own works.
- How this plays out in the journey:
    - Every day we will get just enough food for that day
    - We cannot store any up for future use, as it will rot and stink.
    - On the sixth day God will give us enough food to carry us through the Sabbath day so that we don't have to work.
- This is the most basic level of relationship with God
    - It requires the least level of commitment to God and the least level of trust in God. We don't even have to be faithful to God to get this provision.
    - It is adequate, but the least glorious experience.

Sabbath year (Leviticus 25:2-6)

- In the Sabbath year, our needs are met for a year. That is one year of not relying on our own works. God causes the land to produce an extra amount of harvest in the 6th year to carry us through the 7th year.

- ◆ Unlike the manna, this fruitfulness can be stored and will become seed that we cultivate for ourselves in years to come.
- ◆ It is a time of increasing fruitfulness gifted to us apart from our works.
- ◆ This is a year of rest for the land, not the man. The man keeps working at other tasks. He just doesn't work the land.
- How this works out in the journey:
  - ◆ The Sabbath year will only be experienced by those who enter the Land.
  - ◆ When we enter the Land, the manna will stop and be replaced with fruit of the Land.
- This is the next level of relationship with God
  - ◆ It requires faith (to enter the Land).
  - ◆ It requires increasing commitment to God and an increasing trust in God.
  - ◆ It is a more glorious experience.

Jubilee year

- The Jubilee year is the 50th year following the seventh Sabbath year. It is counted as a Sabbath in its own right, making two Sabbath years back-to-back on the timeline.
  - ◆ In the Jubilee year, our needs are met for three years. A double portion of fruitfulness in the 6th year will carry us through to the beginning of the 9th year.
  - ◆ It marks complete rest from work and enemies.
  - ◆ It requires the release of captives and debts.
  - ◆ It is the time for claiming or reclaiming the inheritance.
- How this works out on the journey: there is no record that this level of Sabbath has ever been experienced in the history of Israel. It should have been experienced when they finished taking the Land from the Canaanites, but they never achieved that goal. It wasn't even celebrated in Solomon's day at the height of the kingdom.
- This is the final level of relationship with God
  - ◆ It represents living in oneness with God.
  - ◆ It requires a high level of faith in God's provision.

- It requires full commitment to God and full trust in God.
- It is the most glorious experience.

The Sabbaths represent a spiritual growth chart. Each level represents a point of growth in our trust in the Lord and commitment to Him. Each is a new and distinct level of experience, a next step toward glorification and increased oneness with God. In fact, you can even see us growing from glory to glory toward that oneness with God in this model.

The writer of Hebrews is referencing the Sabbath model. It is an experiential model. The difference from one state to the next is not in your spiritual status (saved or unsaved). The difference from one level to the next reflects your spiritual experience of God's glory. We all entered this journey as believers, but some will only achieve a basic Sabbath-day relationship whereas others will experience a more glorious Sabbath Year-experience. The goal is to be progressing toward the Jubilee level of experience.

The Timeline

The Sabbath represents a timeline. The wilderness journey is also a timeline. So let's overlay those two timelines and see how they match up.

The command to keep the Sabbath is part of the Law, and the giving of the Law falls in the same year as our coming out of Egypt. So both timelines have the same starting point.

We should have entered the Land in the second year out of Egypt. We would have come into the Land and taken the fruit of it. In the third year, we would have given a tithe of the fruit to the Levites for their food according to Numbers 18 (cr Deut. 14:28, 26:12). From then on, every seven years we would have followed the Sabbath year schedule.

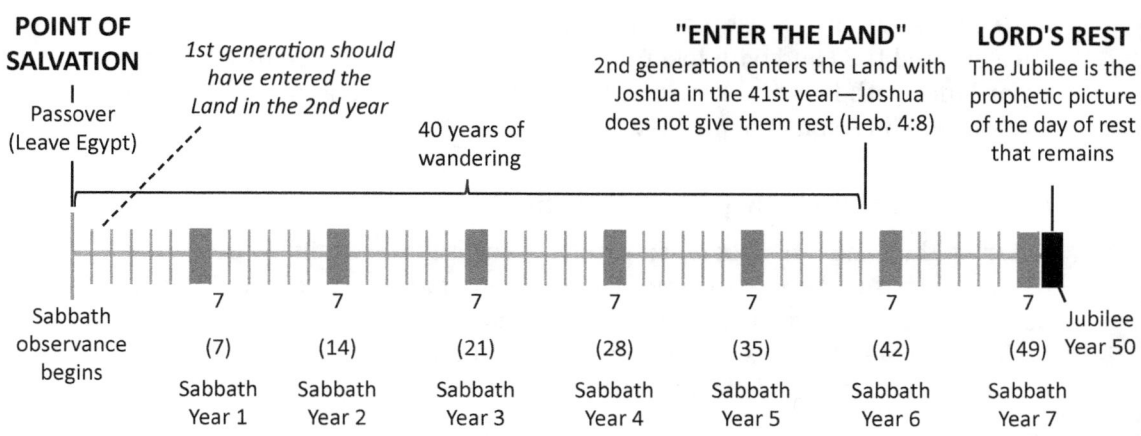

Because of our failure to enter the Land, we will spend a full 40 years in the wilderness (starting from when we left Egypt). In the middle of that 40th year after the first census generation has died, the curse will come to an end and the next generation will begin moving toward the Land. In the 11th month of that 40th year, we will come to the plains of Moab on the edge of the Land.

Reckoning from the day we left Egypt, we will enter the Land specifically on the 10th day of the first month (Jos. 4:19) of the 41st year. Notice where that puts us on the Sabbath timeline.

We are entering the Land in the 41st year. That is the 6th year of the Sabbath schedule, the year of extra fruitfulness that precedes and is provision for the Sabbath year. In this year of preparation before the Sabbath year, the Lord causes the land to grow an abundance of fruit beyond what was cultivated. We come into the Land in this year of gifted fruitfulness. We will gather and eat fruit that we have not planted ourselves and it will become the provision for the Sabbath year and seed for the following years.

The next year, the Sabbath year, will be a year of rest for the Land but not for us since we will be engaged in warfare with the Canaanite nations this year and for many years to come. Coming into the Land does not equal coming into a rest. Joshua did not give them rest.

Entering the Land is about reaching that milestone on our spiritual journey, the Sabbath year, that should launch us into a new level of experience of God's glory, but the promise of another rest remains. The Jubilee will include a rest from work, a rest from enemies, a double portion of fruitfulness from the land to carry us through the Jubilee year, and the claiming our inheritance.

The Jubilee rest is the prophetic picture of the Lord's rest being spoken of in Hebrews 4. It is the rest that remains even after the children of Israel have entered the Land with Joshua, and has yet to be observed by Israel in accordance with Levitical law. It translates into the rest that remains for us as believers on a spiritual journey.

Entering the Land in Regards to Salvation

Entering the Land does not mean receiving salvation. We talked about why the Lord was so adamant that every man should participate in the Passover before beginning this journey, to the point that He even had us celebrate a second Passover for those who missed the first one. Everyone entering this leg of the journey has identified with that Passover Lamb, which for us was

Christ at the cross. Salvation was already accomplished at the start of the journey, and having been accomplished, is assured and no longer a factor.

Entering the Land happens at a much later place on the journey than the point of salvation. It is a completely separate event. Therefore, entering the Land doesn't have anything to do with our salvation. Failing to enter the Land doesn't have anything to do with our salvation. Salvation is not a factor at this point.

Entering the Jubilee rest happens at the end of the journey. Entering the rest doesn't have anything to do with our salvation. Failing to enter the rest doesn't have anything to do with our salvation. So the correct equation is:

Not entering the land ≠ not entering into the rest ≠ losing one's salvation

The writer of Hebrews is not talking about losing our salvation when he speaks of entering the Lord's rest. He is referring to the Sabbath as an experiential model. It doesn't have anything to do with your spiritual status (saved or unsaved) but with the levels of intimacy you have with God based on increasing faithfulness. By pairing the Sabbath model with places on the Wilderness journey, we understand that he is talking about failing to enter the Lord's rest in terms of losing levels of intimacy with the Lord as a result of unbelief and disobedience.

Doctrine of Rewards

When we look at this timeline, we can see that different levels of Sabbath experience are tied to physical places on this journey. The wilderness wandering outside the Land is paired with the Sabbath-day level of experience. Entering into the Land is paired with the Sabbath-year level of experience. We enter the Land under Joshua, but the kingdom still has to be claimed. Coming into our inheritance in the kingdom and having rest from enemies in the Land is the final Jubilee-level experience. That is the Lord's rest.

When Jesus speaks about the kingdom in His parables, there is a similar pairing of levels of reward with places in the kingdom. He talks about those who will come into the kingdom with varying levels of reward and those who will be sent to the outer darkness where there is weeping and gnashing of teeth. I think we will agree that is pretty apt description of what happens in the Wilderness journey. The wilderness is to the Land what the outer darkness is to the Kingdom.

There is even another example of an "outside" designation that will come up in Lesson 12, but I will mention it here. Once we enter the Land, we begin to set up cities, and in relationship to a city there is the designated place outside the gates where the defiled are sent, similar to being put outside the camp.

Jesus talks about servants coming into the Kingdom with varying levels of reward as well as those who suffer the loss of everything. Some will become rulers with various levels of authority in the Kingdom while others will be sent out of the Kingdom. There are those who enter into the wedding feast and those against whom the gates are shut. In Jesus' parables, there is this pairing of certain levels of experience with specific places in the kingdom.

The Kingdom is like the Land. It is an environment that the Lord creates. He places Himself in that environment, and then His people are situated in that environment relative to Himself. There is a closeness to Him that is reserved for those who persevere in faithfulness. There are places attached to the Kingdom that represent degrees of separation reserved for those who are less faithful. Outside the camp, outside the gates and outside the Land are places as far from the Lord as possible yet they do not cross over into the realm of Hell and its permanent disassociation with God reserved for unbelievers.

As I discussed in Lesson 2, we all begin this physical journey to the Land with an initial allotment for our inheritance. Based on our faithfulness on the journey, our inheritance ranking will change. At the end of the journey, there will be an accounting and those who were faithful and increased will get more in terms of inheritance in the Land. Those who decreased will have their allotment taken from them, to be given to those who have increased.

What is true of the physical journey is true of the spiritual journey. Based on our faithfulness, whatever level of experience we achieve and its corresponding place is going to translate into the level of experience we will have in the Kingdom of Christ and its corresponding place, as Jesus indicates in His parables.

Another name for this teaching is the Doctrine of Rewards.

If salvation once attained cannot be lost, then in these parables where He is speaking of believers' experiences in the Kingdom, we must consider what it means for believers to be sent outside the gates. The doctrine of rewards incorporates this idea, teaching that within the Kingdom there is a place of separation for believers who have become unfaithful, equated with being put outside the gates or sent to outer darkness. It is a place of separation, and yet not equated with Hell, which is the place reserved for unbelievers.

This is not a teaching that many churches espouse, but it is one that my church teaches and of which I am convinced, based on both New Testament teachings and the model I see here in the book of Numbers.

Entering the Land, in Terms of Fruitfulness

Entering the Land has nothing to do with gaining or losing salvation. Entering the Land has to do with the experience of fruitfulness that comes with a deepening relationship and trust in the Lord.

Sabbath year fruitfulness is a physical fruitfulness provided by the Lord through the Land. It is fruitfulness beyond our own cultivation effort. It is gifted to us. Receiving this fruitfulness was meant to build trust over a longer period of time than just one day. We don't have to rely on our works for an entire year to come. The fruitfulness becomes the seed we plant for future harvests.

The New Testament equivalent of Sabbath year fruitfulness is spiritual fruitfulness provided by the Lord through the Spirit, and it is gifted to us apart from works. We don't have to rely on our own works to experience this fruitfulness. It is a renewable resource that we experience, store up and then begin to cultivate and increase in our life.

Fruitfulness is a reward of faithfulness. It goes hand in hand with Camp Rule #2 and the picture of the unfaithful wife. As a result of unfaithfulness, we will watch the first generation begin to waste away and become unfruitful. She is not put away by her husband, according to the Law, but she ceases to experience fruitfulness in that relationship.

The Perils of Not Progressing

The chapter heading for Hebrews 6:4-12 in my Bible reads "The Peril of Not Progressing" and it is particularly appropriate to the discussion of failing to enter the Land in our Numbers journey. So far in this physical journey, we have a proven history of God's power and faithfulness behind us. Now we have come to the place where witnesses have shown us the fruit and we may have tasted it for ourselves. The experience is real. The proof is tangible.

If we refuse to believe and turn back to Egypt at this point, it will be in denial of the reality of all that has happened. If we return to Egypt at this point, we devalue the death of the firstborn at our redemption. Their death will be for nothing. If we return and become slaves again, what will purchase our redemption the next time? If we return to Egypt, we put the Lord to open shame in the face of His enemies, for they will say He is a God who is unable to bring His people out of their slavery.

If we make that decision to turn back, there will be no turning around again. There is nothing left for the Lord to do that He hasn't already done to bring us into the Land.

The writer of Hebrews draws this same parallel to the spiritual journey.

> *"For it is impossible for those who were once enlightened, and have tasted the heavenly gift, and have become partakers of the Holy Spirit, and have tasted the good word of God and the powers of the age to come, if they fall away, to renew them again to repentance, since they crucify again for themselves the Son of God, and put Him to an open shame." Hebrews 6:4-6*

Again, these passages in Hebrews are not speaking about losing our salvation. I think the use of the word repentance here is in keeping with the Hebrew understanding of the word, which carries with it the idea of turning around. If we turn back at this point, it will be our last turning. God is not going to walk through all this journey with us a second time.

This generation has refused to enter the Land. They are not going on to that next level of glorious Sabbath experience. They have opted to remain in the lowest level of Sabbath experience, the daily subsistence on the Lord's provision of manna and water. If you think this is the easy life, think again.

Ask someone who lives paycheck-to-paycheck how easy life is for them. Ask them how easy it is waiting on that next installment, knowing before they even get it that it has already been spent. Ask them about the leanness and stress in their life. That is how God is going to give us manna in the wilderness. Always just enough but never with anything left over. No savings. No cushion. No rest.

I think a lot of Christians opt for the lesser relationship with the Lord without realizing how much more difficult it really is to live that way. Their needs will be met faithfully, and very little effort will be required of them besides just walking the daily walk. But as we will see in this journey, these same believers will come to a point in their lives where they are dissatisfied because the walk has become fruitless to them. They will see the walk as just trudging through sand for a lifetime, and they will often formally depart from the faith. Their dissatisfaction is a consequence of not stepping up to the next level of relationship with God when He asked them. That was a decision they made, and a failing on their part, not God's, just as the failing was on the part of the children of Israel at this point.

God will not let us return to Egypt. If we do not go forward into the next level of relationship with God, then we will remain at the base level of relationship for the rest of our lives with eternal consequences. Unfaithfulness does not result in permanent separation from God, but it does result in permanent unfruitfulness, which is the next point the writer of Hebrews makes.

> *"For the earth which drinks in the rain that often comes upon it, and bears*

herbs useful for those by whom it is cultivated, receives blessing from God; but if it bears thorns and briers, it is rejected and near to being cursed, whose end is to be burned." Hebrews 6:7-8

We are like land that the Lord has cultivated for His use, and as a result we were meant to receive a blessing of fruitfulness. But despite His cultivation, some have produced thorn and briers. They are not cursed but near to it.

Therefore, the writer of Hebrews exhorts us,

"And we desire that each one of you show the same diligence to the full assurance of hope until the end, that you do not become sluggish, but imitate those who through faith and patience inherit the promises." Hebrews 6:11-12

New Camp Rules (Numbers 15:22-41)

We covered the first half of Numbers 15 already. Now I want to finish going through the rest of the laws in Numbers 15:22-41. Before I begin, I just want to reiterate our New Covenant stance on the Law of Moses.

For Israel, living in Old Testament times before Christ, the standard is the Law. The Law represents a relationship with God based on works—the things you had to do to keep yourself physically holy and clean to maintain that relationship with Him.

We, as believers today, relate to these laws differently. Christ has come. His death on the cross is the substitute for the sacrificial system. Our cleanness or uncleanness is determined by our spiritual relationship with Christ and not our physical condition. These laws require a physical Tabernacle or Temple and a physical priesthood to carry out the penalties for sin and cleansing from sin. We are not called on to recreate the Old Testament physical environment to keep these laws.

We have entered a more glorious relationship with God through Christ. Life lived by the laws represented a very basic and fruitless relationship with God because of our inability to keep the laws in their perfection. We do not return to the lesser relationship that we had with God through the Law, which was just a shadow of what we now experience. The more glorious relationship was meant to replace the less glorious one, just as the fruitfulness of the Land replaced the manna of the wilderness. The old ends, the new begins.

That being said, these laws working in this environment create physical relationships that were meant to teach us a spiritual relationship with God. We are studying the relationship aspect. As we work through Numbers 15:22-

41, I am going to take from these laws some principles for congregational living relevant to camp life and future lessons on this journey.

Camp Rule #6: Be Others-Focused.

I am going to add this to our camp rules because it is very much part of the physical and spiritual journey we are on. This isn't actually in the text, but it is implied by the fact that the first generation will never enter the Land. Being barred from the Land, the first generation is now engaged in training their children to occupy it. They are no longer living for themselves but others.

Camp Rule #7: Learn to Judge One Another Rightly

This camp rule is taken from the laws concerning unintentional and presumptuous sin in Numbers 15:22-31. This rule is about learning how to judge sin, how to discern the difference between unintentional sin and presumptuous sin, and how to execute judgment accordingly.

Note that just because we are under punishment for sin and have been exiled to the wilderness, that doesn't mean that life ends. The journey keeps going. God is still with us, caring for us, and teaching us. He is even lifting us up. The relationship with God and each other keeps developing and maturing. We have now moved into a higher level of relationship. We are responsible for judging each other and for carrying out penalties, even death penalties.

What was true of the physical journey is true of our spiritual journey today. Even though we don't execute capital punishment on people the way the Old Testament demands, we are still called to discern the difference between unintentional and presumptuous sin, and hold each other accountable for our relationship with God, because sin will affect the spiritual health of our congregational body. We are still called to judge one another according to God's word, so we need to remember God's word, if we are to judge rightly.

In Numbers 15:22-31, we are given the definition of each type of sin.

Unintentional sin is breaking the commandments without meaning to or without realizing you have done so. It is not a deliberate act. It is done out of ignorance or oversight. The penalty is to offer a burnt offering, a sin offering, and a grain or drink offering in order to re-establish your communion with the Lord. There is forgiveness for unintentional sin.

Intentional or presumptuous sin is deliberate breaking of the laws. You knew you were breaking the commandments but you did it anyway. The penalty is being cut off from the congregation. There is no forgiveness for presumptuous sin.

Immediately on the heels of these laws comes an opportunity to practice them in the case of a man collecting sticks on the Sabbath (Numbers 15:32-36).

What class of sin is it? This is a presumptuous sin. The man knew that such a thing was forbidden and he did it anyway. We have been talking about how the Sabbaths reflect different levels of relationship with God, the Sabbath day being the least glorious. This man has scorned even the least level of relationship. His actions fly in the face of God because the Sabbath is His day of blessing.

What is the punishment? Death.

Who carries out the punishment? The people do. This is the first time in this entire journey that we are executing the death penalty on someone for breaking the Law. Up to now, the Lord and Moses have been the one dealing out death penalties.

If we are going to judge rightly, we better remember the standard God has given us for judging which brings us to the next camp rule.

Camp Rule #8: Wear Tassels

Numbers 15:37-41 details the commandment to wear the tassels (tzitzit). First and foremost, they are a reminder to us (as Old Testament Israel) of our responsibility to keep the Law and the penalty for breaking it. We were never to forget that we had a responsibility to God for judging, teaching and living out that relationship with Him.

The blue thread carries an additional significance. In ancient times, blue denoted royalty, especially God's kingship which is why blue was used so much in the Tabernacle fabrics. The blue thread within the white tassels was also similar to the blue cord that the high priest wore on his white turban. By wearing these tassels we are to remember we are identified with priesthood and also royalty.

A Royal Priesthood

Those white tassels with their blue thread invoke the picture of a royal priesthood. This is a new dimension in our relationship with God and a more glorious identification with Him. It is a reminder that even though we have been unfaithful, we are still a holy people with God in our midst. He still loves us. He is still lifting us up. He is still working with us and increasing our relationship with Him, just in a different way.

This identity as a royal priesthood translates into New Testament teachings as well. 1 Peter 2 talks about being royal priesthood and the responsibility we have to maintain correct relationships with the authorities God has placed over us.

> *"But you are a chosen generation, a royal priesthood, a holy nation, His own special people, that you may proclaim the praises of Him who called you out of darkness into His marvelous light; who once were not a people but are now the people of God, who had not obtained mercy but now have obtained mercy.... Therefore submit yourselves to every ordinance of man for the Lord's sake, whether to the king as supreme, or to governors, as to those who are sent by him for the punishment of evildoers and for the praise of those who do good. For this is the will of God, that by doing good you may put to silence the ignorance of foolish men—as free, yet not using liberty as a cloak for vice, but as bondservants of God. Honor all people. Love the brotherhood. Fear God. Honor the king." 1 Peter 2:9-10, 13-17*

Can being identified with a royal priesthood go to our heads? You bet.

Does being one of the royal priesthood mean you can take liberties and challenge authority that God has put in place? No.

This new identity of being a royal priesthood certainly goes to the heads of Korah, Dathan and Abiram, as we will see in the next lesson when they challenge Moses' and Aaron's authority.

The Journey from Different Perspectives

When we came to this lesson in class, I had to change what shoes I was standing in, since the first generation isn't going to finish the journey of the book of Numbers. I asked everyone to pick one of the two groups to identify with—either Caleb and Joshua or the children of the second generation.

We could easily have stepped into the second generation's shoes and discussed the events from their perspective—how they were affected by their parents' decisions, what they learned from their parents (or failed to learn), and what part of the journey they experienced that their parents did not.

My class decided to stand with Caleb and Joshua, and that is what I will present here. For the rest of the study we will walk through the events in the shoes of Caleb and Joshua, looking at this experience from their perspective. So what is that perspective?

Caleb and Joshua only have passive roles in the Numbers narrative from here on out. Caleb's name only comes up as part of the second census and receiving an inheritance. Joshua will be inaugurated at the next leader of Israel to replace Moses in Numbers 27, and he is assigned the task of dividing the Land by inheritance once they enter in. But neither are directly involved with any of the events that take place from here on. That doesn't mean they are not in the picture, though.

They will enter the Land, but the rest of their peers, the first generation, will not. Even though they are not under judgment for unfaithfulness, they are not exempt from the journey. They still have a role to play. Our role going forward in the physical journey is the same as we have in the spiritual journey.

- We are going to come alongside the rest of our suffering kinsmen as co-laborers. We will suffer with them in their defeats, share in their griefs, and rejoice with them in their victories. We will struggle with them. It will seem like we are covering the same ground over and over with them.
- We will watch the second generation go through many of the same lessons and failures that their parents did. We will be learning some lessons with the second generation that we did not experience with our own generation, and we will be tested with them to see if we persevere in our own faith.
- We are also leadership in training. We will observe Moses and take lessons from leadership, both good and bad. We will learn something about the people we are going to be leading and how to deal with them.

For the rest of this study we will join Caleb and Joshua, walking the journey ourselves and observing what happens to the first and second generations during this time of wandering and testing.

In our next lesson, we will be looking at Korah's Rebellion and we will see how the identity of a royal priesthood can get twisted toward the Enemy's purpose.

Overview of Camp Rules to Date

Camp Rule #1: What gets you put out of camp: Uncleanness and defilement from death gets you put out of camp. You cannot return to camp with out someone coming outside camp to cleanse you.

Camp Rule #2: Accountability between one another: Sin against others is counted as an act of unfaithfulness to God. If you have sinned, confess your sin and make restitution, to the man first and then to God.

Camp Rule #3: Accountability between husbands and wives: Unfaithfulness will result in unfruitfulness. If faithfulness is in question, it will be tested by a trial by ordeal.

Camp Rule #4: Accountability between individual and God: Self-control is a voluntary practice that expresses a desire to be closer to God. Abstinence is a choice.

Camp Rule #5: The Priestly Blessing: Love one another to be a conduit for God's love and blessing.

Camp Rule #6: Be others-focused

Camp Rule #7: Learn how to rightly judge one another: Discern between unintentional sin and presumptuous sin and execute judgment accordingly.

Camp Rule #8: Wear the tassels as a reminder of your responsibility to know the Law and judge each other rightly. Remember that you are becoming a royal priesthood.

LESSON EIGHT

The Wilderness of Paran: Korah's Rebellion

CHAPTERS 16-19

Korah's Rebellion takes place in the Wilderness of Paran, somewhere in the 40-year wandering, but the place and time are not mentioned. It is the only event noted during the wandering, but it is a significant one. In the midst of this desolate wilderness, we will watch a showdown as a group of men contend with Moses and Aaron over the right to rule the camp.

As we stand on the sidelines with Joshua and Caleb as leaders in training, watching this go down, we will take some lessons from Moses as he answers this challenge. We are also going to see a tremendous amount of prophetic imagery play out.

This rebellion is covered in chapter 16, but the effects of it continue on in chapters 17-19. I want to keep all this content together because there are pictures that span the full breadth of these chapters, so I am going to break this study into these major sections:

- We will walk through the Korah Rebellion in Numbers 16:1-40 and talk a little about how we end up with "Korahs" in our own lives.
- In Numbers 16:41-50 the rebellion continues as the rest of the congregation complains over the death of Korah and his company which then brings the Lord's wrath down on them as well. We see a dramatic turn of events as Aaron assumes the intercessor's role in making atonement for the people.
- In Numbers 17 God will validate His High Priest with the budding of Aaron's rod.
- Numbers 18 gives us another series of laws tucked into our narrative. I want to highlight a few of these which add to the picture of the priesthood, and set us up for lessons to come.
- Numbers 19 deals with the Laws of Purification in the Red Heifer Sacrifice which contains an important prophetic picture.
- As we wrap up our study of this particular incident, we will make some comparisons between Korah and Aaron which will take us into Romans 5.

Korah's Rebellion (Numbers 16:1-40)

Numbers 16:1-17 gives us the opening exchange between Moses and the opposition. A group of rebels have risen up and laid a charge at Moses and Aaron. The text specifically names Korah, and he is joined by Dathan, Abiram, On, and 250 unnamed men. Let's examine who these rebels were and what we know about them from Scripture.

Korah, son of Izhar, son of Kohath, son of Levi (v1)

Korah is the ringleader of the rebellion. He is a Levite from the tribe of Kohath. He is the first named son of Izhar (Exo. 6:21) which probably means he is the firstborn son. Being of the Kohathites, he has a particular family relationship with Aaron and Moses.

Lesson 2 (setting up camp) discussed the housekeeping duties of the Levites (Num. 4) and how the family of Kohath was divided. Let's have a quick refresher.

From Amram, the firstborn son of Kohath, came Aaron and the line of the priesthood. Aaron was the firstborn son of the firstborn son. Aaron's son Eleazar was in charge of the Kohathites who carried the holy articles.

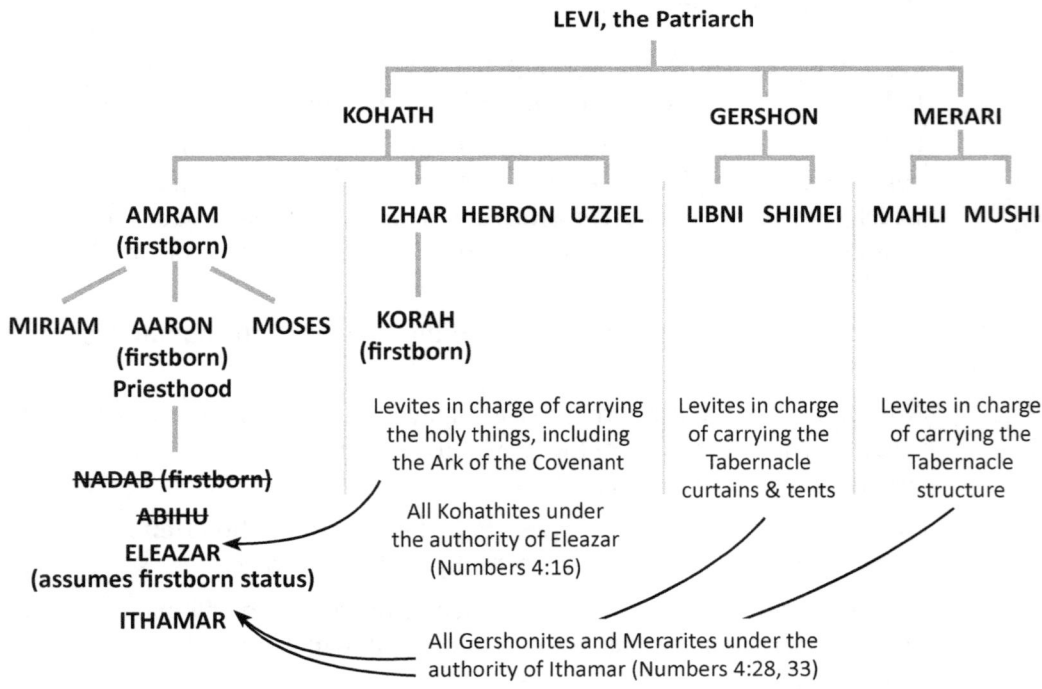

From Izhar, the second born son of Kohath, came Korah and his brothers. Korah is the firstborn son of the second-born son. He shares firstborn status with Aaron in terms of family standing, but in terms of service to the Lord, Korah must submit to the authority of his nephew, Eleazar, because it is Korah's task to carry the holy articles on the daily walk. He may even have been one to carry the Ark of the Covenant as it sets out ahead of the armies.

We see here in Numbers 16:10-11 that Korah has a grievance specifically with Aaron in that he desires to be High Priest with his own priesthood. In terms of family standing, he is nearly equal to Aaron, and yet Aaron has been honored and Korah has not, which rankles Korah's vanity. I think that is part of what is spurring Korah's grievance. In addition to that, don't forget that everyone in camp has all been given a newly exalted status of being judges of one another and being told to wear the tassels. We talked about that in the last lesson. I think this identity with a royal priesthood has gone to Korah's head. He is now lifting himself up and challenging the authorities in the camp.

250 Leaders from the Tribes

A self-proclaimed priesthood stands behind Korah, made up of representatives from among the tribes. In the Hebrew they are called princes of the assembly. They are men of renown—men of reputation and standing—and yet they are not honored with names in the text. It doesn't even mention what tribes they were from. This omission is a mark of the Lord's scorn for them.

Dathan and Abiram and On

Dathan, Abiram and On are sons of Eliab and Peleth, chiefs of the house of Reuben. On is only mentioned here once and then disappears from the narrative. Dathan and Abiram come to the forefront as they join ranks with Korah.

We should note something characteristic of the line of Reuben. The line of Reuben has a bit of a history of challenging authority.

Reuben was the first-born son of Jacob. He should have been preeminent among the tribes and his sons should have been kings among the princes. But Reuben lost preeminence among the tribes because he lay with his stepmother, Bilhah (Gen. 35:22). He usurped his father Jacob's authority and place, and as a result, he lost his standing when Jacob handed out the blessings to his sons in Genesis 49.

Reuben challenged his own father's place and authority in a most appalling way, and his descendants resist authority as well. Remember the spy Shammua who brought a bad report of the Land and agitated for new leadership? That was another son of Reuben. Now we have Dathan and Abiram challenging Moses. There is a particular lack of restraint, and a lack of a sense of boundaries, that runs in the tribe of Reuben.

The Charge

> *"They gathered together against Moses and Aaron, and said to them, 'You take too much upon yourselves* [assume too much for yourselves], *for all the congregation is holy, every one of them, and the LORD is among them. Why then do you exalt yourselves above the assembly of the LORD?'"* Numbers 16:3

The opening salvo begins with the charge that Moses and Aaron have presumed to take authority over the congregation because of their "holiness." Korah says all the congregation is holy, making Moses and Aaron no different from the rest. In truth, Korah's argument is aimed more at Aaron than Moses. Let's pick through this argument a little more deeply.

Where does Korah get that idea of the whole congregation being holy? We are indeed all called to be a holy people. Besides that, seventy elders from among the tribes now have the same Spirit in them as Moses has (Chapter 11), and all the people have been identified with a royal priesthood (Chapter 15). All called on to act as judges of each other now, to discern presumptuous sin from unintentional sin, and execute judgment accordingly.

In chapter 15, we studied the difference between unintentional sin and presumptuous sin. Which kind of sin is Korah accusing Moses and Aaron? Presumptuous sin. They charge Moses and Aaron with presumptuously assuming a level authority that they have no right to claim. What would be the penalty for that sin? Being cut off from the congregation (Num. 15:30)—a death sentence.

If the charge against Moses and Aaron proves to be false, what will happen to their accusers? If the charges brought against someone are false, and intentionally false, then the punishment the false accusers wanted to execute on the accused will be visited back on them (Deut. 19:16-20).

Korah and company lay the charge against Moses and Aaron for having assumed the leadership by their own will. In this charge we see a worldly mindset on how leadership is chosen. The world chooses leadership by numbers, by popular vote, by birthright, or by a show of force and violence. Korah and company see themselves as having the greater right according to numbers and birthright (and if necessary, by their ability to take leadership by force). They view Moses and Aaron as self-appointed leadership—but they are picking a fight with the wrong people.

Leadership is chosen among God's people *by God Himself*. God is king over all His people, and He decides what role each will play and where their places are. The right of leadership and authority does not belong to Moses and Aaron based on their holiness or ranking among their brethren, but based on God's will.

The rebels are quick to point out that the Lord is among the people, but they completely ignore the fact that He is the one in authority over them. They don't give Him His rightful place. They call themselves God's people, but downplay a personal relationship with Him. They only see themselves in physical relationship to Moses and Aaron, and not in spiritual relationship to God. It is almost as if they have objectified God as being just a figurehead without any say in the matter.

Squabbles arise among God's people over status or place when God the King is cut out of the picture. God the King puts His people in their various positions and tasks. He defines their freedoms and boundaries. No one has the right to challenge those authorities or boundaries, not even members of the royal priesthood.

We, as a royal priesthood (1 Pet. 2:9), can get caught up by the "fleshly lusts" that war in our hearts. These lusts include the glorious perks and benefits of status. We covet the glory of the position, but do we really understand the level of responsibility, commitment, sacrifices and restraint the position also demands? Does God lift us up that we should take power and glory for ourselves, or does He lift us up that we might serve and glorify Him?

At the heart of the rebels' complaint is the fact that they haven't acknowledged God as King over them. They have disdained the place they have been given among the Lord's people. When they look at Moses and Aaron, they covet the power and glory. They set themselves up as equal to Moses and Aaron and, therefore, able to take the leadership at will.

Beware of people who push their agenda by riling people up instead of calming them down. Beware of leaders who lead by emotion. Beware of people who try to sway your reasoning with emotionally-charged rhetoric. Beware of letting character assassination sway you.

Lift your heads and understand what is going on.

Keeping in Perspective

We have a Kohathite who would be a priest (a spiritual leader) but isn't.

We have men who would be kings (political leaders) but aren't.
We have men who would be a priesthood but aren't.
We have men who are unhappy with their place in camp. They want greater glory for the wrong reason.

Are these rebels going to enter the Land? No, the kingdom has been taken away from them personally and given to their children. They are already doomed to die in the wilderness. Is that reality going to change with someone different in leadership? No, and I think they know it. So what do Korah, Dathan and Abiram hope to accomplish by ousting Moses and Aaron?

Korah and Dathan and Abiram have said to themselves, "There is no hope of entering the kingdom, so we will be kings and priests within the limits of this wilderness into which we have been cast." That is a very satanic line of thinking. It is the same rationale driving Satan toward his end.

He will have no place in the Kingdom to come, so he will pursue the kingship over this realm, this world to which he has been cast down. We know kingship over this world will be his pursuit through the end of time, and in the end times, he will raise up a political leader and a spiritual leader to help him. This is the beginnings of a shadow image of end times events. We will come back to this picture after we get through the narrative. Moving on . . .

Moses Speaks to Korah and Company

In Numbers 16:5-7, Moses addresses Korah and all his company, meaning the 250 men of renown from among the tribes.

Moses' challenge is this: take censers, put fire in them and put incense in them before the Lord. Let the Lord choose the holy ones. Imagine how Aaron would react to hearing such a challenge. Aaron has already lost his sons Nadab and Abihu when they presumed to offer profane fire before the Lord, and they were legitimate priests (Lev. 10:1-3). These 250 men who are presuming to offer incense are from among the tribes. They are not even of the priesthood. Aaron knows exactly what is going to happen if they do this. These men should remember what happened to Nabab and Abihu as well, but the arrogance of our old-man nature is marked by a certain blindness.

The showdown will be tomorrow morning. Moses tells them they have one night to think it over.

- One night to consider the reason why you are doing this and who will be glorified by your actions. Are you serving God or yourself?
- One night to remember what happens when you approach the Lord in

any way other than the way He has ordained. Men who presume to be kings and priests should know the Law.

- One night to remember what happens when people overstep their place.
- One night to remember the last time the people tried to replace Moses and Aaron.
- One night to remember Miriam's leprosy for challenging Moses' authority.
- One night to remember Nadab and Abihu's death for their presumption.

Moses Speaks to Korah Personally

Having addressed the company, Moses now addresses Korah specifically in Numbers 16:8-11. He asks Korah why he is unhappy with the place God has given him. In his heart, Korah doesn't like playing second fiddle to his cousins. Korah thinks he has a right to be a priest, even a High Priest as Aaron. He is unhappy with the place God has given him among his brethren. He counts it a small thing, something unworthy or unvalued. We get no answer from Korah here.

Dathan and Abiram's Response

Finally Moses summons Dathan and Abiram but they won't come. Cravens. Instead they shout invectives back at Moses.

Let's pick apart their argument in Numbers 16:13-14. The same old Enemy strategies are a play here as well.

> *"Is it a small thing..."* That is a contemptuous parroting of Moses' words to Korah. This is the beginning of the skewed comparison.

> *"...that you have brought us up out of a land flowing with milk and honey..."* Are they talking about Egypt? Since when was Egypt ever the land of milk and honey? That was how the Land was described. By comparing the Promised Land with Egypt, they are setting Egypt up as an equal option to the Promised Land. And don't forget who brought them out of the Egypt. That was God, not Moses. So God has been cut out of the picture entirely.

> *"...to kill us in the wilderness..."* Whose fault was it that people are going to die in this wilderness? It is certainly not Moses' fault. Again, we see the focus on being victims. The hope of entering the Land and the inheritance remains to the second generation. It is only lost to those of the first generation who are unfaithful in the journey.

> *". . . that you should keep acting like a prince over us? . . . Will you put out the eyes of these men?"* That is a stab at the fact that Moses had been a prince in Egypt, and implies his authority over the people is based on that earlier ranking. We aren't in Egypt anymore. Does Moses expect the people to keep following him blindly?
>
> Is Moses the one who has blinded them and concealed these things from them? When we turned away from the Land, the Lord blinded us from seeing the way. Who is suffering blindness at this point?

Dathan and Abiram have taken all the glory that should have gone to God, turned it into a bad thing and then blamed it all on Moses. They have lifted themselves up in the eyes of the people, and determined to take the leadership from Moses. They have used all the strategies that this world uses. They have created an issue based on a skewed argument, false witness, and character assassination. They have offered themselves as the better option, as the politically correct choice, backed by force.

Have you ever had someone right there in your face, spouting absurd accusations about you? What is the natural response to that?

Moses' Reaction to Dathan and Abiram

Remember we are standing with Caleb and Joshua. We are leadership in training, so we need to take some lessons from Moses' reaction here. I love how Moses reacts in verse 15.

Moses knows God is right there with him, hearing this, witnessing this great slap in the face he is receiving from Dathan and Abiram. Moses does not waste time arguing with them. It's an absurd argument. He does not try to vindicate himself to other people who are listening. He immediately appeals to God's glory.

It is clear that these men have no respect for God, let alone Moses, so Moses asks God not to respect their offering in return. *Note:* the offering here is not referring to a blood offering for sin or trespass, but to something like a peace offering or free will offering—a tribute offering. In other words, Moses is saying that any tribute these men might bring to the Lord is hypocritical at best.

Moses points out that he has not taken one donkey from them nor has he hurt them. Taking a donkey would be considered a receipt of tribute by a ruler. Rulers of this world demand such gifts as their right. Moses has not lorded over them in this way, nor has he used his authority to harm them for his own personal vengeance, as rulers of the world are want to do to those who oppose them.

He simply rebukes them and leaves them in God's hands.

The Showdown (Numbers 16:16-22)

So let's set the stage. Korah has sent out a call and gathered all the people—the armies of the North, South, East, and West—around the door of the Tabernacle against the camp of Aaron and Moses. The 250 princes from among the tribes of Israel have gathered at the door of the Tabernacle, carrying their censers with incense burning in them. Moses and Aaron are standing before the Tabernacle. Aaron has his censer in hand.

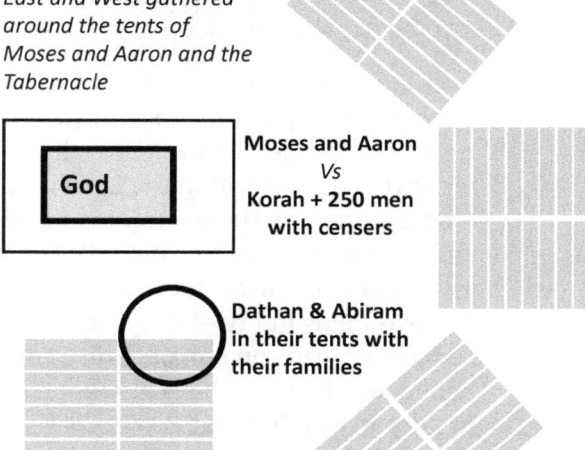

Armies of the North, South, East and West gathered around the tents of Moses and Aaron and the Tabernacle

Moses and Aaron Vs Korah + 250 men with censers

Dathan & Abiram in their tents with their families

We have the ringleaders: Korah, who has presumed to be the new spiritual leader, with Dathan and Abiram, who have joined him in this bid for power. Dathan and Abiram are in their tents camped just to the south side of the Tabernacle next to Korah's tent. Then the glory of the Lord has appeared to all the congregation at the Tabernacle.

Last Chance for Grace

It's amazing how Moses could ask for grace for the people in this moment.

> *"And the LORD spoke to Moses and Aaron, saying, 'Separate yourselves from among this congregation, that I may consume them in a moment.' Then they fell on their faces, and said, 'O God, the God of the spirits of all flesh, shall one man sin, and You be angry with all the congregation?'" Numbers 16:20-22*

Here the Lord is offering to wreak divine vengeance on all these complaining, ungrateful people who have persecuted Moses from the beginning, and instead of glorying in the Lord's vengeance, he asks for grace on some. Moses intercedes on behalf of those who have not joined with the rebels. Let's look at this statement more closely.

> *"El, Elohiym of the spirits of all flesh . . ."* a name denoting Most High God at His most powerful, most supreme, authoritative role, one who rules the spirits within man, not just the physical man of flesh. This is giving glory where glory is truly due. This appeals to His majesty and sovereignty, and it comes from a very deep unshakable understanding of who He is.
>
> *". . . shall one man sin, and you be angry with all the congregation?"* I assume that the "one man" Moses is referring to is Korah as the representative leader of the rebellion. Even though Korah is the instigator, it is clear that the Lord is angry with the lot of Israel. To Moses it appears He is condemning all the people for the sin of one man, and judging them as one man. Moses and Aaron see Korah and company as being the culprits and worthy of wrath, but they don't see the entire camp as being guilty of sin, at least not after the likeness of Korah's sin. So Moses pleads on behalf of the individuals who seemingly have not joined Korah. In this he is also appealing to God's character because it is to the glory of God that He shows grace to His people. If He were to kill them all, then it would bring shame on Him as their God.

Because Moses has upheld the name of God, God's glory and God's kingship in front of everyone, God honors Moses' request in dealing with the rebels. God is going to restrain His wrath, even though He knows that the hearts of the people are unfaithful to Him and His anointed leaders. He is going to deal with the children of Israel as a whole shortly after this, but in this moment, He lifts Moses up in the eyes of the children of Israel by agreeing to Moses' request.

> *"So the LORD spoke to Moses, saying, 'Speak to the congregation, saying, "Get away from the tents of Korah, Dathan, and Abiram."' Then Moses rose and went to Dathan and Abiram, and the elders of Israel followed him. And he spoke to the congregation, saying, 'Depart now from the tents of these wicked men! Touch nothing of theirs, lest you be consumed in all their sins.'"*
> Numbers 16:23-26

Korah, Dathan and Abiram brought trouble to God's doorstep. Now God is going to bring calamity to them.

Moses takes the 70 Spirit-filled elders and they face off with the camp of Dathan and Abiram. Every man in the congregation is given the choice at this moment as to whom he stands with: Korah, Dathan and Abiram, or God, His anointed leadership and the elders.

Get away from them, cut them from the congregation. Do not be part of their presumptuous sin. Take nothing of theirs. They have been given over to God for utter destruction. Korah, Dathan and Abiram have become *cherem*, meaning "under the ban." *Cherem* applies to their property as well, which is wholly given over to the Lord for destruction. It is not to be sold or redeemed, or in any way counted as gain or spoil of war. That is what this crisis has brought us to, the brink of open warfare within the camp. But this is not a war that Moses is going to fight. God is going to deal with the rebels Himself. The glory will be His and the spoil will be His when He puts His enemies beneath His feet.

> *"So they got away from around the tents of Korah, Dathan, and Abiram; and Dathan and Abiram came out and stood at the door of their tents, with their wives, their sons, and their little children." Numbers 16:27*

Now the greater part of the congregation withdraws from Korah, Dathan and Abiram. Dathan and Abiram are left standing in the doors of their tents, with their wives, sons and little children. Korah is also there and he has loyal supporters with him, but we should note the judgment that is about to fall on them is not going to include Korah's sons. Korah had three sons, Assir, Elkanah, and Abiasaph (Exo. 6:24), and in the second census it will be noted that the sons of Korah did not die with their father (Num. 26:11), unlike Dathan and Abiram's sons.

> *"And Moses said: 'By this you shall know that the LORD has sent me to do all these works, for I have not done them of my own will. If these men die naturally like all men, or if they are visited by the common fate of all men, then the LORD has not sent me. But if the LORD creates a new thing, and the earth opens its mouth and swallows them up with all that belongs to them, and they go down alive into the pit, then you will understand that these men have rejected the LORD.'" Numbers 16:28-30*

I love how God upholds Moses in this moment. God has not told Moses by what means He will take vengeance on Moses' enemies. It almost seems as if God is allowing Moses to dictate how his accusers will be dealt with. Moses chooses a way that brings glory only to God and establishes God's sovereign power over His people and His creation.

He does not ask for personal vengeance. He does not ask that he be allowed to kill the rebels himself or have his supporters do it. He does not ask for any spoil or personal gain from this.

He asks that they be dealt with immediately, and not just allowed to die naturally. When you are faced with arrogant rebellious people who have challenged your authority, don't you just wish that God would smite them right there on the spot? How often do we ache for swift justice? So often the wicked go on to live long and abundant lives and we try to console ourselves with the thought that our enemies will eventually die and face judgment. If

Moses is going to have any authority over the children of Israel in the future, he is going to have to establish who God is in their eyes. An immediate response is needed in this case.

Moses asks for God to do a "new thing" by having the earth swallow them. It has to be something that bears witness of God's glory and sovereignty over His creation.

> *"Now it came to pass, as he finished speaking all these words, that the ground split apart under them, and the earth opened its mouth and swallowed them up, with their households and all the men with Korah, with all their goods. So they and all those with them went down alive into the pit; the earth closed over them, and they perished from among the assembly." Numbers 16:31-33*

The earth opens its mouth and Korah, Dathan and Abiram (and their families) go down into the pit. Whenever I think of a pit swallowing the rebels, I always imagine a sinkhole. You hear of sinkholes opening up in many places around the world today, some large and some small. There was reported in the news some years back one sinkhole that had opened up under a man's house but only the floor of his bedroom gave way. He went down into the pit and was lost while the rest of his house remained standing. Such was the case here, I think.

The world today can offer any number of scientific reasons why the earth should "open its mouth" and swallow people. These sinkholes tend to happen when soil erodes away and collapses into underground caverns. The Wilderness of Paran is full of underground caverns. But what scientists cannot explain is how a sinkhole manages to close itself back up again. That remains an act of God.

I do not believe that sinkholes today are necessarily sent as divine judgments on people, and yet you cannot look at one without fear and dread rising inside you, and a desire to flee.

With the pit comes the fire. Fire consumes the 250 men with the censers. Just as it happened to Nadab and Abihu, so it happens to these men when they offer profane fire. It must be a poignant moment for Eleazar who now has to pick up the purified censers, just as he had to pick up his brothers' censers. History is repeating itself.

> *"The censers of these men who sinned against their own souls, let them be made into hammered plates as a covering for the altar. Because they presented them before the LORD, therefore they are holy; and they shall be a sign to the children of Israel." Numbers 16:38*

Verse 38 in the NASB is rendered: "As for the censers of these men who have sinned at the cost of their lives," which is a better translation in this case. You don't mess with boundaries set for the priesthood. You don't challenge boundaries a sovereign God sets to maintain His holiness in this camp. You cross those boundaries at the cost of your life.

The Reminder

These censers are now hammered out as a covering for the bronze altar of sacrifice as a memorial that *"no outsider, who is not a descendant of Aaron, should come near to offer incense before the LORD."* Every time the children of Israel come to offer a sacrifice for their sins, they are to remember the Korah rebellion. They were to remember who was allowed near the Lord, that there was a boundary they cannot cross without forfeiting their lives. When you take glory away from the Lord and exceed the realm of authority you have been placed in, it won't go well with you.

Being Happy as a Kohathite

This rebellion began with Korah's resentment over the level of authority and boundaries God has given him. He wanted entrance into the private world of the priesthood, to go behind the veil. He wanted more intimacy with the holy vessels than the Lord had allotted him.

Lesson 2 walked through the duties of the Kohathites in Numbers 4, and drew some parallels between ourselves as believers and the holy vessels. I talked about the boundaries and levels of accountability to protect the set-apart status of God's holy vessels, and how we, as believers, are also holy vessels for the Lord's use. We have boundaries and levels of accountability in our lives to help protect our set-apart status in relationships with others on our daily walk. We also have our own version of Kohathites and priests.

So what happens when the Kohathites in our lives decide they are unhappy just being our burden-bearer, and try to take a greater level of intimacy or familiarity than they should? Well, that is how we end up with our own versions of Korah in our lives.

Boundaries are a little harder to define now that we no longer have many of the physical representations. There are no veils, no fences, and no altars with hammered coverings. But boundaries still need to be observed in our relationships to others and our submission to authority. It is very easy when you are in a Kohathite role to want to demand a greater level of intimacy than you have been given. When you push yourself into the middle of relationships or try and assume authority that you have no right to, you cause friction with very bad consequences.

Back at Kibroth Hatta'avah, we talked about the frustrations of dealing with unrealistic or out-of-place expectations. We talked about how people in our lives—our Kohathites—can assume a level of authority or intimacy in our lives that crosses a boundary. They may think they are in the right to demand that level of equality with our inner circles, whether because of their position in the greater family or because they feel morally obligated to step in and direct our paths in life. In truth, there is some self-gratification for them in challenging those boundaries.

When they try to become part of our inner circle, they can cause friction and warfare with those who are rightly in our inner circle—our husbands or wives, our leadership, and even with Christ. They can become our Korah's in life.

If you have a Korah in your life, you will need to re-establish those boundaries. And there is going to be a confrontation. Ask for help from your fellow Kohathites. Ask for help from your inner circle. Above all, ask help from God. You give Him glory when you ask for help in these moments and sometimes He can resolve the situation in ways that you cannot.

The Prophetic Rebellion

Before we move into the second half of this incident, I want to mention the parallels between an end times rebellion and this confrontation between Korah and Aaron.

> "Now when the thousand years have expired, Satan will be released from his prison and will go out to deceive the nations which are in the four corners of the earth, Gog and Magog, to gather them together to battle, whose number is as the sand of the sea. They went up on the breadth of the earth and surrounded the camp of the saints and the beloved city. And fire came down from God out of heaven and devoured them. The devil, who deceived them, was cast into the lake of fire and brimstone where the beast and the false prophet are. And they will be tormented day and night forever and ever."
> Revelation 20:7-10

The Enemy is driving Korah, Dathan, and Abiram in this rebellion, just as he is the driving force behind the nations in the end times. In the Revelation account we see this gathering of nations from the four corners of the earth to surround the camp of the saints and the beloved city, whereas in the Numbers account we see a call being sent out by Korah to the armies from the four corners of the camp to gather around the tents of Moses and

Aaron and the Tabernacle compound. Just as the fire of the Lord comes out to devour the rebels in Revelation 20, so His fire also consumes the 250 men who tried to overthrow Aaron and the priesthood. It is also noted in Revelation 20 that the beast (a political leader) and the false prophet (a false religious leader) have been consigned to the lake of fire and brimstone, an echo of Korah, Dathan and Abiram being sent down into the pit.

When we sketch the basic element of the rebellion, we see a distinct End Times picture playing out. There is definitely a picture of the satanic rebellion from Revelation 20, but also a foreshadowing of the gathering of the nations against Jerusalem in the call to Armageddon (Rev. 16:13-16).

The Rebellion Continues (Numbers 16:41-50)

Even though Korah and company have been dealt with, the rebellion continues.

> *"On the next day all the congregation of the children of Israel complained against Moses and Aaron, saying, 'You have killed the people of the LORD.'"* Numbers 16:41

Not even a day has passed since the judgment of Korah. The people can still hear the ringing as the altar is plated with bronze censers. Why has none of this made a difference?

The word, *complain*, used here means "to murmur" with the added sense of digging in ones' heels and refusing to budge. It implies a hardening has taken place. This is the hardening that the writer of Hebrews talks about:

> *"Do not harden your hearts as in the rebellion, in the day of trial in the wilderness, where your fathers tested Me, tried Me, and saw My works forty years. Therefore I was angry with that generation, and said, 'They always go astray in their heart, and they have not known My ways.' So I swore in My wrath, 'They shall not enter My rest.'" Hebrews 3:8-11*

Their hearts have been hardened and God knows it. God knew even during Korah's Rebellion that the corruption went through and through the lot of them.

Moses and Aaron asked for grace for those who did not sin after the likeness of Korah's sin, and the Lord relented for the moment. But it didn't change the hearts of the people, because now the children of Israel are complaining again, saying *"You have killed the people of the Lord!"*

Are they seriously calling these rebels "people of the Lord"?

Remember the wicked spy Ammiel, the man whose name meant "kinsman of God" but did not reflect his relationship with the Lord? Can you really call yourself a kinsman of God if you reject the Lord, stage a coup against His appointed leadership and try to set up your own kingdom without Him? Again with the twisted argument and the focus on victimization! Those "people of God" sinned against their own souls and brought their own death down on their heads.

We have already been down this path before. This time the Lord is not going to restrain Himself. Just as the mob begins to wind up, the glory of the Lord appears in the Tabernacle and, boom, the plague goes out to the people. Again God says to Moses and Aaron:

> *"'Get away from among this congregation, that I may consume them in a moment.' And they fell on their faces." Numbers 16:45*

Does Moses ask for grace on the people this time? No, he doesn't. Moses' eyes have been opened. He realizes he has made as much intercession as he could but it was not sufficient. It has not had any effect on turning the people's hearts away from sin. Even though these people did not sin in the likeness of Korah and company, nevertheless, death in the form of the plague had come to reign in the camp. In order to stop this reign of death, a different kind of intervention is needed apart from what Moses and the Law can provide.

> *"So Moses said to Aaron, 'Take a censer and put fire in it from the altar, put incense on it, and take it quickly to the congregation and make atonement for them; for wrath has gone out from the LORD. The plague has begun.'" Numbers 16:46*

This time, Aaron the High Priest intervenes.

> *"Then Aaron took it as Moses commanded, and ran into the midst of the assembly; and already the plague had begun among the people. So he put in the incense and made atonement for the people. And he stood between the dead and the living; so the plague was stopped." Numbers 16:47-48*

It is important to note how Aaron makes atonement for the people. It says he puts incense on the fire in his censer, runs into the midst of the plague-stricken population and makes atonement.

From what we know of the Law, a blood sacrifice is required to make atonement for sin. But we don't see Aaron running to the altar to perform sacrifices. All he brings is a censer and incense. Can burning incense alone make atonement for sin? No. That is never the purpose of incense. According to the Law, incense is used in two distinct ways.

First, incense is burned on the golden altar before the veil as a sweet aroma to the Lord. It is Aaron's job to burn the incense before the Lord as he is tending the lamps in the morning and evening.

> *"Aaron shall burn on it sweet incense every morning; when he tends the lamps, he shall burn incense on it. And when Aaron lights the lamps at twilight, he shall burn incense on it, a perpetual incense before the LORD throughout your generations." Exodus 30:7-8*

We know that the burning of this incense represents the prayers of the people being lifted up to God.

The second use of incense is when the high priest takes it in hand as he goes behind the veil on the Day of Atonement. The Day of Atonement is the judgment day when the sins of the nation must be atoned for (which is exactly what in needed in this moment in Numbers).

> *"Then he shall take a censer full of burning coals of fire from the altar before the LORD, with his hands full of sweet incense beaten fine, and bring it inside the veil. And he shall put the incense on the fire before the LORD, that the cloud of incense may cover the mercy seat that is on the Testimony, lest he die. He shall take some of the blood of the bull and sprinkle it with his finger on the mercy seat on the east side; and before the mercy seat he shall sprinkle some of the blood with his finger seven times." Leviticus 16:12-14*

The blood, not the incense, is what is required of the High Priest for atonement, yet the incense plays a very important role in this act of atonement. There is a prophetic picture in this.

Elements of the Picture

Aaron's actions here are a pantomime of the actions of the High Priest on the Day of Atonement. He is making atonement for the nation. He is presenting incense before the Lord in the same way he does on the Day of Atonement when he goes behind the veil.

There is a departure from the Law, however, in that he is not performing the atonement in the Tabernacle. He is not where he is supposed to be. Instead, we see him running out into the midst of the stricken congregation. The people do not come to him. He goes out to the people. Also, the blood of the animal sacrifice is missing. We don't see Aaron running to the altar and slaughtering bulls on behalf of the people to make atonement for them. Aaron simply takes the censer and incense and goes.

When we look at this picture of Aaron with his censer of incense standing between the living and the dead, we are seeing a prophetic picture of a new order of High Priest. This future High Priest is not necessarily one who ministers behind the veil in the Tabernacle like the Levitical High Priest does, even though He makes atonement as a High Priest. Instead of offering animal sacrifices, He offers himself as a covering for the people to hide their sin and turn away God's wrath. The atonement He offers is sufficient to stop the reign of death, whereas the intercession performed by Moses proved insufficient.

This future High Priest creates a boundary that is not physical but spiritual in nature. Remember back when we were setting up camp, I talked about boundaries that were in place and how the physical boundaries often had a human counterpart associated with them. The Tabernacle veil was one of those boundaries that separated God from the people and it was specifically associated with the High Priest.

The curtains that separated the Holy of Holies from the rest of the Tabernacle had a gap in them. The veil performed the function of standing in the gap between the side curtains in order to complete that wall and yet provide a way into the Holy of Holies. I told you that at some point the physical veil that stands in the gap would transfigure into a man who stands in the gap. The Lord looks for that man to stand in the gap, as He says through Ezekiel:

> *"'So I sought for a man among them who would make a wall, and stand in the gap before Me on behalf of the land, that I should not destroy it; but I found no one. Therefore I have poured out My indignation on them; I have consumed them with the fire of My wrath; and I have recompensed their deeds on their own heads,' says the Lord GOD." Ezekiel 22:30-31*

In this moment, Aaron is not officiating through the veil. He has become the veil, even the veil with incense burning before it. He is the picture of a future High Priest who will become that veil in order to turn away the Lord's wrath. The incense He offers are His prayers and supplications to God. The writer of Hebrews explains fulfillment of this picture for us:

> *"Therefore, brethren, having boldness to enter the Holiest by the blood of Jesus, by a new and living way which He consecrated for us, through the veil, that is, His flesh . . ." Hebrews 10:19-20a*

> *". . .who, in the days of His flesh, when He had offered up prayers and supplications, with vehement cries and tears to Him who was able to save Him from death, and was heard because of His godly fear," Hebrews 5:7*

So let's summarize the picture in Numbers 16:41-50. We have a picture of a High Priest who:

- Makes a form of atonement for the nation that stops the progress of death. It brings an end to the reign of death in the camp at this moment. Even though this act of atonement is a departure from the Law, it is acceptable to the Lord.

- Offers himself as covering for the people instead of an animal sacrifice.
- Has become the embodiment of that picture of the veil with incense burning before it, as one who stands in the gap to stop the Lord's wrath.
- Brings an end to death and then returns to the Tabernacle (v50).

Aaron is painting a picture of Christ at His death, offering prayers to His Father in Gethsemane as He prepares to make atonement on the cross with His own body. Having made that atonement, He then returned to presence of His Father in that heavenly Tabernacle. What a magnificent picture!

From here we move on into Numbers 17, where God glorifies and justifies His High Priest. Tracking along with same passages in Hebrews, we read:

> *". . . no man takes this honor [of being High Priest] to himself, but he who is called by God, just as Aaron was. So also Christ did not glorify Himself to become High Priest, but it was He who said to Him: 'You are My Son, today I have begotten You.'" Hebrews 5:4-5*

The Budding of Aaron's Rod (Numbers 17)

Having performed the atonement and brought an end to death, Aaron then returns to his place with Moses and God at the Tabernacle (Num. 16:50) Now God is going to lift Aaron up and glorify him before his brethren with this picture of a rod (that is, a branch) that was once considered dead but will return not just to life but to fruitfulness, and even a fruitfulness that is out of season.

In Numbers 17:1-13, there are three things to note out of this incident. First, the preeminence of Aaron's rod comes not from Aaron's will but God's.

Remember Korah's accusation of Aaron and Moses that they took their authority by their own power and will? Here, God chooses the rod. Aaron himself did nothing to bring this rod back to life. The transformation took place while the rod was out of Aaron's power.

Secondly, the fruitfulness of Aaron's rod comes from God's works, not Aaron's. God could have chosen any number of things to do with that rod to make it stand out from the others. This was the same rod that Aaron threw down in front of the Egyptian court and it became a snake (Exo. 7:9). This is the rod that turned Egypt's waters to blood and brought the plagues of frogs and lice on the land (Exo. 7:19-20, 8:5, 16-17). This time God chooses to make it fruitful with a particular kind of fruit, the almond. It came back to life in the form of an almond branch with buds, blossoms and fruit, all three at one time. This is usually a six-month process, but here it happens overnight.

Of all the varieties of fruitful life, God chooses the almond with a purpose. The shape Aaron's rod takes is similar to the almond branch that the golden lampstand is modeled after. God produced in Aaron's rod a likeness of the golden lampstand in the Tabernacle, of which the High Priest himself is keeper (as we are reminded of back in Number 8.) So we have this developing association between the light in the Tabernacle, the High Priest, and the rod that has come back to life and produced fruit—all symbolic of a future Christ.

Finally (and this hearkens back to our camp rules) we see that fruitfulness is the reward for faithfulness. Aaron's obedience has born fruit in a way that none of the other's have.

Just like the bronze censers that are now a covering for the altar of sacrifice, Aaron's rod is also going to be kept as a reminder. It will be placed in the Holy of Holies with the Ark of the Covenant, along with a pot of manna and the tablets of the commandments.

More Laws (Numbers 18)

Following the Rebellion and the budding of Aaron's rod, we have the introduction of another set of laws in Numbers 18. They are, in part, fallout of the rebellion. Their purpose is to reestablish the place and duties of the priesthood and Levites. I will not go through these thoroughly, but here are some important highlights.

In Numbers 18:1-3, the High Priest is told that he and his house will bear the iniquity for the sanctuary and the priesthood. The Levites are joined with them, but cannot approach the articles of the sanctuary (they are restricted to the courtyard). If they do approach, then they will die, and *"you also"* (v3). The priesthood is held accountable for the Levites handling of the Tabernacle's holy things. The priest and Levite will die if the holy things are mishandled. This is going to be brought to bear in the next failing on this journey.

Numbers 18:8-20 defines how food is provided for the Levites—what offerings they can eat and what offerings their families can share.

Numbers 18:21-32 defines how the people are to support the Levites with tithes. This is the tithe of the third year from the fruits of the Land, and will not be practiced until the people actually come into the Land.

The people tithe to the Levites. The Levites tithe to the priesthood.[1]

The Laws of Purification and Red Heifer Ritual (Numbers 19)

The Laws of Purification and Red Heifer Ritual is tucked into the end of the discourse on the priests' duties. The message has been rammed home that God's priesthood is to be considered inviolate. One of the driving factors of Korah's Rebellion was the desire to have an active role in priestly functions. Korah and the 250 men of renown went too far in their bid for the priesthood, yet there remains for the rest of us here in camp the command to wear the tassels and an implied identification with a royal priesthood.

Just because the priesthood is the official intercessor with God does not mean that the children of Israel don't have a part, too. This law will clarify the role we as the body play in interceding for and purifying our kinsmen. We don't have to be part of the priesthood proper to perform certain acts of a priestly nature. This passage on the Laws of Purification is going to outline our role in this.

This purification ritual is prescribed specifically for cleansing after a person has been defiled by something dead. There has been a lot of death in the camp. No one escapes defilement of this nature when so much death is happening around us.

I am first going to outline the ritual and the facilitators in Numbers 19:1-22, and then we will walk through the process.

The Ritual

- We begin with one red heifer, solid red without blemish or defect, and having never been yoked (v2).
- Eleazar, son of the High Priest, officiates its sacrifice outside the camp because it is classified as a sin offering (v4).
- Its blood is sprinkled toward the Tabernacle, later the Temple (v4).
- The sacrifice must be wholly burnt with the elements of hyssop, cedar wood, and scarlet dye (v6). Hyssop is an herb used for cleansing, but also considered a symbol of lowliness in contrast to the cedar wood, which is an Old Testament symbol for something being exalted or lifted up. These two elements together present an opposing picture.

---

1   Hebrews 7:1-10 adds an interesting note that even though the priesthood didn't tithe to anyone, their ancestor, Abraham, tithed to the Priest-King Melchizedek. So in that sense, the priesthood tithed through their father Abraham, who was their representative.

How can something be considered lowly and be lifted up at the same time? The scarlet dye is symbolic of blood.

- The ashes are gathered and stored outside the camp in a clean place for future use (v9). There is a unique aspect to the ashes themselves. Unlike blood or water which degrade and become contaminated with long-term storage, ashes can be stored forever and not degrade. So long as they exist, they can be used to purify generation after generation. Given that a completely red heifer meeting all the requirements was something of a biological anomaly, only nine red heifers have ever been offered in the history of the Jewish people, and yet these served the purification requirement for all the generations of Jewish people up to the time of Christ.[2] In some Jewish circles, it is believed that Messiah will facilitate the tenth sacrifice. (He did, just not how they expected.)

- When needed, the ashes had to be mixed with living (running) water in order to be applied (v9, 17). The mixture is referred to as the water of purification or the water of separation. The mixture must be sprinkled with a hyssop branch on the unclean person and on the tent and vessels if needed (v18) on the 3rd and 7th day or the cleansing is not accepted. (v12)

The Facilitators

In order to perform this cleansing, all facilitators have to be clean.

- Eleazar, son of the High Priest, officiates on behalf of his father, the High Priest. This cannot be performed by the High Priest himself because he is holy and not allowed to make himself unclean under any circumstance. It has to be performed by his son and it is a one-time act. So long as those ashes last, another sacrifice is not needed. After the sacrifice, Eleazar becomes unclean until evening and must wash his clothes and body (v7).

- The burning can be done by any third party. The one who burns the sacrifice becomes unclean until evening and must wash his clothes and body (v8).

- The one who gathers the ashes can be any congregant. He becomes unclean until evening and must wash his clothes and body (v10).

- The one who mixes the ashes with the water or touches the water

---

[2] Parsons, James J. (2018). The Tenth Red Heifer. [online] Hebrew4christians.com. Available at: http://www.hebrew4christians.com/Articles/Tenth_Red_Heifer/tenth_red_heifer.html [Accessed 29 Jun. 2018].

of purification can be any congregant. Both become unclean until evening (v21).

- The one who sprinkles the unclean with the water can be any congregant. He must wash his clothes only but he himself is not considered unclean (v21)

The Red Heifer sacrifice is unique in terms of its mediation. Whereas the sin offering is solely mediation by fire (wholly burnt), the red heifer sacrifice combines aspects of purification by fire and by water. The ashes represent a sacrifice that has been purified through fire, the refining process by which impurity is removed, but is applied to the person by the vehicle of water.

Anything that has been defiled by a dead body must be put through fire for purification. Anything that cannot withstand refining by fire must be put through water containing a representative of the refining process, that is, the ashes (Num. 31:23). When a person is sprinkled with the water and ash, the refining process (the substitutionary ashes transferred by the vehicle of water) is attributed to him to make him clean.

Picture of Christ in the Red Heifer Sacrifice

Jesus, the Son of God, offered Himself as this sacrifice. He was perfect, without blemish or defect. He was put to death by the Romans (a third party, not the priests) outside the gate. His death included the hyssop, wood, and a scarlet stain. The purpose of His death was to purify us from sin and cleanse us from the condemnation of death.

Just as ashes transformed by fire no longer decay, so Jesus now lives eternally in a glorified body that no longer decays. As long as He lives, His sacrifice facilitates the cleansing for all who are defiled by death. He is both the sacrifice and the living water that washes us (Eph. 5:25-17, Titus 3:4-7).

He arose on the third day, the day when the application of the sacrifice was deemed acceptable by the Father.

Glory in Humility

Notice how many of these tasks associated with this sacrifice fall to the general congregation. The priest is only involved in the initial act of atonement at the point of sacrifice. His role is a one-time act. Once the sacrificial requirements are met, then it remains to the rest of the congregation to perform the application of the waters on an as-needed basis. The only qualification for the facilitators is that they be ritually clean; and yet in the process of administering the purification, they become unclean. This begs the question, "Why would you volunteer to do something you knew would make you unclean?"

It would depend on how well you understand glory from God's perspective. The idea of glory in humility challenges us with an opposing picture, just as the pairing of hyssop and cedar in the ritual.

There is a glory in status as being one of the priesthood. There is authority and status and power that comes with those stations. There is the sense of being very close to God and achieving the pinnacle of cleanness and holiness before God. This was the glory and status that Korah tried to take for himself.

Korah set his sights on being the High Priest which would have exempted him from the dirty act of facilitating this sacrifice. He would not have coveted the inglorious job of going outside the camp into the world of defiled and dying people and ministering to them. Doing this for a brother means sacrificing your own status and your own purity, making yourself ritually unclean. This level of humility and care of others comes from a desire to see a brother lifted up, even at the cost of your own status. Korah would have seen no glory in that—*but God does* because such an attitude aligns itself with His character and His desires.

Sacrificing Personal Status and a False Sense of Purity

Pride and status seeking within the body is one of the biggest pitfalls we experience as believers. Learning to see glory in humility and to be others-focused is part of the journey toward a mature relationship with God.

Our mission is not to keep ourselves inside the camp in our holy huddle. Our mission is not to serve God only within church walls. Sometimes Christians can hang on to a false sense of "purity" in demanding that all activities go on only with the church, and their whole focus is on getting people to the church instead of taking Christ out to the community.

We can project a false sense of purity by whom we are seen with. Heaven forbid we sit on a park bench with a "sinner"! What would other Christians say about the people we are associating with? Being one of the "clean" people is still a status symbol to some Christians. This is a false sense of purity and it does not give glory to God.

We are called to go "outside the camp" and bear the same reproach Christ bore, even when it is reproach from our own peers.

> *"For the bodies of those animals, whose blood is brought into the sanctuary by the high priest for sin, are burned outside the camp. Therefore Jesus also, that He might sanctify the people with His own*

blood, suffered outside the gate. Therefore let us go forth to Him, outside the camp, bearing His reproach." Hebrews 13:10-13

Camp Rule #9: Be willing to go outside the camp to restore a brother, even if it means a loss of your own personal status and "cleanness." This act is an expression of loving your brother.

Korah is to Aaron as Adam is to Christ

There is one last picture that comes out of Korah's Rebellion that I want to discuss. It is the contrast of Korah to Aaron. If we were studying this the way Jewish scholars do, we would note that both of these men are firstborn sons and they are set closely together in the incident, which indicates that a comparison should be made between them. So let's do that.

Before we get to the comparison, I want to draw our attention back to Numbers 16:22, where Moses asks this question, *". . . shall one man sin, and You be angry with all the congregation?"* This is a very important question, and I want to draw two points from it. First, Moses points out that the Lord is treating all of Israel as one man; and secondly, the sin of one man, Korah, is being attributed to the whole, making all of them guilty of the one man's sin.

Moses does not understand why God is seeing the nation of Israel as being guilty of one man's sin when they haven't sinned after the likeness of Korah's sin. He is grappling with a picture of God's nature that is half-hidden from him.

When I read Moses' question, *"shall one man sin, and You be angry with all the congregation,"* in my mind I answered, yes, He can. As a New Covenant believer, I have Paul's commentary in Romans 5 that provides an answer to Moses' question.

> *"Therefore, as through one man's offense judgment came to all men, resulting in condemnation, even so through one Man's righteous act the free gift came to all men, resulting in justification of life." Romans 5:18*

From where we stand today as New Covenant believers, we understand the concept of one man being representative of all men, and we know that Paul is speaking here of the contrast between Adam and Christ. But in the wilderness, Christ is unknown. So how does God convey to us an understanding of the future relationship between Adam and Christ when Christ is veiled?

The Law tutors us by giving us a shadow picture that has a similar relationship to the future fulfillment. We know that Moses is speaking of Korah when he says *"shall one man sin."* Korah stands in opposition to Aaron. There is a relationship between these two firstborn sons that is going to explain the relationship Paul describes between Adam and Christ.

Korah is a type of the first man whose offense brought judgment on all, and death to the camp. Aaron is a type of the (veiled) Christ, whose righteous act of intercession and atonement for the people brought life.

I am going to walk through the Romans 5 passage and consider it next to this picture of Korah and Aaron because it really is a perfect match to Adam and Christ.

> *"Therefore, just as through one man sin entered the world, and death through sin, and thus death spread to all men, because all sinned . . ." Romans 5:12*

Korah was the instigator of the initial rebellion. Following his action the whole nation of Israel has now sinned and is condemned because they have identified with Korah in saying *"You have killed the people of God."* Korah himself died for his sin, but now death has spread throughout the camp.

> *". . .For until the law sin was in the world, but sin is not imputed when there is no law. Nevertheless death reigned from Adam to Moses, even over those who had not sinned according to the likeness of the transgression of Adam, who is a type of Him who was to come." Romans 5:13-14*

Just because one man sins, does that mean condemnation falls on all? Legally, no (Deut. 24:16), but in practice, it certainly has played out that way, just as God knew it would. Moses and Aaron saw Korah and company as being the culprits and worthy of wrath, but they didn't see the entire camp as being guilty of sin, at least not after the likeness of Korah's sin. Moses saw Korah's sin as an isolated case. God saw what Moses and Aaron did not see. He saw Korah's sin but also that the people had identified with Korah and the corruption infected all the people. The plague God sent is merely an outward manifestation of the inward condition.

> *"But the free gift is not like the offense. For if by the one man's offense many died, much more the grace of God and the gift by the grace of the one Man, Jesus Christ, abounded to many." Romans 5:15*

Aaron, God's righteous High Priest, is a type of Christ to come. Even though Aaron does not die at this point as Christ did, he nevertheless offers himself as a covering for the people. He does this of his own free will. It is not his lawful duty. It is a gift.

"And the gift is not like that which came through the one who sinned. For the judgment which came from one offense resulted in condemnation, but the free gift which came from many offenses resulted in justification. For if by the one man's offense death reigned through the one, much more those who receive abundance of grace and of the gift of righteousness will reign in life through the One, Jesus Christ..." Romans 5:16-17

Aaron stands as representative of all of them and as covering for all of them. The sins of the many, condensed into a single representative man, are now atoned for and forgiven. And so we conclude:

"Therefore, as through one man's offense judgment came to all men, resulting in condemnation, even so through one Man's righteous act the free gift came to all men, resulting in justification of life. For as by one man's disobedience many were made sinners, so also by one Man's obedience many will be made righteous." Romans 5:18-19

Korah and Aaron are an excellent illustration of what Paul is talking about in Romans 5. This is the purpose of the Books of Moses, to give us the pictures that go with the New Testament teachings. God uses Korah's catastrophic failure and Aaron's righteous intercession to teach His people something about their spiritual relationship to Himself through a coming Messiah (a relationship that not even Moses understood, or he would not have asked that question *"shall one man sin, and You be angry with all the congregation?"*). God orchestrated these events to highlight the contrasting examples of these two firstborn sons.

Conclusion

So we see many pictures of Christ throughout this incident in Numbers:.

- A large part of the book of Hebrews follows a parallel track with Numbers 16-19 in its commentary on Christ, the more glorious High Priest.
- Korah and Aaron become types of the relationship between Adam and Christ that Paul explains in Romans 5.
- The budding of Aaron's rod foreshadows the picture of a resurrected Christ, the heavenly High Priest, whom the prophets call the Branch.

―∞―

Next we will move on to the Wilderness of Zin, where the pictures of Christ reach a crescendo. The Wilderness of Zin will be the moment of our greatest discouragement, and yet it will also hold the greatest pictures of hope in a future Messiah. When we are at our worst, God's glory is at its greatest.

LESSON NINE

The Wilderness of Zin

CHAPTERS 20–21

Thirty-nine years ago we left Kadesh and we have been wandering in the Wilderness of Paran. Now, at the start of the 40th year, the Lord is going to bring us back to Kadesh, on the border between the Wilderness of Paran and the Wilderness of Zin. We are not going to take the original route north as we were supposed to the last time. That path is closed to us. From this place we turn east and begin our trek through the Wilderness of Zin.

The Wilderness of Zin has some unique geological features. There are a series of flat, barren valleys encompassed by ragged saw-tooth cliff on all sides, very much like the American Grand Canyon in their sculpted rock formations, except these formations were made by wind, not water. In the Hebrew, they are called the Maktesh, the grinding bowls.

The lessons we are going to experience in this wilderness in the last year of the journey are going to make us feel like we are indeed in the grinding bowl. As we journey through this area, we are going to find ourselves in hot, windy, waterless places, and it will be an extreme test of our trust in God and faithfulness to Him.

In this leg of the journey, we are going to begin at Kadesh and work our way through the Maktesh until we come out on the flood plain of the Arava River Valley. Here we will run up against the mountains of Edom.

Highlights on this leg of the journey include:

- Miriam's death at Kadesh (20:1)
- Moses' personal failing at Kadesh (20:2-13)
- Our impasse with the kings of Edom and Moab (20:14-20)
- Aaron's death on Mount Hor on the edge of the Wilderness of Zin (20:21-29)
- An engagement of the enemy in battle (21:1-3)
- The Bronze Serpent incident (21:4-9)
- The death of the last of the first generation

The narrative of chapters 20-21 gives us a string of incidents involving the enemy within (our own internal camp problems and personal testing) and the enemy outside (battles that we fight). In this lesson we will work through the internal problems, specifically Moses' error at Kadesh, the death of the High Priest and the Bronze Serpent incident. In the next lesson we come back through these chapters and address the challenges of engaging the enemies outside.

Let's begin with our internal problems.

Discouragement

The greatest challenge that is going to hit us on this part of the journey is discouragement. Discouragement comes over time and from having fought the same battle against the same enemy for too long. It comes from trying to move forward and hitting obstacle after obstacle that hinders our progress.

Discouragement comes with a sense of fruitlessness.

Fruitfulness is what makes the journey bearable. Those moments in our spiritual walk when we get tastes of the peace, the rest, and the joy—those are what urge us on and keep us going. Those are the little rewards that keep the promise of the greater reward alive in us, and make the relationship with God something to be yearned for and pursued. But you have to commit to that greater level of relationship with God to get that reward.

We are standing with Caleb and Joshua. For us, this wilderness journey has been difficult, but not unbearable because the hope is still alive in us of seeing that land and receiving our promised inheritance. But for the rest of our kinsmen from the first generation, there will be no hope for a more fulfilling experience.

At this point, discouragement sets in.

Discouragement is an issue that often develops over time in both the physical and spiritual journey. It is a consequence of unfaithfulness and a lack of trust in the Lord.

In the Wilderness of Zin, we have come to the grinding bowls, both physically and spiritually. The grinding bowl moments hit all of us at some point in life. Mature believers will struggle at these times along with immature believers. The only way to keep ourselves from being overwhelmed by discouragement is to remain focused on God. The grinding bowls are the ultimate test of our faithfulness, how well we understand who God is in His glory, sovereignty, and power, and how deeply we trust Him to carry us through this place. If we try to get through this time by our own effort, will, or wisdom, we will sink into discouragement and bitterness.

Hope

The Lord can take the most inglorious moment for men and transform it into something of surpassing glory for Himself. He is the master of these kinds of reversals. Out of the depths of discouragement in this wilderness will come great hope. Out of our weakness, God will reveal His strength. Out of the lowest point on our journey, the picture of the Savior will reach a new height. This will be a place of great death but also a place of great release.

In this place, the Lord is going to bring us to the deep understanding of our sin and the need for salvation, and then He is going to paint picture upon picture of a future Savior who will die to atone for our sin. This current generation will not see the hope, but through their lives, future generations will come to understand it.

I am going to work through the events that happen as we pass through the Wilderness of Zin, look at how the children of Israel came to this point of discouragement, how it plays out in the narrative, and then draw some parallels to our own spiritual journey. We are also going to examine the pictures of Christ that come out of this grinding bowl experience.

Moses in the Grinding Bowl (Numbers 20:1-13)

We see in Numbers 20:1 that it is the start of a new year. We come into the Wilderness of Zin in the first month, which means we will celebrate the Passover here. There is no water. There is no food. The people begin to complain, again.

How many times has this happened, and how many times has the Lord been faithful to us?

Starting back to the early days when we first came out of Egypt, in the Wilderness of Sin, we complained about the bitter waters of Marah; the Lord made them sweet (Exo. 15:22-25). We complained of no food; God gave us manna from heaven (Exo. 16).

We complained of no water again at Rephidim; God gave us water from the rock. That place of failing was then renamed Massah Umeribah (Massah and Meribah) meaning tempting and contention (Exo.17:1-7).

Now, in the Wilderness of Zin, some complain of no water at Kadesh. God gave us water from the rock before, and He is going to give us water from the rock now (Num. 20). This will be a place of failing for some of us, and also for Moses who responds the wrong way. For this reason, this place will be renamed Meribah Kadesh.

There are two places now named Meribah—Massah Umeribah in the Wilderness of Sin to the west and now Meribah Kadesh here in the Wilderness of Zin, to the east. They are a great distance apart in terms of the physical journey, and yet it is almost as if we are back at square one in terms of our spiritual journey. There has been no progress at all in our relationship with God.

Here at Kadesh, Moses is in the grinding bowl. These people have been grinding away at him for 39 years now. He has led them, provided for them, prayed for them, interceded for them, and yet their constant eroding complaints continue.

In verse 3, they begin by complaining for not having died with their brethren. What brethren are they talking about? Those who went down into the pit with Korah? Those who died by fire before the Lord? Those who died by plague because of the corruption within them?

In verse 4 they complain about Moses bringing them into this wilderness where they and their animals will die. Has any person (or animal, for that matter) ever died for lack of food or water on this journey? No. Notice there is the inclusion of animals dying here. I think that reflects the sheer barrenness of the Wilderness of Zin. It was even without vegetation for animals. It is interesting how the sense of victimization has progressed through this journey from everyone, to women and children, and now to animals. Yet the only people who are going to die in this wilderness are those who are unfaithful.

In verse 5 they complain about being brought out of Egypt to this evil place where there is no grain or fruit or water to drink. Have they forgotten why we were brought out of Egypt? The Lord brought us out to show His glory to us and through us, and so He would in turn lift us up as His people. How did we end up in this evil place? We were all meant to enter the Land. Their failing has brought us to this place. They chose this path in life because they refused to give glory to God and accept the glorious life He had planned for them. What are they missing in their lives? Grain, figs, grapes, pomegranates. Fruitfulness. This journey has become a fruitless endeavor.

The sad thing is, their life did not need to be completely fruitless, even in this wilderness. After failing to enter the Land, the Lord re-purposed their life so that they should not live for themselves but for their children. Their hope is not in entering the Land themselves, but in their children entering the Land. Their hope is not to realize physical gain for themselves, but a spiritual gain for their children.

If they had taken responsibility for the path they chose, submitted to God's will and embraced this new purpose He gave them, I think they would have realized a little bit of fruit from it. Not in a physical sense, but in a spiritual sense. There would have been a purposefulness about life. And yet it seems they have failed to embrace this task also. They are still focused on themselves and their own lack of physical fruit and water.

God is going to solve the water problem, but not the fruit problem. He provides for necessities, but not the abundance.

God's Command

God is going to command Moses to bring water from the rock, but this is not the first time. There is another instance of Moses bringing water from the rock recorded in Exodus 17:5-6, and it would be good to compare these two records because there is a picture of Christ in them.

Let's begin with Exodus 17:5-6 and then come back to Numbers 20:7-8. I want to pay close attention to the rock and the rod in both.

> *"And the LORD said to Moses, 'Go on before the people, and take with you some of the elders of Israel. Also take in your hand your rod with which you struck the river, and go. Behold, I will stand before you there on the rock in Horeb; and you shall strike the rock, and water will come out of it, that the people may drink.' And Moses did so in the sight of the elders of Israel." Exodus 17:5-6*

"Take your rod with which you struck the river..." That is the rod that struck the river in Egypt and turned it to blood. It is also the rod that parted the Red Sea and then brought it back down on the Egyptians. It is the rod of judgment.

"Strike the rock and water will come out..." The word for "rock" here is the Hebrew word, *tsur*. *Tsur* is used to describe a foundation rock or boulder from a quarry or cliff, a base or lowly rock. It is a place of refuge in a time of siege or warfare because it stands in spite of being battered and struck.

> *"Then the LORD spoke to Moses, saying, 'Take the rod; you and your brother Aaron gather the congregation together. Speak to the rock before their eyes, and it will yield its water; thus you shall bring water for them out of the rock, and give drink to the congregation and their animals.'" Numbers 20:7-8*

"Take the rod..." Verse 9 says that Moses takes this rod from before the Lord. This verse is cross-referenced in my Bible to Numbers 17:10, where it speaks of Aaron's rod that was placed in the Tabernacle with the Testimony as a reminder of the High Priest's authority and glorification. This is not a rod of judgment but a glorified rod.

"Speak to the rock..." and water will come out. The word for rock here is the Hebrew word, *cela*. *Cela* describes a lofty rock that you must lift your eyes to see, a craggy peak, a stronghold that cannot be breached. It is a glorified rock.

Between these two accounts, the Lord is painting a picture of Christ. Christ is the rock, as Paul explains in 1 Corinthians 10.

> *"Moreover, brethren, I do not want you to be unaware that all our fathers were under the cloud, all passed through the sea, all were baptized into Moses in the cloud and in the sea, all ate the same spiritual food, and all drank the same spiritual drink. For they drank of that spiritual Rock that followed them, and that Rock was Christ." 1 Corinthians 10:1-4*

The picture of Christ, the Rock, in Exodus is a different picture from the one in Numbers. In Exodus, the rock is a lowly rock being struck with the rod of judgment. That is Christ on the cross. In Numbers, He is a glorified rock, and the presence of Aaron's rod—the rod that came back to life and bore fruit— adds to that picture of a resurrected and glorified Christ. In Numbers, He is not to be struck with the rod. Moses is commanded just to speak to Him and He will provide the life-giving waters. Ask and you shall receive.

Moses' Response

In Numbers 20:9-11, Moses is going react to the people's grinding on him. He is going to say something wrong, and then he is going to do something wrong. Of the two, his words will get greater condemnation than his action.

> *"So Moses took the rod from before the LORD as He commanded him. And Moses and Aaron gathered the assembly together before the rock; and he said to them, 'Hear now, you rebels! Must we bring water for you out of this rock?' Then Moses lifted his hand and struck the rock twice with his rod; and water came out abundantly, and the congregation and their animals drank." Numbers 20:9-11*

Remember earlier in this study, we talked about the tongue getting us into trouble. But the tongue isn't really the problem. The problem is the heart, and the tongue is simply the means of revealing the heart attitude. From Moses' words in verse 10, *"Hear now, you rebels! Must we bring water for you out of this rock,"* what is in Moses' heart right now? Anger, frustration, bitterness...

As Moses is walking to the Tabernacle to get Aaron's rod, and then walking over to the rock, I imagine he is remembering all the times these people have contended with him as if he personally was responsible for their predicament.

> Why does everyone blame me? God is the one doing this. God led them here. God is the only one who can provide these things. Do they think He is blind and deaf, that He doesn't see or hear their needs? What can I do?

> *"If only we had died when our brethren died before the LORD..."* Yes, why couldn't they all have died in Korah's rebellion? God wanted to consume them all then and there, but I had to open my mouth and intervene. I didn't want to see innocent people suffer for the sin of one man, but all they did was turn on me. I should have kept my mouth shut and let God consume them.

> Water, water, water. The rod, the rod, the rod. Strike the river with the rod and turn it to blood. Part the Red Sea with the rod. Put a branch in the bitter water to turn it sweet. Strike the rock with the rod and it will give water. Now God says get the rod and *speak* to the rock. Forty years I've been doing this, and still these people contend with me. How they have provoked me! They want water? I'll give them water!

When we started this journey, Moses was displeased with our complaining over the craving for meat. He became incensed with Korah and company when they rebelled. Now Moses has finally reached his boiling point, and he bubbles over. Let's dig into the words he is using here.

"Hear now, you rebels!..." The Hebrew word for rebels here is *marah*. *Marah* is a very evocative word to use. In one use, *marah* means to be rebellious or contentious in the sense of lashing out or striking. Moses calls them *marah*—rebels—because they have rebelled against God but also because they have given him grief now these forty years. They have provoked him, and struck at him without cause, and now it's his turn to lash back at them.

But *marah* has a second meaning in the Scriptures. It is often used as a proper name, but comes from the root meaning bitter, usually in regards to water but also to tears of anguish over personal failure. Here are some examples:

- Marah is the spring of bitter water that Israel came to at the outset of the journey. The waters of Marah (Exo. 15:23) were undrinkable because of their bitterness, but were turned sweet when Moses touched them with the branch of a tree. Marah was the first test of Israel's faith and the place of their first failing.
- Marah describes a bitterness or anguish of heart that come with the

realization of hopelessness or failure. Tears of anguish are marah—bitter waters.

- According to the Law, the bitter water will bring a curse on a married woman who has strayed from her husband, as we read in Numbers 5. If she has been unfaithful, the bitter waters will reveal it by causing her to lose fruitfulness the rest of her life. She will have no children. The *marah*—bitter waters—are part of that test of faithfulness.

Let's consider how *marah* applies to Moses.

Moses calls the rebels *marah*, because that is what they are. They are rebellious and contentious, lashing out at him, provoking him and the Spirit within him.

He calls them *marah* because they have become a source of bitterness and anguish to him. Here in the depths of the grinding bowl, he has reached a point of being thoroughly worn down by their constant complaint. There is no hope in dealing with these unfaithful rebels. They have not progressed in faith from the first time they were tested at the waters of Marah. They failed then, and now they have failed again to trust in the Lord. It is like they haven't learned a single lesson. Contentions like this that remain unresolved become rooted in bitterness over time.

Moses Strikes the Rock

Moses doesn't speak a single word to the rock itself. His anger and bitterness have so clouded his judgment that he has failed to do what the Lord commanded him. His verbal lashing at his kinsmen follows through into a physical lashing. He lashes out at the rock as if it were some cursed thing. Not once but twice, just for good measure. This is a horrific thing Moses has done. This life-giving rock is the very embodiment of the Lord before His people, and yet Moses strikes it as he would strike a man. Symbolically, he has crucified Christ again. He has corrupted the picture that God was creating of a glorious, resurrected Messiah who would give living water.[1]

Remember what the writer of Hebrews says about this:

> "For it is impossible for those who were once enlightened, and have tasted the heavenly gift, and have become partakers of the Holy Spirit, and have tasted the good word of God and the powers of the age to come, if they

---

1   I want to note that one of the purposes God gives Israel is to keep the prophetic pictures of Christ intact until they are fulfilled. Whenever they corrupt those pictures, judgment falls on them. It falls on Moses for this reason. Another example would be the judgment that falls on Jeroboam when he corrupts the keeping of the feasts of Israel (1 Kings 12-13).

fall away, to renew them again to repentance, since they crucify again for themselves the Son of God, and put Him to an open shame." Hebrews 6:4-6

It is a testament to God's great love and grace that He allows the water to burst from that rock abundantly, in spite of Moses' failing. God's children are thirsty after all, and He is merciful to them and their animals. But Moses has put Him to open shame publicly, and that has made a rift in their relationship that cannot be overlooked. It is the public nature of the act that is so galling.

A Lesson from Leadership

It is one thing to blow off steam with the Lord in private. God grants grace in those moments of wrestling. It is another thing to do it publicly.

It isn't the first time Moses has done his own share of complaining, and has shown some attitude in the presence of God. Remember back in Numbers 11 with the quail issue when Moses speaks to the Lord in almost a sarcastic manner? God was forbearing in that moment perhaps because it was done in private between Moses and Himself. This time Moses publicly lifts himself up in a disrespectful manner in front of everyone, and such public display requires the Lord exert His own authority for the sake of His own glory. If He is going to be hallowed in the eyes of Israel, He is going to have to rebuke Moses publicly. And that is how the Lord hallows Himself before Israel in this moment, by lowering Moses in the presence of Aaron and the rest of Israel.

Here in the depths of the grinding bowl, Moses' own faithfulness is on trial. This is his trial by ordeal, like the wife of a jealous husband. Just as the bitter waters reveal the unfaithfulness of the wife, so the waters that comes from this rock are going to become a bitter lesson in Moses' life. His flood of rash words bear witness of the bitterness within him. Just as the bitter waters rob the unfaithful wife of future fruitfulness, Moses is going to lose the reward of fruitfulness in the Land as a result of his unfaithfulness at this moment.

As soon as Moses strikes that Rock, God lays this judgment on him: Because he didn't hallow the Lord in the eyes of Israel, he will not bring the assembly into the Land (v12). *"Because you did not believe Me"* can also be translated as "because you did not confirm Me" or "because you were not faithful to Me." Why are Moses' words counted as an act of unfaithfulness to God? Pay close attention to what Moses says.

"Must we bring water for you out of this rock?" Who exactly is the "we" in this statement?

Are Moses and Aaron the ones bringing water from the rock? Well, technically, yes. Moses is the one who is bringing water from the rock, but the way Moses says this implies that he and Aaron are doing this by their own will and power. The tone and attitude are all wrong, and there is a distinct lack of acknowledgment of God.

What God told him to do is to speak to the rock, not answer back the children of Israel. God asked Moses to focus on doing what God wanted him to do in this moment because He is painting a very important picture here. He needed Moses to facilitate that picture for Him.

Instead, Moses focuses on his own hurt and his own desire to justify himself to these rebels. He has been provoked severely, the Holy Spirit within him has been provoked severely (Ps. 106:33), and all the bitterness and anger that has been buried for a long time has built to the brink of eruption. In this moment, Moses forgets his purpose, forgets to give glory to God, forgets who the rock represents, forgets humility, and rises to the bait.

Instead of lifting God up, Moses lifts himself up and lashes back at their accusations in a way that justifies himself and builds himself up in their eyes. Instead of lifting God up and hallowing Him in the eyes of Israel, Moses has now sunk to their level by lifting himself up. There is anger, and a little bit of grandstanding in Moses' words. *"Must we bring water for you out of this rock?"*

Do we do this in our own lives today? Do we have our grinding bowl moments when we get so distracted by the affront to our own pride or ego that we end up in a verbal fight with someone instead of doing what the Lord has asked us to do? Do we respond in a way that takes glory back for ourselves in these moments instead of giving glory to God? Do we forget our purpose in being the Lord's representative? I don't know about you, but I stand guilty as charged.

It is for his words more than his actions that Moses stands condemned. David speaks of this incident in Psalms, saying,

> *"They angered Him [God] also at the waters of Meribah, so that it went ill with Moses on account of them: because they rebelled against His [God's] Spirit, so that he [Moses] spoke rashly with his lips." Psalm 106:32-33*

The Spirit in Moses had been stirred up because of their rebellion, but instead of letting the Spirit lead him and letting the Lord have command of the situation and glory for it, Moses lost his temper and spoke rashly. That word, "rashly," means to babble, to run off at the mouth with unprofitable words.

Do we do this, especially when we get angry, frustrated or bitter?
Does it ever go well with us as a result?

Maybe we keep our temper at the first slight, or the second, but what about the twentieth or thirtieth time? We may put up with the digs for a while but eventually it becomes personal. Then we get angry. It may be a righteous anger or a self-righteous anger, but in that moment we fail to remember whose glory is actually being trampled on and whose Person we represent. We have our grinding bowl moment as well. When we have been severely provoked, it can be almost impossible to restrain the urge to lash back. We should all understand what Moses is going through here, but we can also see that his words did not bring glory to the Lord or accomplish His purpose. *"For the wrath of man never produces the righteousness of God."* (Jam. 1:20)

These are grinding bowl moments. Even the most mature Spirit-filled believers can fail at moments like this, but it is a failing nonetheless. There are a few things that can help us override our natural tendency.

1) We need to identify with the Lord so much that we let go of self. We have to die to self, and make a habit of it, so that when grinding bowl moments come, a mindset of humility is already at work in us. This has to be an ongoing practice if it is going to help in moments of stress.

2) We need to understand that Christ has redeemed us and we are precious to Him, regardless of what the world tells us. It is easier to let go of self when we understand that the Lord knows our value and will glorify us. Remember that every slight or hurt that we receive, the Lord sees and will remember. In His own timing He will deal with them more thoroughly than we ever could. Pour out the rage and the hurt to Him in private, and let Him deal with the rebels. We don't have to take glory for ourselves.

3) We need to remember that we have a spiritual purpose that runs throughout our physical life. The spiritual purpose is actually more important than the physical one. That spiritual purpose is to paint a picture of Christ as we live our lives. All Moses had to do physically was hold a rod and speak to a rock, but those actions had a spiritual purpose in painting a picture of a future Messiah. As we go through our lives, we are asked to do so in a way that confirms and supports that picture. We are also asked to glorify Christ and not bring shame on His name. That is the job of a faithful bride.

When you are in the grinding bowl moment, if you can stay focused on your spiritual identity and spiritual purpose, they will help you keep the right perspective and bring glory to God. So lift your head and bite your tongue!

Death of Aaron (Numbers 20:22-29)

> *"And the LORD spoke to Moses and Aaron in Mount Hor by the border of the land of Edom, saying: 'Aaron shall be gathered to his people, for he shall not enter the land which I have given to the children of Israel, because you rebelled against My word at the water of Meribah.'"*
> Numbers 20:23-24

Who is the "you" in that verse? The rebellion is most certainly attributed to Moses' rash words and his striking the rock. The Lord was painting a picture of the Messiah for His people with the glorified rod and rock, and Moses corrupted that picture with his actions. But what was Aaron's part in all this? There is no record of his words or actions throughout the incident. He was present, but his role appears to have been a passive one, much as it was when he stood with Miriam against Moses. In that incident, the Lord only turned His face from Aaron while Miriam received the brunt of the punishment for her rebellion. So why would such harsh judgment fall on Aaron now for a rebellion that was mostly Moses' fault?

Is it fair that one man should die for another's sin? No, but isn't that part of the picture that the Lord is orchestrating of a future Savior?

This is the glory of the Lord that one man's sin (Moses' sin) has created the opportunity for the Lord to present yet another picture of a future Messiah. The Lord can take the worst moments of utter failing and discouragement and turns them to His purpose to give us hope. There is not a single moment in our lives, whether we are acting faithfully or unfaithfully, that the Lord cannot turn to His glory. He will shine as the glorious, merciful God of grace who rewards those who seek Him, or He will shine in fierce glory as King and Judge of the wicked. The only difference is the consequence we will experience as a result.

I imagine this was another blow for Moses, knowing that his brother was going to die on account of that incident at the rock. Imagine having to take your brother outside the camp, go up on Mount Hor in the eyes of all Israel, strip him of his robe and give it to another. In this case, it is given to Aaron's son, Eleazar, who will assume the place of High Priest. Then you get to watch him die, knowing it was because of you.

Our High Priest has been through this entire journey with us. He has been tempted as we were tempted, suffered as we suffered, interceded on our behalf after the rebellion of Korah to stop the plague, to stop the death and affliction. He has done mighty works before our eyes, and now he himself has gone outside the camp to die for another's sin. What a magnificent picture of the death of Christ, our High Priest, even down to the details of being taken outside of camp to a high hill and stripped of His robes before all of Israel.

We are given a few more details of Aaron's death in Numbers 33:38-39 that I will mention here. Aaron was 123 years old when he died. He died on the first day of the fifth month, in the 40th year after coming out of Egypt. We previously discussed how the fifth month of Av is a month known for tragedy in Israel. Years later, both the first and second Temples would be destroyed in this month and it would mark the beginning of the exile. But here at this moment, the tragedy doesn't mark the beginning of exile. It marks the end of it. Interesting twist, isn't it?

The High Priest is not the only person to die in this 40th year. All the remaining men of war who were numbered in the first census will also die. This is the year of Israel's reaping. The last of the old will be cut off and a new generation will begin. All the death associated with that curse will come to an end after the death of the High Priest and with it comes Israel's release.

One final event happens before the death of the first generation is complete and that is the incident with the bronze serpent in Numbers 21:4-9.

The Bronze Serpent (Numbers 21:4-9)

Our High Priest has died. We have mourned him for thirty days, and now we are on the way to the Promised Land. We are at the end of this long trial and we are tired. Tired of walking aimlessly in circles, tired of eating manna, tired of death. Tempers have become short. We are impatient and frustrated and just want this ordeal to be finished.

Numbers 21:4 says we have become discouraged. The Hebrew word for discouraged here is *qatsar* which means to be short or impatient, or to be grieved. But the word has a much broader use. It can also mean to be cut short or be shortened, as in one's length of days.

How the word is used here in verse 4 is an atypical use of the word. *Qatsar* most often means to be reaped—to be shortened or cut off the way stalks of grain are cut off in reaping, or as reaping cuts off the growing season. In regards to the journey, the last of the first generation of Israel will be reaped here shortly. They are going to be cut off permanently in death and a new generation will take their place.

Qatsar is most often used in regards to reaping something that has been sown, whether physically or spiritually. It also means to shorten. Here are some examples to give you a sense of how the word is used in Scripture:

> *"Even as I have seen, those who plow iniquity and sow trouble reap the same."* Job 4:8
>
> *"The days of his youth You have shortened; You have covered him with shame. Selah."* Psalm 89:45
>
> *"He weakened my strength in the way; He shortened my days."* Psalm 102:23
>
> *"Those who sow in tears shall reap in joy."* Psalm 126:5
>
> *"The fear of the LORD prolongs days, but the years of the wicked will be shortened."* Proverbs 10:27
>
> *"He who sows iniquity will reap sorrow, and the rod of his anger will fail."* Proverbs 22:8
>
> *"They have sown wheat but reaped thorns; they have put themselves to pain but do not profit. But be ashamed of your harvest because of the fierce anger of the LORD."* Jeremiah 12:13
>
> *"They sow the wind, and reap the whirlwind . . ."* Hosea 8:7a
>
> *"Sow for yourselves righteousness; reap in mercy; break up your fallow ground, for it is time to seek the LORD, till He comes and rains righteousness on you. You have plowed wickedness; you have reaped iniquity. You have eaten the fruit of lies, because you trusted in your own way, in the multitude of your mighty men."* Hosea 10:12-13

Qatsar can describe a physical reaping that parallels a spiritual consequence. So it is for Israel at this point in the journey. Keep in mind, this time of year is the time of harvest in the Land. If we had been in the Land of Israel at this point (somewhere around the 7th month), we would have been reaping a tremendous physical harvest now and celebrating the Feast of Tabernacles under vine-covered booths. But here we are still living in these rough little wilderness booths, eating manna. Instead of experiencing a physical harvest, we are going to go through a reaping of our own, as the last of the congregation will be cut off. This is bitter fruit indeed.

Numbers 21:5 shows we are complaining again, this time about the worthless bread called manna that we have been living on these 40 years. There goes our tongue again. James reminds us:

> *"But no man can tame the tongue. It is an unruly evil, full of deadly poison."* James 3:8

These are poisonous, biting words aimed at God and Moses, and in the next moment, God bites back, returning venom for venom. He sends fiery serpents to bite the people and the venom kills many (v6).

And during all this Moses says—nothing. Moses keeps his mouth shut. He doesn't try to intercede or intercept God's wrath even after the deaths begin. This time Moses holds his tongue until the people cry for intercession. This is an important point. We can spend much of our lives trying to intervene for immature people to keep them from getting into trouble. That is not a bad thing necessarily, because it shows we have developed a sense of mercy. Mercy exercises those fruits of the Spirit such as kindness, goodness, and faithfulness. But there is a down-side to being constantly merciful, because it does not encourage growth on the part of the immature person. Sometimes consequences are needed to drive home the lesson. Sometimes it just requires holding our tongue.

Moses has repeatedly interceded for the people when God was ready to deliver punishment, much as a parent intercedes on behalf of their child when facing authorities. At times Moses himself has dealt out punishment, as a parent would to a child. As a result, their relationship with Moses has grown, but their relationship with God has not.

Now, in this moment, Moses has stepped out of the way. This time Moses waits until they admit they need intercession before he goes before God on their behalf. He waits for them to ask for prayer. Then he prays (v7).

The healing can't begin until the people admit they have sinned, and not just that they have sinned but an acknowledgment of how they have sinned. Do you realize that this is only the second time in this journey that they have admitted to sin? The first time was when they refused to go into the Land, and then turned around and tried to go up that mountain without God. When they didn't like the consequences of our action, they recanted with a flippant response, like saying, "Sorry. My bad. I'll be good now." That was not repentance at all. That response is why they lost the battle at Hormah the first time. What should have been a victory became a defeat. This time there is a true confession and a specific request to the Lord that the serpents be taken away. This is a sign of ripening spiritual maturity. Even though they have failed, they have had a spurt of spiritual growth!

Once again, the corruption that was on the inside has manifested in the form of sickness. The venom that came out of the heart has made us sick. The sin is embodied in the infirmity. God does this with His people over and over again, which is why sin and sickness are paired in Jewish thought.

Now the Lord tells Moses to present another picture of a future Messiah who will take away our sin and heal our infirmity. He tells Moses to make a fiery serpent of bronze and lift it up on a pole (v8-9).

So Moses obediently makes a fiery serpent, a *saraph*. In the Hebrew, *saraph* means burning, as from the poison or fire. The same burning quality is what characterizes the seraphim that attend to the Lord. What Moses actually makes is a bronze version of the serpents that have bitten the people. Bronze has to be put through the fire to be worked into a shape, and I imagine that the image of the serpent came out of the fire glowing white hot.

Bronze has another significance because it is associated with the altar where the sacrifices were burnt as payment for sin. This bronze serpent raised up on a pole was going to be what covered our sin. If they would look at it with faith and believe, they would be healed.

Why the serpent, of all figures, to raise up on the pole? The serpent in this case was representative of the particular sin and consequential sickness. It was the symbol of our suffering.

It is also symbolic of the curse of sin. The serpent on the pole parallels the serpent in the garden of Eden, the catalyst that brought the curse of death for sin. Christ on the cross would take that sin upon Himself —become the embodiment of sin—and suffer the penalty of that curse on our behalf, that we might have life.

Beyond this, I think the serpent was just an awful image to look at. A serpent is a disgusting, repulsive, fearful thing. It is something unclean to be struck at and avoided, killed and disposed of. It is something to put away from yourself. Yet here they are being asked to lift their heads and look at this detested thing as a savior that would heal them, if they would have faith and believe. The inner revulsion must have warred with the desire to be healed.

We know this is a picture of Christ, as it says in John's Gospel,

> "And as Moses lifted up the serpent in the wilderness, even so must the Son of Man be lifted up, that whoever believes in Him should not perish but have eternal life." John 3:14-15

I think Israel's reaction to seeing that serpent on that pole was the same reaction they would have to Christ as He hung on that cross. I think the Lord deliberately orchestrated it that way as part of the picture.

> "He is despised and rejected by men, a Man of sorrows and acquainted with grief. And we hid, as it were, our faces from Him; He was despised, and we did not esteem Him." Isaiah 53:3-4

The vision of this serpent on the pole was something that caused us to turn our eyes away and yet it was something that bore our sin and takes away our infirmity.

The pictures of Christ's death and resurrection really reach a crescendo in these chapters. Out of the depths of our discouragement and failure comes this magnificent promise of hope, redemption and release.

The grinding bowl of the Wilderness of Zin has taken its toll on everyone, and it has done its job in cutting deeply into our marrow to divide the faithful from the unfaithful. It is tempting to just give up when life brings us to the grinding bowl. But the journey doesn't end just because we have failed at some point. We must keep moving forward.

Keep Moving Forward

In chapter 20:1-13, Moses made a grievous error at Kadesh that cost him his entrance into the Land. After coming all this way and suffering this entire journey with a complaining, balking congregation, it would be completely understandable for Moses to decide not to go any further. Why continue the journey if you are not going to get into the Land?

Even though he failed in faithfulness to the Lord in one moment, it is a tribute to Moses' humility and continuing faithfulness that he keeps moving the people forward. The journey isn't done. He must bring them as far as the Lord will let him.

In chapter 20:14-21 Moses sends a request to the King of Edom to pass through his land, but we are refused passage through Edom, even the use of the Kings Highway. The Kings Highway is an ancient caravan route used for trade. It runs through the mountains of Edom, up through Moab and all countries north, and connects all the watering places along the way. Edom has stationed a border guard along their mountains, and so we have been denied access to even the public right of way.

This is a set-back. But the journey doesn't end because of set-backs. We must keep moving forward.

In chapter 20:22-29 Moses takes us through the Wilderness of Zin and into the Aravah Valley, to Mount Hor on the border of Edom. There on Mount Hor the High Priest dies. We camp at Mount Hor 30 days while we mourn the death of our High Priest.

This is a set-back. But we must keep moving forward.

From Mount Hor, we come up against the mountains of Edom, and we are faced with a dilemma. We have to go one direction or another to get around Edom. We wanted to take the broad and easy Kings Highway that all the rest of the world travels. But that would take us through Edom and death waits for us if we go that way.

Instead of taking the broad highway, the Lord leads us through a winding, difficult way around Edom that threads its way through enemy territory. There is a little lesson in this that Jesus comments on:

> *"Enter by the narrow gate; for wide is the gate and broad is the way that leads to destruction, and there are many who go in by it. Because narrow is the gate and difficult is the way which leads to life, and there are few who find it."* Matthew 7:13-14

I think it is interesting how the order of these events are presented in the narrative and reflect the unfolding gospel message. Having come to Mount Hor and the death of the High Priest, we are now faced with this decision over which path to take in the journey. Do we follow where the Lord leads or take the path the rest of the world follows?

We are heading for the plains of Moab in Amorite territory. It is going to take about six months to get there. On the way, we will begin to engage the enemy. We should note that the Lord never intended us to fight some of these battles we are going to fight. If we had not turned back from the Land, we could have avoided the confrontation with the Edomites. We might have avoided some of the future trouble with the Moabites and Midianites and the sin we fall into on account of them.

Once we get off the path the Lord originally planned for us, we end up having to face obstacles and difficulties we would not have had to deal with otherwise.

Next lesson: battling the enemy outside.

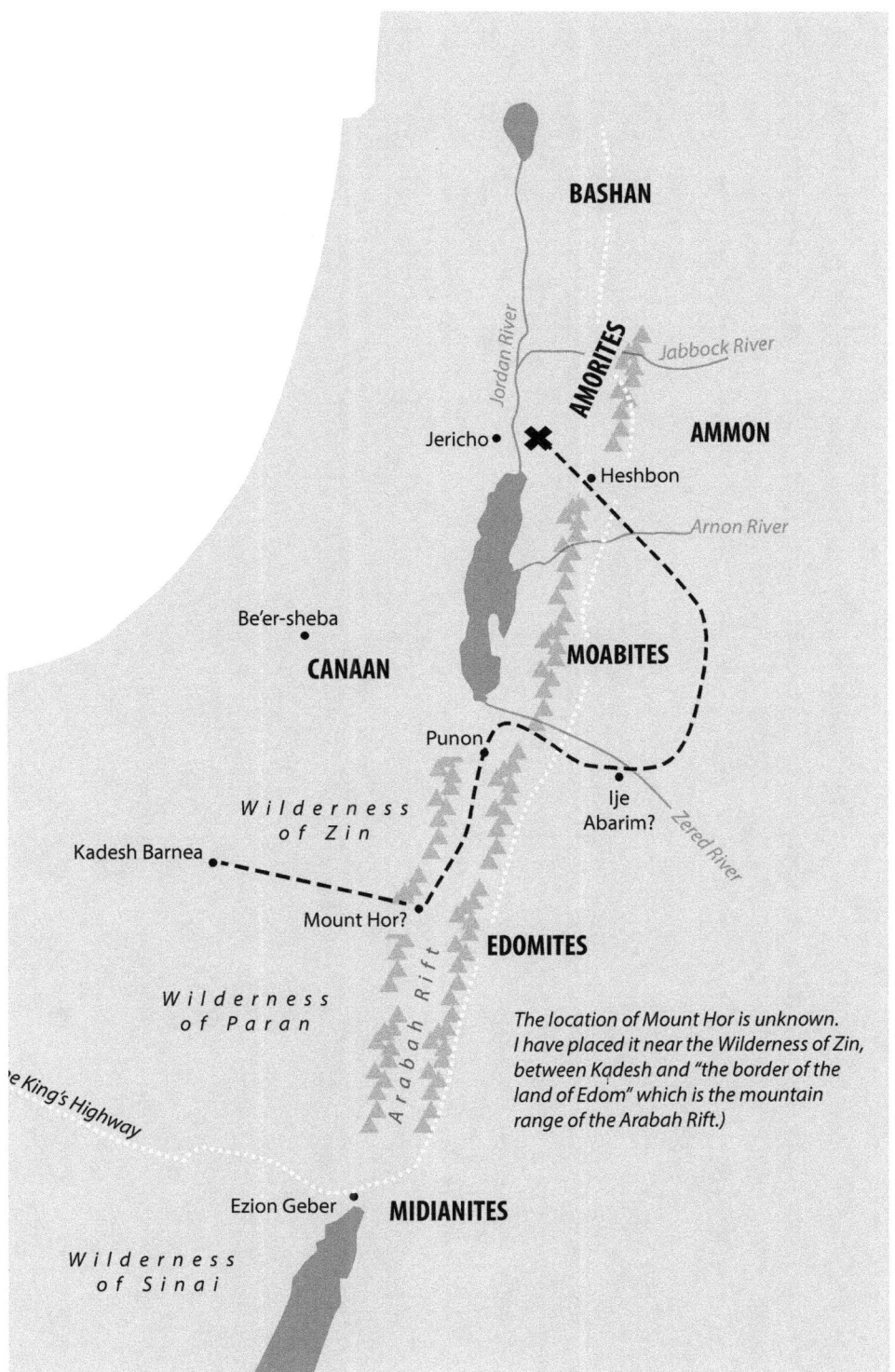

LESSON TEN

Into Enemy Territory

CHAPTERS 20–24

In this lesson we are going to focus on engaging the enemy outside the camp. We are revisiting Chapters 20 and 21 to cover the passages we skipped, and then moving on to Chapters 22-24.

The enemies we will be studying today are:

- King Arad of Canaan at Hormah (21:1-3)
- King Sihon of the Amorites (21:21-32)
- King Og of Bashan (21:33-35)
- King Balak of Moab (22-24)

Hormah (Numbers 21:1-3)

As we turn north from Mount Hor and begin to make our way around Edom, we are going to meet an enemy who defeated us once before. Numbers 21:1-3 gives us the details.

So here is our first battle, revisited. The Canaanite king hears we are coming north. He remembered the spies came up through his land forty years before, and now the whole nation is on the way. So he makes a show of force by attacking us and taking some of us prisoner. This appears to be another defeat, just like last time (Num. 14:39-45).

Hormah was a bitter lesson to learn, so we do things very differently this time. There are no complaints. There is no charging up the hill to deliver the prisoners. This time we go to the Lord first to ask for deliverance. We vow to align ourselves with the Lord's agenda which is to destroy and drive out the Canaanites from the Land. We vow not to take the spoils of victory for ourselves but give it over for destruction. And then we wait for the Lord. That is a big difference from last time.

In response, the Lord listens and rewards the request by delivering the Canaanites into our hands. We set the prisoners free and utterly destroy the cities, making good our vows.

God has given us a second chance, and this time we gave Him the glory and asked for His help, and in return He lifted us up and gave us victory. Lesson learned. That is how this relationship is supposed to work, and it has now borne a little bit of fruit. We are making progress at last, not just physically but spiritually.

A side note: While the army at this point may be mostly the second generation, this is really a redeeming moment for those who are left of the first generation. This is the first and last battle they will fight and a very poignant moment. Here at Hormah they failed in faithfulness to the Lord the first time, but now Hormah has become a moment of victory. It is almost like the Lord allows them to prove their faithfulness to Him.

We should also note that their first failure happens before the death of the High Priest, while this second confrontation happens after the death of the High Priest. Taking this into a New Testament context, there is an interesting parallel with Peter and Jesus in John 21. During Jesus' trial, Peter denied Him three times in a heartbreaking act of unfaithfulness. But in the days after Jesus' death and resurrection, He came to Peter again and offered him a chance to redeem himself with a confirmation of faith, expressed three times. Peter had his Hormah victory.

I think the Lord also gives us, as believers, second chances like this sometimes. He brings us back to a similar circumstance where we once suffered a defeat because we handled it the wrong way, maybe by our own strength, or our own will or our own judgment, but definitely in a way that did not bring Him glory. I think He brings us to those places to see if we will respond differently, in a more mature manner. If we do, He rewards that.

Setting Prisoners Free

The purpose of this battle is not to take the land, but to set prisoners free. It follows closely on the heels of the death of the High Priest, which is a prophetic picture of Christ's death that sets us free from the bondage of sin. Though we are now free of that bondage, we can fall back into the hands of the Enemy again and need rescue. When some of our brethren fall back into bondage, it is our task to engage in battle to set those prisoners free.

Moving on

From Hormah we will continue our trek north toward the Dead Sea, encamping at Zalmonah, Punon, and then turning east to camp at Oboth (Num. 33). Most of these places cannot be located on current maps except for Punon which has been a copper mining area since antiquity. Turning east, we follow the Zered River that is the border of Edom and Moab. We will cross the Zered River at Ije Abarim (Num. 21:10) and head north again around the east side of Moabite territory until arriving at the Arnon River. The Arnon is the boundary between Moab and the Amorites, although we find out later that Amorite lands once belonged to Moab (Num. 21:26).

After we cross the Arnon, we will be in Amorite territory which will eventually become the lands inherited by the tribe of Reuben.

Deuteronomy 2:4-25 gives us a little more info about this part of the journey. As we have been walking, the Lord has been telling us a little about the people of these lands. As we are passing by Edom, He says, Oh, by the way, the Horites (cave dwellers) used to live here, but when I gave this land to the descendants of Esau, the Edomites took the land from the cave dwellers (v4-8, 12). When passing by Moab, He says, Oh, by the way, giants called the Emim used to live here, but when I gave this land to the descendants of Lot, they destroyed the giants and took the land (v9-11). As we pass into Amorite land, He points out the hills of Ammon to the east of us. He says, Oh, by the way, giants called the Zamzummim used to live here, but when I gave this land to the descendants of Lot, I destroyed the giants and gave the land to the Ammonites, just like I destroyed the Horites in Edom (v19-22). Then He mentions other giants called the Avim of Gaza were destroyed (v23).

What is the point of God talking to us about all these giants?

The reason the first generation didn't enter the Land was because of the fear of giants, and we are going to be battling giants before this lesson is over. The Lord is encouraging us and preparing us for these battles.

King Sihon of the Amorites (Numbers 21:21-32)

Numbers 21:21-26 pairs with Deuteronomy 2:3-37 to give us an account of the battle with King Sihon of the Amorites. This is the first battle that the new generation fights on their own.

Just as with Edom, we send messengers and are refused passage even via the Kings Highway. Just like at Hormah, the Lord delivers the enemy into our hands. We take the main city of Heshbon with the unfortified villages and utterly destroy them, men, women, and children. This time we take the livestock and material goods as spoil. We stop short of entering Ammonite territory because its borders are fortified (Num. 21:24).

We have now come into an area called the Plains of Moab. This land will become Reuben's inheritance. We are going to continue to press northward along the Jordan River to take the lands from Bashan.

King Og of Bashan (Numbers 21:33-35)

Numbers 21:33-35 pairs with Deuteronomy 3:1-11 to give us an account of the battle with King Og of Bashan. This time we don't send messengers. The Lord says go, and we go.

Again the Lord delivers the enemy into our hands. Again we take the cities and utterly destroy them, but these cities present more of a challenge. There are sixty cities, all fortified with high walls, gates and bars in addition to many rural towns. We destroy all the men, women, and children, and take the livestock and material goods as spoil. Oh, and by the way, King Og of Bashan was the last of the giants (Rephaim) in the area. We have battled giants and won.

This land will become Gad and Manasseh's inheritance.

The Enemy We Don't See

There is a physical enemy that we can see, although we may not realize they are the enemy at first. Then there is the Enemy who is the spiritual power behind our physical enemy—Satan himself. Both of these enemy agents are going to be working in tandem to get God's people off the journey from here on out.

We have conquered the territory as the Lord has told us and now we settle down on the Plains of Moab on the east side of the Jordan across from Jericho. Here we are going to stay from now until Joshua leads us over the Jordan into the Promised Land. So for a couple months, we are going to have a short rest from battle while Moses gives us the review of the Law.

Just because we have rest doesn't mean the battle has stopped. In reality, the Enemy is still out there, stalking us like a lion, and he never rests. He is going to use enemies like Balak of Moab for his purposes. While we are resting, the Lord Himself is fighting the battle against this unseen Enemy, tripping him up, frustrating him and restraining him in the most maddening and glorious fashion. In this moment, the glory of the Lord truly shines, which is why I think this episode of Balak and Balaam is given a place in Numbers. So often we forget just how glorious and sovereign the Lord is because we cannot see all the work in which He is engaged on our behalf.

Chapters 22-24 are a distinct departure from the rest of the book because the focus shifts dramatically away from Israel and gives us a narrative of what is going on in the enemy camp in Moab.

Balak, King of Moab (Numbers 22-24)

Moab's territory once included the Amorites' land until the Amorites took that territory away from Moab. Now Israel has taken it away from the Amorites and sits on Balak's border. Balak, King of Moab, son of Zippor, climbs one of the hills to get a better look at Israel. They seem to fill the plains of Moab, and he becomes sick with dread.

Balak judges only by what he sees and he sees a lot of people. Balak judges strength by numbers—how many men of war they can muster, how much wealth they have amassed, and how much land they have conquered. Israel has grown strong in number.

If Balak had known anything about God, he would have known there was nothing to fear. The Lord told Israel that He had given Moab their own land, and it was not to be infringed upon (Deut. 2:9). Israel has no intention of invading Moab, but Balak imagines they do. If he were in their place, that's what he would do.

If Balak had known anything about God, he would have understood that the Lord Himself gave Moab to Balak. Balak thinks the land became his by birth, and he keeps it by strength and cunning. In reality, the only reason Balak has been allowed to keep his land is because God is faithful to His promises, even to men who are unfaithful and unbelieving of Him. In Balak's eyes, his security is only in his own strength and wealth and influence, and when he looks at Israel, he knows it's not enough. He is scared and threatened. If he had known anything about God, he could have rested in security and peace.

If Balak had known anything about God, he would have understood that God is the one who has brought Israel out of Egypt. God is the one who has lifted them up. God is the power behind Israel, and God is the power that Balak faces when he lifts himself up against Israel. He is getting ready to go head to head with the God of Israel.

If he had known anything about God, the fear of Israel would not have overwhelmed him. Instead, the fear of Israel's God should have made him reconsider this fight.

The saddest part of this is that God never intended Balak to feel threatened. Misplaced fear has taken Balak, and he is going to pick a fight with Israel over an imagined threat. Balak has judged his own strength and wealth and influence against Israel, and he knows it is not enough. He needs support, so he turns to Midian and proposes an alliance (Num. 22:4).

This is an odd thing. Why did the King of Moab seek out the elders of Midian as possible allies? The Edomites are right next to Moab and next in line for battle if Moab should fall to Israel. The land of Midian is far removed from this conflict, being far south on the other side of Edom. So why Midian?

I think Balak has done a little spying himself and come upon the fact that Israel's leader, Moses, has ties to the Midianite elite. Remember Moses' history with Midian?

When Moses fled from Egypt, he went to the land of Midian. He ended up living with Jethro, the priest of Midian, and marrying the priest's daughter Zipporah. Moses has two sons by Zipporah. Jethro was mentor to Moses. When Israel prepared to leave Sinai, Moses wanted these Midianites to come with them. He begged his brother-in-law Hobab to come with them (Num. 10:29-32). Moses has also made some promises and a tentative alliance with Midian.

Trust in these old loyalties will create a vulnerability for Moses and Israel.

Balak thinks he has everything to lose at this point which makes him a little desperate. If he engages Israel on his northern border, Midian might attack him on his southern border if they come to the aid of Moses. Strategically, he faces the possibility of a battle on two fronts. He has to be sure of Midian's position in regards to Israel, so he approaches the Midianites, sowing seeds of antagonism against Israel. It wasn't such a difficult thing to get Midian to change sides after all. Midian has very little to lose and possibly something to gain in this arrangement. A new alliance is formed.

Balaam, Son of Beor

Balak has judged Israel by its physical numbers, and has found his own numbers lacking. So to begin with, Balak is going to try a little supernatural leverage by having Israel cursed. He is going to hire Balaam to go head to head with the God of Israel (Num. 22:5-6).

Why Balaam?

Balak has purposely sought out a foreigner to do the job. The name, Balaam, means "foreigner" or "not of the people." He comes from Pethor in Mesopotamia, near the Euphrates River, which is about as far removed from the whole Israel/Moab situation as you can get. Balak assumes that because Balaam has no ties or allegiance to Israel, he will be loyal to Moab for the right price. Faithfulness is something to be negotiated and bought in Balak's mind. It is true, Balaam is without any allegiance to Israel, or Israel's God, but then, he has no loyalty to Balak either, as Balak will discover.

Balak assumes this soothsayer has the power to curse Israel. Mind you, he doesn't ask for a super duper whammy of a curse to knock Israel out completely. He just wants something to weaken them enough so he can defeat them. After all, he doesn't want all the glory to go to Balaam.

Balak says to Balaam *"...he whom you bless is blessed, and he whom you curse is cursed."* Balak credits Balaam with a lot more power and authority than Balaam actually has. Balak has lifted Balaam up to the place of God in asking him to curse Israel, while at the same time he assumes Balaam's power can be bent to his own will in this. Balak attributes the power to Balaam, but assumes the right to direct that power how he sees fit. In reality, Balaam cannot do anything without God's permission, regardless of what he leads Balak to believe.

Balak assumes that Balaam has integrity, which I think is hilarious. Balak has no qualms in dealing with Israel in a devious, backhanded manner, but he never considers the possibility that Balaam will deal treacherously with him. Balaam knew from the beginning how this was going to play out, but he strings Balak along anyway. First he says "no," he won't go and refuses the fee (Num. 22:13). Then Balak ups the reward and promises honor and wealth and power, and Balaam says "yes, but no promises." Throughout this episode, Balaam continues to remind Balak that he never made any promises, and yet Balak clings to that hope blindly.

Over and over again, Balaam makes Balak jump through hoops, having him build seven altars and offer sacrifices to a God Balak doesn't even believe in, and then Balaam makes a show of going off to inquire of God as if the answer may be different each time. Each time the prophecy goes against Balak, Balak trots Balaam to the next high place, trying to get Balaam to "see" the problem. It's Balak who doesn't "see" the problem. Balaam already knows what is going on. God has blessed Israel and there is nothing Balaam can say to change it. Balaam is restrained by a higher power. All that comes out of his mouth is glory to God and prophecies of a future Messianic King.

The Glory of God and His People: Balaam's Prophecies

Balaam delivers four prophecies that are a resounding praise and lifting up of God and His people. The first declares the glory of Israel (23:7-10), as a nation blessed by God that does not reckon itself among the nations. The glory of God's people is never about their standing among the nations but in their identity with God. Balaam sees a future where Israel is so blessed, they are beyond number.

Balaam's second prophecy (23:18-24) declares the glory of God. God is faithful to do what He says He will do, and He has said He will bless Israel. God is sovereign, the King of Israel. God is strong, as strong as a wild ox. When you look at Israel, you can only say, "Oh, what God has done!" Whatever glory Israel has, they have because of their identity as God's people. They are a people who have been lifted up.

There is a reference to a lion rising in verse 24, which pairs with the imagery of the king in verse 21. The combined imagery echoes back to Jacob's blessings on his son, Judah, in Genesis 49:9, who is described as a lion and from whose lineage the king will arise. Whereas Jacob's blessing describes a lion that has come to rest, Balaam's words describe a lion rising up to devour its prey. That should have struck fear in Balak's heart.

In verse 21, Balaam says that God has observed no iniquity or wickedness in Israel, which is a little surprising considering our track record so far. The reason for the Lord's favor is not because Israel is free of sin, but because Israel's sins have been covered. Their righteousness is counted by that covering and not by their works. This is cross-referenced with Psalm 32:2, where David says,

> "Blessed is the man to whom the LORD does not impute iniquity, and in whose spirit there is no deceit." Psalm 32:2

In regards to the immediate context, there is certainly deceit in the spirit of Balak and Balaam. Balak is the aggressor, attacking Israel without reason and in a covert way. Israel is not guilty of anything against Moab in this conflict. The Lord sees this and indicates that He has imputed iniquity to Moab that He has not imputed to Israel. This is reminiscent of God's judgment against Miriam and Aaron when they spoke against Moses. There God declared Moses faithful, with the implication that Miriam and Aaron weren't.

Balaam's third prophecy (24:3-9) describes Israel in her ultimate glorification. "How lovely are your tents . . . like valleys . . . like gardens . . . like aloes . . . like cedars beside the waters . . ." The words God puts into Balaam's mouth are like something out of the Song of Solomon, a paean of praise to His beloved.

Again the royal imagery is repeated. There is a particular reference to King Agag, a future king of Amalek. The mention of Amalek has cropped up a couple times in the journey. The Israelites were first attacked, unprovoked, by the Amalekites at Rephidim back in Exodus 17:8-13. God defeated them there and promised to utterly blot out Amalek from under heaven. The Amalekites were also the ones who chased the first generation out of Hormah in Numbers 14. In the future, Amalek will join with Moab in attacking Israel in the days of the judges (Jdg. 3:13) and continue to be enemies of Israel through the days of David's kingship, after which they decline as a nation. The spies reported that the Amalekites lived in the southern part of the Land that Judah would inherit, thus the Hebrew king who comes from Judah in the future would literally supplant the king of Amalek in the Land. Balaam prophesies that such a king is coming, and his words in verse 9 are the words of Jacob's blessing on Judah, verbatim.

Balaam's third prophecy ends with a divine parroting of Balak's own words in Numbers 22:6, only this time spoken as a blessing on Israel.

> *"Blessed is he who blesses you, and cursed is he who curses you."*
> *Numbers 24:9*

At this point Balak is incensed with Balaam wants no more prophecies, and refuses payment; but Balaam gives him one gratis, which is really God ramming the message home. Where his third prophecy is of a most glorious Israel, Balaam's fourth prophecy (24:15-24) is wholly about the most glorious of the Davidic kings, the Messianic King, whose coming is described in vivid detail.

> *"I see Him, but not now; I behold Him, but not near; a Star shall come out of Jacob; a Scepter shall rise out of Israel, and batter the brow of Moab, and destroy all the sons of tumult." Numbers 24:17*

The reference to the sons of tumult is repeated in the prophecy of Jeremiah, describing the judgment of Moab in the latter days (Jer. 48:45). "Tumult" is a rather derisive description of an uprising that is more noise and posturing, bluff and bluster, rather substantial strength. The kings of Moab will roar, not as the Lion of Judah roars, but as drunkards roar.

The Lord doesn't just deliver the judgment on Moab. Balaam's prophecy goes on to include judgment on Edom, Amalek, and also on the Kenites (which are the clan of Midianites from whom Moses' wife Zipporah comes). The Midianites will perform an unprovoked act of treachery in the next chapter for which the Lord will exact vengeance, and Balaam himself actually plays a part in that treachery as we will see.

Balaam's prophecy ends with the resounding acclaim to God Almighty. *"Alas, who shall live when God does this?"* He isn't just God over His people. He is God over all people. What a magnificent tribute to a glorious God and His glorious people from the lips of a wicked, heathen, false prophet hired by a deceitful, arrogant, enemy king. It is to Israel's shame that such praise of God must come from such a man and not from His own people.

Without our lifting even a single finger, God has glorified His people above and beyond anything we have deserved, and revealed to the nations His grand plan beyond what we ourselves have even imagined so far.

This strategy of Balak's has failed miserably, so now he is going to change tactics and come at us a different way. In the next lesson we are going to look at Israel's harlotry with Moab which turns into a war with Midian.

LESSON ELEVEN

Into Enemy Territory: The Final Battle

CHAPTERS 25–30

This going to be a long lesson. I could find no easy way to break up these chapters as they are so entwined with one another. I have broken the sections into these divisions:

- Israel's Harlotry with Moab (Chapter 25)
- A Break in the Narrative Timeline (Chapters 26-30). Chapter 25 ends with the Lord's command to harass the Midianites. Chapter 31 begins with nearly the same command, telling us to take vengeance on the Midianites. Sandwiched between these two bookends are important events and laws that break us away from the timeline of the narrative but are relevant to it. I want to make a high-level pass through these to give us a sense of their content and the possible reason for their placement between chapters 25 and 31.
    - The Second Census (Chapter 26)
    - Zelophehad's Daughters and the Commissioning of Joshua (Chapter 27)
    - Offerings for the Sabbath, New Moon and Feasts of Israel (Chapters 28 and 29)
    - Laws Concerning Vows (Chapter 30)
- War with Midian (Chapter 31)
- Prophetic Picture of Christ (Chapter 24-31) and how Numbers tracks with the narrative of the book of Revelation

Before we get to Numbers 25 and our harlotry with Moab, I want to review Israel's current condition. Remember, we are standing with Caleb and Joshua as the only members of that first generation who will enter the Land.

We are standing with a generation that has grown up insulated by the wilderness life. We remember the oppression and idolatry of Egypt, but it has been forty years now since we have been under the thumb of a foreign master and forty years since idolatry was last seen in Israel. Many of the second generation may have been too young to understand or remember it. Those born in a third and fourth generations on this journey (which are noted in the second census) will have no knowledge of it.

Throughout this journey, we have been learning and living the Law. These truths have been taught to us, and we have been living with the consequences of not obeying the Lord's commands for the last forty years. This new generation has been tested in little things. They should be prepared for the challenge, and yet, when they are called to put that knowledge into practice in their personal life and take a stand against the enemy, they are going to fail. All that knowledge and preparation goes in one ear and out the other. Where they should have had discernment, they utterly fail to recognize what is going on—or maybe they do recognize what is going on and let it happen anyway.

They have heard about idolatry and been warned against it. This encounter with the Moabite women will be the first time they have come face to face with idolatry in a real life situation. The challenge is to see if they recognize idolatry as a counterfeit worship and whether they will remain faithful to the Lord or choose to follow a counterfeit path.

We have been through forty lean years since we left Egypt and its "variety." This generation hasn't known anything but manna and water. We are coming into a fruitful land and foreign pleasures. The Enemy is going to make full use of this opportunity to tempt us away from God's definition of glorious living.

We think we know our enemies. We took King Sihon's land. We took King Og's land. We have battled giants and won. It never occurred to us that Moab would be our enemy. In as much as it depended on us, we are living at peace with Moab. It never occurred to us that Midian would deal with us treacherously.

New Enemy Tactics

In Numbers 22-24 Balak tried one scheme and it failed spectacularly. He hired a man to curse Israel and ended up totally frustrated. So now in Numbers 25, he is going to change his tactics. If you can't beat them, get them to join you. This time he is going to use women to do the job. There are more ways to weaken people than by outright force.

Balak's new tactics are:

- Infiltrate their ranks and compromise them.
- Play to their cravings.
- Draw them outside their camp with the promise of glorious living.
- Bring them into slavery to their lusts.
- Then bring them into slavery to his god.

We should know better than to fall for this. It is the same tactic that the Egyptian rabble used on the first generation at Kibroth Hatta'avah. They got us focused on the food we didn't have at the moment and tempted us with their glorious alternatives.

The circumstances now are different. The physical enemy is different. The cravings are different. This time it is women instead of food (although the women are going to offer us food). But cravings are cravings, whatever form they take. The unseen Enemy is the same, his tactics and goal are still the same. That goal is to sever our relationship with our God.

God is our identity. Without God we are just numbers.

God is our freedom and strength. Without God, we are powerless slaves.

Harlotry with Moab (Numbers 25)

Our harlotry with Moab is recorded in Number 25. We find out after the fact (31:6) that using the women was actually Balaam's idea, and Balak sends them. They are beautiful, exotic, and inviting. They come to us in the wake of our victories, when we were still flush with triumph over battling giants. Our guard was down, and we had become complacent.

They come to us almost like a reward. There is an expectation of the glorious living we will come into when we enter the Land, and the arrival of the Moabite women coincides with our taking of the Land. The Enemy's timing is impeccable.

The women come to us offering pleasure and glorious living, *outside the camp*. Notice we have to go outside the camp to participate in their activities. They offer a release from abstinence. After all, we are entitled to a little pleasure after all these years of abstinence. We're entitled to let our hair down a little. Right?

Some of us begin to commit harlotry with the Moabite women (v1). That phrase "began to" is the Hebrew word, *chalal*, and it is used to indicate when people have begun down the path to profaning themselves or being profaned. Just to give you a feel for how it is used in Scripture, here are some examples:

- In Genesis 6:1-2, the men began to multiply on the earth and the sons of God took their daughters as wives. There was a chalal-ing moment that started a profane lineage.
- In Genesis 9:20-21, Noah began to be a farmer which lead to planting a vineyard, which led to drinking wine and becoming drunk and uncovered in his tent. The chalal-ing moment was not a bad thing, but it was the point of origin for the sin that followed. It provided the opening.
- In Genesis 11:6, the people began to build the tower of Babel, and their effort would not have been stopped without the Lord confusing their tongues.

Chalal indicates an action characterized by throwing off restraint, abandoning self-control, or giving way to desires. There needs only be an opportunity, an opening, for the corruption to begin. That is what *chalal* means, to make a beginning in the sense of opening a way for corruption, to pierce or make a hole in something and thus ruin the perfection or health of the whole.

It also means to be wounded or pierced and thus to be violated, profaned or polluted, in the way an infection begins in an open wound and defiles the body. This word carries a sense of being both sexually and ritually profaned.

In its most figurative use, *chalal* means to play the flute (a flute being an instrument pierced with holes). The sound of the flute is an enticement to a pleasant thing, an invitation. The sound of a flute paired with the movement of a woman's body is enchanting. The urge to join that dance is strong. The invitation is accepted. Moab played the flute for Israel, and Israel danced.

The men of Israel begin to take their pleasure of the women of Moab. Then the women of Moab begin to explain that this is how they serve their god, Ba'al of Peor. The word, Ba'al, means husband and master. For these women, the offering of their bodies is their way of serving their husband-god. Sex for them is an act of worship, a way of glorifying their god. Sex and sacrifice.

Suddenly the men of Israel are no longer just taking the pleasure of the women. Now they are up to their necks in idol worship. They are eating the sacrifices given to idols and performing profane acts of worship to Ba'al, at the enticement of these cult prostitutes. They have engaged in the violation of women without realizing it is their own bodies that have been violated. They have now joined themselves in a very physical way with Ba'al of Peor, and the corruption has entered them (v2-3).

There is one other aspect of the word *chalal* that I want to show you. *Chalal* is very similar to another Hebrew word, *halal*, which means to praise or glorify. *Halal* is the word we get hallelujah from.

One applies to true worship, one is the counterfeit. The counterfeit is a pretty good likeness. When you see these words written in Hebrew, there is only one small difference between them. See if you can spot it.

הלל   Halal: to praise or glorify

חלל   Chalal: to begin down a path to being profaned

The only difference between these two words is in the first character on the right (the small symbols beneath are vowel points, not actual characters). In *halal*, the left leg doesn't quite join the rest of the letter as it does in *chalal*. The joining of the leg to the rest of the letter changes the character of the letter. A little joining of the leg and we have ceased giving praise to God and are on our way down the path to profaning ourselves.

The defining difference between the praise and the profane is who is being given the glory—God or His rival.

Recognizing the Counterfeit

The words sound nearly the same. At first glance, one even looks a lot like the other. That is the way the counterfeit works. The words they say will sound almost right. The way they act will look much like what we expect.

The Moabite women tell us their god is like a husband to them. Doesn't our God identify Himself with a husband, even a jealous husband?

The Moabite women give their bodies in holy worship and service to their god. Doesn't our God expect us to see our bodies holy and for His service? Doesn't our God expect us to worship Him with our bodies? (Ah, but how they use their bodies is very different from what the Lord has told us to do. That should be a red flag.)

They come during a time of rest and victory. They offer an abundance of pleasures. Hasn't our God promised us rest and reward and abundance in the Land?

They offer a release from years of restraint. Hasn't our God told us that the lean years of our wilderness wandering were only temporary?

Some of us have been led away by the counterfeit. A little joining of the leg with the women of Moab, and now they are neck deep in idolatry. God's holy people have joined themselves to a profane priesthood.

Recognizing the counterfeit is the new challenge we are facing at this point in the journey. It is a test of our understanding of God if we can recognize the counterfeits.

In the physical journey, the Moabite women invite us to counterfeit worship. In the spiritual journey, the counterfeit worship is introduced by false prophets, false teachers, and false apostles. Their purpose is the same in both cases.

Their purpose is to deceive. Their words may sound right, but their actions will be wrong. The inconsistency between their words and actions reveals their deceitfulness and corruption.

Their purpose is to exploit. Their lifestyle will often revolve around the pursuit of sensual pleasures. They will use worship as a cloak for pursuing vices.

Ultimately, their purpose is to bring us into bondage.

The New Testament writers warn us of the false teachers and leaders to come and their purpose.

> *"Beware of false prophets, who come to you in sheep's clothing, but inwardly they are ravenous wolves." Matthew 7:15*

> *"...false brethren secretly brought in (who came in by stealth to spy out our liberty which we have in Christ Jesus, that they might bring us into bondage)," Galatians 2:4*

> *"Beloved, do not believe every spirit, but test the spirits, whether they are of God; because many false prophets have gone out into the world." 1 John 4:1*

2 Peter 2 gives us the best parallel to the picture presented here.

> *"But there were also false prophets among the people, even as there will be false teachers among you, who will secretly bring in destructive heresies, even denying the Lord who bought them, and bring on*

> *themselves swift destruction. And many will follow their destructive ways, because of whom the way of truth will be blasphemed. By covetousness they will exploit you with deceptive words; for a long time their judgment has not been idle, and their destruction does not slumber." 2 Peter 2:1-3*

The purpose of the false prophets and teachers is to introduce destructive doctrines, words that twist our understanding of God and how we are to live in relationship to Him, even to the point of denying Him. The Moabite women have introduced this idea that there is another husband-god that we can be serving. That is a false teaching that led many into idolatry to Ba'al.

In regards to the level of depravity that marks the false teachers, Peter tells us:

> *"But these, like natural brute beasts made to be caught and destroyed, speak evil of the things they do not understand, and will utterly perish in their own corruption, and will receive the wages of unrighteousness, as those who count it pleasure to carouse in the daytime. They are spots and blemishes, carousing in their own deceptions while they feast with you, having eyes full of adultery and that cannot cease from sin, enticing unstable souls. They have a heart trained in covetous practices, and are accursed children. They have forsaken the right way and gone astray, following the way of Balaam the son of Beor, who loved the wages of unrighteousness; but he was rebuked for his iniquity: a dumb donkey speaking with a man's voice restrained the madness of the prophet. These are wells without water, clouds carried by a tempest, for whom is reserved the blackness of darkness forever." 2 Peter 2:12-17*

Carousing in the daytime. Carousing in their own deceptions while they feast with you. This is exactly the kind of licentious behavior by which the Moabite women have ensnared many unstable souls in our camp. Peter even mentions Balaam by name here, presenting him as a type of false prophet.

Balaam was a false prophet, not because he did not hear from God, but because he loved the wages of unrighteousness. He saw in Balak, King of Moab, the means of pursuing his own desires for riches and glory. Balaam came to Balak with the intent to deceive and exploit the situation under the guise of being a holy prophet, but in the end, Balaam's prophecies went against Balak, and his deception was revealed.

The tactics Balaam used on Balak are the same tactics he suggests Balak use in dealing with Israel. Deceive them with an enticement, bring them into bondage to their lusts, and then exploit them for your own purpose to achieve your own desires.

Peter goes on in describing the deception of the false prophets and teachers, and it is as fitting for the scenario here in Numbers as it is for us as believers today.

> "For when they speak great swelling words of emptiness, they allure through the lusts of the flesh, through lewdness, the ones who have actually escaped from those who live in error. While they promise them liberty, they themselves are slaves of corruption; for by whom a person is overcome, by him also he is brought into bondage. For if, after they have escaped the pollutions of the world through the knowledge of the Lord and Savior Jesus Christ, they are again entangled in them and overcome, the latter end is worse for them than the beginning. For it would have been better for them not to have known the way of righteousness, than having known it, to turn from the holy commandment delivered to them."
> 2 Peter 2:18-21

Under Balaam's counsel, the women have led some of us away from worship of God and into the worship of Ba'al of Peor. They have ceased to praise and glorify the one true God who would be husband to us, and have gone after another husband-god. We were once separated and set apart as God's holy priesthood, but now some have joined themselves to a profane priesthood. They have let their hair down in the most wanton way and thrown off restraints like unfaithful wives.

The Lord's Reaction, Numbers 25:4-5

Now the Lord is angry. Some of His people have committed a profound act of unfaithfulness. They have opened themselves to corruption and the enemy has taken them. God's rage is the rage of a jealous husband toward an unfaithful wife. God commands Moses to search out the unfaithful, kill them, and put their bodies on display like the harlots they have become.

Kill those who were joined to Ba'al. They are to die for their sin and be hung out in the sun, like cursed things. In addition to the specific offenders, a plague from the Lord has also broken out among all of Israel.

The first people on the firing line are the leadership. The judges are the leaders of tens, fifties, and hundreds. It is easy to distance ourselves from this command to judge, because we think of judges as being government level authorities. But Moses doesn't just command the leaders of thousands to execute judgment on the offenders. He is also talking to leaders of 10s. These are small group leaders, heads of households, who are being asked to put someone in their group, even their family, to death for having joined with Ba'al of Peor.

We all know the Law. A couple chapters back we were taught to discern between presumptuous sin and unintentional sin. What our brothers are committing here is presumptuous sin. They know what they are doing is sin, but they are doing it anyway. We know the penalty. If a brother in our accountability group commits a deliberate, presumptuous sin, then it falls to the rest of us to carry out the Lord's sentence on him. Imagine the horror when Moses hands us the sword and the rope and says "Go kill your brother."

The judges are arming themselves to execute judgment. The conflict in camp has escalated to the brink of warfare with brother turned against brother. A plague has begun and people are falling sick. All of Israel is congregated at the door of the Tabernacle, weeping and in mourning. The camp is falling apart.

Yet the Enemy is not satisfied.

Penetrating the Camp

Up until now, Israel's harlotry with Moab has been kept outside the camp. Some went out to the Moabites and defiled themselves in the process, but the boundary of the camp itself has not been violated. God is cleaning camp and keeping it intact. But the Enemy is not content with that. His goal is to get inside our camp, disrupt it, weaken it, and scatter it. If his plan is going to succeed, the next step in the attack must go beyond what our human enemy, Balak, can orchestrate. This is the Enemy at work now.

He knows the quickest way to bring down a people is to attack and compromise its leadership. Strike the shepherd and the sheep will scatter. The lynch pin of the nation is its leadership. Leadership is a source of great strength and also a point of great weakness. Moses is the key leader the Enemy is going after, and he is going to attack Moses at a weak spot.

The Enemy needs an opening to get into the camp and destroy it from the inside out. He is looking for a weak link—someone with position and sufficiently motivated by his own desires and hubris to perform an act of treachery against his own leadership. He is looking for his Judas. When he finds him, the Enemy is going to arm that man with a particularly sharp tool who will open the breach in Israel's defenses and hit right at the heart of Moses.

> "And indeed, one of the children of Israel came and presented to his brethren a Midianite woman in the sight of Moses and in the sight of all the congregation of the children of Israel, who [were] weeping at the door of the tabernacle of meeting. . . . Now the name of the Israelite who was killed, who was killed with the Midianite woman, [was] Zimri the son of

Salu, a leader of a father's house among the Simeonites. And the name of the Midianite woman who was killed [was] Cozbi the daughter of Zur; he [was] head of the people of a father's house in Midian." Numbers 25:6, 14-15

Zimri, Son of Salu

The Enemy finds his man. His name is Zimri, the son of Salu, a leader in the tribe of Simeon (v14). He is not one of the inner circle of leadership, but he has access to it and the ability to impact it.

His father has named him Zimri, meaning "my music" in the sense of a song of praise. Zimri was called to lift up the glory of the Lord in a song of praise, and yet he is a man who has been enticed away by music of another god. The Enemy played the flute for him, and he danced.

His father's name is Salu. Salu means to be weighed, from the root word, *salah*, meaning to make light of, toss aside, or flout (openly disregard, mock, or scorn) something. It implies something that has been weighed, found wanting and rejected contemptuously. Where it is used in the Scriptures, it describes the Lord treading a rebellious people underfoot (Lam 1:15) or rejecting them in scorn (Psa. 119:118).

When we studied the names of the spies of Canaan, we discussed how the names were meant to reflect the gloriousness of God's character but turned into an opposite expression when that glory was taken by men for themselves. Zimri's character should have reflected a man who sings praise to a God who tramples down His enemies in contempt. Instead Zimri's praise and glorying is for himself, reflected in his arrogant contempt of authority and unabashed in pursuit of his lusts. He flouts Moses openly in front of all Israel.

Cozbi, Daughter of Zur

The Enemy's weapon is a Midianite woman named Cozbi (v15). She is a princess, the daughter of King Zur of Midian, and she is part of this effort to draw Israel into the worship of Ba'al. She is going to be the spearhead that the Enemy launches into the heart of the camp to defile it.

Cozbi means "my lie." She poses as a false wife, using her body in the worship of a false god in an act of harlotry. She represents the full picture of sensual, "glorious" living according to the world's definition, but she is also a tool of war. What should have been an act of love between a husband and wife has been twisted and used as an act of treachery against the God of Israel and His anointed leader.

The Scene

All of Israel has just gotten the word of the Lord's judgment for their harlotry. Moses has given the order to kill all the rebels and the plague has begun. The camp is under judgment and in mourning. It is often in the middle of a crisis that the Enemy chooses to make his move. As Moses and the whole congregation stand weeping at the door of the tabernacle, Zimri enters with this woman in tow on the way to his tent in the Simeonite camp (v6).

Zimri's lust has blinded him to the status of the camp. It doesn't matter that judgment has fallen on them. It doesn't matter that God's people are dying around him. He is past feeling, like a leper who has entered the camp and brought defilement with him. He announces his intentions of taking this woman by presenting her to the congregation as if she were his bride, and before God and Israel, he proceeds to get in bed with "the Lie."

Zimri has given himself over to the Lie. His alliance with her is an act of treason because he has forsaken loyalty to his own leadership in his quest for power and allied himself with a foreign king through this relationship with his daughter. She is the embodiment of Midian's treachery against God and Israel. Zimri's actions here are very much along the lines of what Judas did to Christ with that kiss. This is the foreshadowing of Judas' betrayal of Jesus.

Enemy Tactics: Old Loyalties and False Guilt

Zimri's actions are a very pointed thrust at Moses because of Moses' personal relationship with the Midianites. Moses is humble, faithful, Spirit-filled, and has a sensitivity of conscience when it comes to a relationship with God, but he also has a past life before God called him to this glorious purpose. Midian was the place Moses sought refuge. Moses has old loyalties and ties to the Midianites through his wife Zipporah. The Midianites are supposed to be allies. He had treated them as family but now finds out that they are aligned with Moab in this attack on Israel. Why didn't he foresee this?

He missed a warning sign early on. Back in chapter 10, when Moses suggested his Midianite brother-in-law come with us, there was resistance. His Midianite relatives always gave the appearance of being helpful and supportive, but they never once were willing to enter into the journey with us. They worshiped their own god. They never wanted that relationship with our God.

At heart, they were not friends at all but enemies, as Cozbi's treachery has shown. The loyalty Moses felt toward them turned out to be one-sided. Like Moses, we may have close friends and family who are not believers, but give the appearance of being supportive, helpful, and accepting the fact that we are Christians. But there is always a resistance to us under the surface. Any invitation to join our journey in Christ is always declined.

We can hold on to that relationship and overlook the fact that they themselves aren't Christians. If we do, we deceive ourselves. They may be physical friends but they are spiritual enemies. Love these people, keep witnessing to them, but beware of them. In the spiritual battle, they are against you.

It will always be this way with this world. James 4:4 warns us that friendship with this world makes you an enemy of God. Old loyalties can be a weak spot in our lives and create a blind spot in our judgment. Old loyalties can compromise us, and they can be a tool that the Enemy seeks to use against us. Exploiting old loyalties is a classic Enemy tactic.

Do not let old loyalties keep you from taking a stand in moments of spiritual crisis.

Zipporah is Moses' weak spot. Their marriage was done appropriately and is a legitimate covenant. Zipporah has not brought her father's idolatry into the camp, or in any way compromised her husband before the Lord. She is an honorable woman, and yet, in this moment, Cozbi's dishonorable actions cast a taint on Zipporah and her relationship with Moses. Zimri and Cozbi stand before Israel in mockery of Moses and Zipporah. If it was okay for Moses to take the daughter of a Midianite priest as bride, why can't Zimri take a daughter of a Midianite king? It is almost as if Zimri is daring Moses to say something about it.

Have you ever had someone do that to you? Pick something out of your past, perhaps before you came to know the Lord, and fling it in your face as a way of justifying something they were doing wrong? Our children do this to us, simply because they know our history.

"You had sex before you were married, right?" "You drank and did drugs . . ." "You were wild and went to parties when you were my age . . ."

Those words—that wretched remembrance and comparison—can render us powerless in that moment when we should be speaking up. Feelings of guilt, hypocrisy, fear, anger, and self-condemnation swamp us, and it is enough to make us bow our heads in shame. What can we say?

Lift your head! It's a skewed argument! It's an Enemy tactic! Jesus paid the price for those sins and bore the shame. He has lifted you up and given you a new identity as His glorious child. He does not condemn you for those failures. Don't let the Enemy use them as leverage against you.

How does Moses respond? There is no response mentioned in the Scripture. It is Phinehas, the son of the High Priest, who responds and intercedes on his behalf.

Phinehas, son of the High Priest

Keep in mind the nature of Zimri's offense. This son of Israel has *chalal*-ed himself. With his act of harlotry, he has given the Enemy the means of penetrating us, wounding us, and violating us. Cozbi has been the Enemy's spearhead thrust into the heart of the camp. The punishment for that treachery is going to demand a similar response. Phinehas retaliates by taking a javelin and running them both through (v7-9). This is an eye-for-an-eye sort of justice.

Phinehas has identified himself with the person and character of God. His actions are described as zealous (v10), which is interchangeable with the word, jealous. He feels jealous in the same way God feels jealous over Israel.

Phinehas made atonement in the sense that he stepped into the breach and made a covering for the gaping wound in Israel by cutting off the source of corruption. He has in essence separated the nation from sin and made Israel whole again.

His action brought such honor and glory to the Lord, to hallow the Lord in the eyes of the people, that the Lord honors him with a covenant of peace. Peace, in the Hebrew, is the word *shalom* which includes a sense of wholeness and well-being. Phinehas brought wholeness back to the camp and in return is rewarded with a covenant of wholeness. He shall be a priest forever (v10-13).

When we align ourselves with the Lord in such a way that we are heart to heart with Him and seek to put His glory first, there is reward: the fruit of peace, completeness, and wholeness in our lives. Even in the midst of an enemy attack, we can have a peace that passes understanding, which is a taste of fruit to come. Peace and the sense of the Lord's presence with us in this difficult moment carries us forward to deal with the enemy and the lingering consequences.

One man and woman have been the Enemy's agents for introducing this corruption into the body of our camp. With their death, the corruption is cut off and the plague ends. Remember, plague is God's tool for making the inward corruption visible on the outside. All the plague throughout the camp comes to an end with Zimri and Cozbi's death, almost as if they are representatives of the sin. (This is similar to Korah being held accountable for the plague during that rebellion.) By Phinehas' righteous act, many are saved.

This is the second time in this book that we have seen this scenario. It previously played out in Korah's Rebellion between Korah and Aaron, the High Priest. This time it is between Zimri and Phinehas. This time the son of the High Priest is performing the atonement, not the High Priest himself.

Phinehas is going to reappear in the narrative in chapter 31 when he is sent to war against the Midianites, but before we get to that lesson, we need to look at the intervening chapters.

A Break in the Narrative Timeline (Numbers 26-30)

Our harlotry with Moab in chapter 25 will segue into war with Midian in chapter 31, but in between there are five chapters that present necessary details to the narrative and are part of the sweeping overview of the prophetic picture.

- Chapter 26 records the taking of the second census after the plague ends and includes a mention of how the inheritance is to be divided.
- Chapter 27 clarifies a point in regards to the inheritance of daughters. It also records the commissioning of Joshua to succeed Moses.
- Chapters 28 and 29 are an overview of the Sabbath, New Moon and Feasts of Israel with an emphasis on the offerings made during each.
- Chapter 30 is devoted to the laws concerning vows.

I want to make a high-level pass through these chapters to give us a sense of their content and possible reason for their placement in the narrative.

Numbers 26: The Second Census

Lesson 2 covered both the first and second census and the implications of their changing numbers in terms of inheritance allotments. I drew the parallel between the census numbers and Jesus' Parable of the Talents in Matthew 25. The censuses speak of the accounting that is taken prior to entering the Kingdom. Each servant's reward and level of governance is determined by the final accounting, just as each tribe's allotment is determined by the final census.

This second census is much more detailed than the first. The first census only gave us the names of the leaders and the totals for each tribe. The second census records the patriarch's name and all the generations that have now sprung from that line according to their clans and final number who will enter the Land. It is notable to have begun the journey, but the real importance rests on how well we finish and whether we have pressed on toward that reward.

It is interesting to note just how many generations are now included in the second census. This isn't just the second generation that will enter the Land. In the case of Judah, Benjamin, and Asher, two additional generations are noted. In the case of Reuben and Ephraim, three generations are noted. In the case of Joseph's son, Manasseh, six generations are noted. His lineage ends with Zelophehad who died having no sons, only five daughters. Zelophehad is a special case and becomes the focus of chapter 27 over the issue of passing an inheritance to his daughters.

Multitudes upon multitudes are coming into the kingdom, to the third, fourth, even sixth generation.

Numbers 27: The Inheritance of Zelophehad's Daughters

An issue is brought up involving a technicality of Law: a man has died on the journey leaving no sons to inherit the Land. He does, however, have five daughters. The concern is that for lack of a son, the father's lineage would be cut off and his inheritance in the Land could not be claimed (v4).

The question boils down to this: must the inheritance be passed strictly by a blood relationship between father and son, or can it be passed on by right of kinship relationship of a daughter? Isn't a daughter considered offspring as well?

It is interesting that Zelophehad's daughters bring up an accounting of their father's sin in their argument. They make the point that their father was not part of Korah's rebellion but died from his own sin (v3). Why compare Zelophehad to Korah? When it says that Zelophehad died in his own sin, it implies that his sin was his alone and the consequence for it affected only himself. It did not result in others falling into sin or dying on account of his sin, unlike Korah. By comparison, Korah died for his sin, but also drew many into sin and took the lives of many, so greater guilt was laid to his account. The sin of Korah was a grievous one in its rebellion against God, and all involved were counted as enemies of God and cut off from the Land.

Zelophehad stands in this limbo of not having made himself an enemy of God to be cut off from the Land, yet having no sons to claim his inheritance. In the book of Deuteronomy, the Law states that if a man dies without a son, then his widow must marry her brother-in-law to produce an heir to the man's inheritance and thus carry on his line (levirate marriage). According to the Law, a levirate marriage would be required here, but that is not what the Lord determines. The Lord upholds Zelophehad's daughters as heirs to their father's allotment in the Land. The Lord even goes so far as to allow those of distant relationship to inherit on the man's behalf (v8-11). Any relation to the man may claim his inheritance so long as they are of the same tribe. All inheritance must be kept within the tribal lineage of the originating patriarch, hence the emphasis on tracing lineage back to the patriarchs in the second census.

Daughters are of the blood of their fathers, the same as sons. From a physical standpoint, it would seem natural that a daughter be allowed to inherit in the absence of a male heir. This minor point of law over a physical inheritance doesn't seem like it should warrant as much attention as it is given. What does it matter if an inheritance passes through a daughter?

What has passing importance in the immediate physical context has tremendous implications when taken into the spiritual context and considered in light of what we know of Jesus Christ. Let's consider that.

Prophets foretold that a Messiah would come from the Davidic lineage. The inheritance of the throne should have passed through the lineage of Solomon and his sons, but this lineage becomes cursed in the reign of Jeconiah (Jer. 22:28-30) so that no king will come from it again. Yet the promise of a Messianic king remains.

The kingly lineage passes from son to son down to the generation of a man named Joseph, betrothed to a woman, Mary. Even though Joseph is of the kingly line, any son born to him would not inherit the throne on account of the curse. Any claim to such an inheritance must come from another line, apart from the line of the kings. And it does—through Mary, a daughter descended from King David.

In Joseph and Mary, we have both a son and a daughter from a Davidic line, but the inheritance of the throne is passed through the daughter and not the son. In fact, the heir born to Joseph and Mary is born of a virgin birth—*purely through the daughter's line*. There is no physical blood tie between the Messianic heir and Solomon's lineage at all.

The mention of Zelophehad's sin emphasizes the impact sin has on a man's right to an inheritance in the Land. What does sin have to do with inheritance?

What is true of the physical inheritance is true of the spiritual. The sin of one king brought a curse on all his descendants, that they should not inherit the throne. In the same way, the curse of sin that began with Adam is carried to all humankind, separating them from eternal life with the Lord. All who are born of man inherit that sin nature, and it is a curse attributed to and perpetuated through the male lineage. It is an inheritance not attributed to the woman, who was deceived and fell into sin, whereas the man, Adam, sinned knowingly. Christ was born of virgin birth by the woman, apart from the curse on the kingly line but also apart from the sin heritage of Adam and his curse.

In as much as Christ will inherit a physical kingdom—the Millennial Kingdom—so He will inherit a spiritual kingdom. Those who believe in Him become co-heirs with Him based on the spiritual relationship—by faith. In the spiritual kingdom, co-heirs can come from any nation, so long as their relationship is by faith in the Son whose lineage is traced back to *the promise* given the patriarch, Abraham, and not by blood.

Zelophehad's daughters set a precedent for an heir to inherit a kingdom apart from a direct father-to-son blood relationship of Israel. Christ's claim to both the physical and spiritual kingdoms comes through a daughter of Israel, apart from a father-to-son blood tie. I believe this is the greater picture foreshadowed in these laws, consistent with the Messianic pictures that have been building in connecting chapters.

Numbers 27: The Commissioning of Joshua

Chapter 27:12-23 describes the commissioning of Joshua. The Lord has told Moses that his own death is imminent (v12-13), and Moses asks that another leader be raised up in his place. Moses asks for this new leader to be a shepherd to Israel, one who will lead the children of Israel in their coming out and going in (v17), and the Lord chooses Joshua, one of the original generation to come out of Egypt and remain faithful and who has the indwelling Spirit (v18).

Joshua is commissioned before Eleazar and the congregation and a portion of Moses' authority is given to him (v19-20), although Moses' authority continues to have a presence through the Law. Joshua does not have the same relationship to the Lord as Moses in that he does not speak to God face to face, but must inquire of the Lord through Eleazar and the judgment of the Urim (v21).

Joshua will also be appointed overseer with Eleazar in the task of dividing the inheritance among the tribes in Numbers 34:17.

We know Joshua will lead the children into the Land and into that next, more glorious level of relationship with God that involves fruitfulness. He will lead them in taking the Land from their enemies and will divide the Land among them. Yet here in Numbers, all these roles remain in the offing. Joshua is commissioned and yet he does not assume his role immediately.

It is not Joshua who goes to war with Midian but Phinehas.

We know Joshua is a type of Christ. We see him as he will be, but not yet. As Balaam said, *"I see him but not yet."* Joshua remains a sketch of a future leader, a picture of someone yet to come.

Numbers 28–29: Offerings

Chapters 28 and 29 outline the burnt offerings made on various days, including the Sabbath, the New Moon and the days of the Feasts. I won't go into detail about this very lengthy set of laws, except to note that every burnt offering requires an offering of grain and wine, which means these laws can be practiced only after we come into the Land. Grain and wine are not available in the wilderness. These offerings are made as a sweet aroma to the Lord, and they set up a picture of a communion experience yet to come.

The grain and wine details are very specific to this passage. These same feasts are mentioned extensively in Leviticus and Deuteronomy, yet without this incredible attention to the offerings of wine and drink. Why not just include these details in the Leviticus passages?

In the immediate context, these chapters seem oddly placed, but not when we get to the bigger picture that is unfolding. As we will see, this information is put here intentionally, just like Joshua's commissioning, but you aren't going to see the logic of it apart from an understanding of Christ in His second coming and the End Times events explained in the book of Revelation. We will get to that shortly.

Wherever we have found sections of law mixed in with our narrative, I have pulled principles out of them as camp rules for us on this journey. As believers in the Church age, we do not practice the keeping of the Sabbaths and Feasts of Israel as the Mosaic Law demands in terms of sacrifices and daily offerings. The bread and wine of our communion are a memorial of Christ's death on the cross, instead of the foreshadowing that we see in the Old Testament sacrifices. Just as the Old Testament Jews were given this picture to keep until His first coming, so we as believers (Jews and Gentiles alike) are to keep communion until His second coming.

Camp Rule #10: Keep communion until He comes.

Numbers 30: Laws Concerning Vows

Vows are serious with God. What comes out of our lips becomes binding, whether spoken thoughtfully or rashly, in faithfulness or unfaithfulness.

Vows are not something we as New Covenant believers are encouraged to enter into, but they were regularly practiced as part of an Old Testament relationship with God.

We have already studied the Nazirite vow at the beginning of this book. It represented a high degree of accountability between the individual and God. These set of laws follow the same vein. The warning is reiterated. Be careful in making a vow because this action invokes the highest level of personal accountability before God.

I think this section is placed here as a setup for the vows that the tribes of Reuben, Manasseh, and Gad will make in chapter 32. Even though their inheritance is on the east side of the Jordan, they will vow to cross the Jordan and enter the Land to help their kinsman battle the Canaanite enemy to take the Land.

The instructions concerning vows in chapter 30 are as follows:

- If a man vows anything, whatever he vows becomes binding, and the Lord will require it of him (v2).
- If a widow or divorced woman makes a vow, it is as binding as a man's vow (v9).
- If a woman is unmarried in her father's house or married with a husband over her, the conditions change. The father or husband can affirm or override her vow in this way.
  - If she makes a vow and her father/husband hears of it and doesn't say anything on the day he hears it, then her vow stands and she is bound to her agreement (v4, 7, 11).
  - If the father/husband hears the vow, he can overrule it on the day that he hears of it. In that case, the woman is not bound to her vow. The Lord will release her (v5, 8, 12).
  - There is a fine line drawn between a betrothed woman and a married woman in the laws. Jewish sources teach that if verses 6-8 speak of a betrothed woman—a woman who is married in status but not yet living in her husband's house then she stands in a middle ground between her father's jurisdiction and husband's jurisdiction, and both her father and husband must revoke her vows. If one or the other upholds it, it must be honored.[1]

---

1 Rashi's commentary on Numbers 30, Nedarim 67a, Talmud.
   https://www.chabad.org/library/bible_cdo/aid/9958/jewish/Chapter-30.htm#showrashi=true

I hesitate to make a parallel to this in the spiritual walk as I do not know the nature of the vows being made. I know that vows can be made to dedicate something or someone to the Lord, as in the case of Hannah giving her firstborn son Samuel to the Lord (1 Sam. 1:11). According to these laws, Hannah's vow could have been voided by her husband, but it wasn't. This stands in contrast to Jephthah's rash vow in Judges 11:30 that tragically required him to sacrifice his daughter. There was no release for Jephthah from his vow. He was bound to do it.

The only principle I will confirm in terms of our spiritual journey is that it is better not to vow at all than to make a vow and not follow through. You cannot know what the future will bring or if you will be able to perform them. If you vow something, even as believers today, the Lord will require it of you, and it will be counted as sin if you do not honor it. James reminds us:

> *"Come now, you who say, 'Today or tomorrow we will go to such and such a city, spend a year there, buy and sell, and make a profit'; whereas you do not know what will happen tomorrow. For what is your life? It is even a vapor that appears for a little time and then vanishes away. Instead you ought to say, 'If the Lord wills, we shall live and do this or that.'"*
> *James 4:13-15*

> *"But above all, my brethren, do not swear, either by heaven or by earth or with any other oath. But let your "Yes" be "Yes," and your "No," "No," lest you fall into judgment." James 5:12*

That is a quick overview of the intermediate chapters that fall between chapters 25 and 31. They seem a little scattered in theme and random in placement, but there is a reason which we will see when we get to the big prophetic picture. Before we discuss that, however, we need to cover the war with Midian in chapter 31.

War with Midian (Numbers 31)

I think it is interesting how the Lord goes after the Midianites and not the Moabites for all of Balak's scheming. All this started with Balak of Moab and Balaam. They were the ones who sent in the women to entice us out, and succeeded to a certain extent in getting some of us to defile ourselves. Even so, they never crossed the line into the camp.

It was the Midianites who crossed that line. They crossed that line physically when Zimri brought Cozbi into his tent, bringing plague to the camp. They crossed the line in their level of treachery, having once been counted as friends and coming to us in the guise of brotherhood, and turning an act of love into an act of war. Their offense against Moses has reached heaven.

Phinehas and the Elite Task Force

In Numbers 31, Moses selects 1,000 men of war from each tribe, making 12,000 total (v3-5). Keep in mind, these are the men of war from the second census. They were the ones who had kept themselves from the women of Moab and not gotten in bed with the Midianite lie, so they were spared the plague of the Lord for those sins. Now they have become an elite task force under Phinehas to go to war with Midian.

It is Phinehas, the son of the High Priest, who leads this foray, not Joshua. I would have expected it to be Joshua who has led them in battle in the past, and will lead them into battle once they enter the Land. But in this instance it is Phinehas who goes to battle.

Phinehas takes his elite force, with the holy articles and signal trumpets in hand, and goes to war with the Midianites (v6). They kill all the men of Midian, including five kings: Evi, Rekem, Zur, Hur, and Reba. Balaam, the false prophet, is also killed by the sword in this battle (v7-8). They take the women and children captive, as well as the cattle, flocks and material goods, then burn all the cities and forts. This is a partial fulfillment of Balaam's prophecy against the Kenites in Numbers 24:21-22.

Balaam's prophecy specifically targets the Kenite clan of Midian, which is the clan that Zipporah's family is from, yet it seems that Zipporah's family survives this battle perhaps because they splinter off from the clan and associate themselves with other people. They are mentioned specifically in the book of Judges.

> "Now the children of the Kenite, Moses' father-in-law, went up from the City of Palms with the children of Judah into the Wilderness of Judah, which lies in the South near Arad; and they went and dwelt among the people." Judges 1:16

> "Now Heber the Kenite, of the children of Hobab the father-in-law of Moses, had separated himself from the Kenites and pitched his tent near the terebinth tree at Zaanaim, which is beside Kedesh." Judges 4:11

So we can see Zipporah's family is spared by some divine orchestration in being absent from the location where the judgment is commencing.

In regards to the kings of Midian, we should note that there are seven Midianite kings mentioned in Scripture. Five kings fall in battle to Phinehas but this doesn't completely end Midian. Two more Midianite kings rise in the time of the judges and are put down by Gideon. After that Midian is finally dissolved as a sovereign nation. Five will fall; two are to come. Keep that in mind.

Return from War

In Numbers 31:12-14, we see that Israel did everything right in this battle except for one thing. They spared the women of Midian and their young sons. When they arrive back at camp with the captives in tow, they are met outside the camp by Moses, Eleazar, and the congregational leaders. When he sees what they have brought back, Moses is furious with the officers who should have known better (v14-16).

Have they learned nothing? How is it that they failed to make the connection between the problem with Zimri bringing Cozbi into camp, and the problem with themselves bringing Midianite women into camp? It seems like a no-brainer.

These men were not guilty of the sin of Zimri the first time around, but now they are on the verge of committing the exact same mistake. How often do we see consequences play out in other people's lives and yet we fail to take a lesson from them and apply it to our own lives? More often than we like to think! If it was wrong for them and brought judgment on them, then it is wrong for us and will bring like judgment on us.

The officers are commanded to put to death all the male children as well as the women who have known a man intimately (v17-18).

Earlier we studied the word, *chalal*, which means to make a beginning so that corruption may enter—to pierce or wound something so that it compromises the health and purity of the whole. A *chalal*-ing occurred when Israel committed harlotry with Moab and when Zimri brought Cozbi into camp.

There is a second usage of the word *chalal*. It can also mean to slay or wound, usually by piercing with a sword. That is the *chalal*-ing that Phinehas visited first on Zimri and Cozbi, and now his officers perform on the women and male children of the Midianites. In the Hebrew, the male children are called the *zakar*, the remembrance. There are many names for man in the Hebrew, and I think this is one is used purposely to indicate the Lord's intent of wiping out the memory of the Midianites that would have been carried on in their male progeny. In regards to the women, all the women who have been known by a man intimately are also to be killed. Only the Gentile women who are whole and undefiled will join the camp.

One act of *chalal*-ing by Midianites on Israel has reaped a whirlwind of *chalal*-ing by God on Midian.

The next task for the returning army is the cleansing of any person or thing that has been defiled by death as a result of battle. Anything that has touched something slain cannot be brought back into camp without being cleansed first (v19).

Verses 20-24 give instruction for purifying different things. Anything that can endure the fire must pass through the fire. This includes all metals such as gold, silver, bronze, iron, tin, and lead. Anything that cannot endure the fire must be put through the waters of purification that have the ashes in them, the ashes being a representative of the refining process of fire. This is the process we discussed in back in chapter 19 with the Red Heifer sacrifice.

Division of the Plunder

The rest of Numbers 31 involves the division of the plunder. The men of war all took plunder, but they are not allowed to keep it all for themselves. They are required to share half of it with the congregation.

By giving half the spoil to the congregation, the men of war are being asked to acknowledge the rest of the camp's place in this war. The reason for the war was to avenge the treachery of Midian on Israel as a whole, not just for personal vengeance for an elite group. Those men represent Israel as a whole. The booty gained from despoiling of the enemy also belongs to Israel as a whole, not just the men who go to war. The men are not to take glory solely for themselves but for God and all of Israel. God has lifted them up in giving them victory, and now they in turn are being asked to lift their kinsmen up as well, which requires a little bit of humility and letting go of ego.

The plunder to be divided includes captives, cattle, donkeys, and sheep. The men of war also took gold, but that is not part of the initial tally.

Half of the plunder remains with those who went to battle. From their half is taken a tribute (tax) to the Lord. One out of every 500 captive, cattle, donkeys, and sheep are given to the priests.

The other half goes to the congregation who remained back at camp. From their half, one out of every 50 captive, cattle, donkeys, and sheep is given to the priests. Though the plunder is split evenly between the men of war and the homefront, the priests take a greater percentage from those who stayed home than from the men who went to battle.

There is one other offering mentioned, which is made by the captains of thousands and hundreds with whom Moses was angry for having kept the Midianite women alive. Out of thanks to the Lord for not having lost one man in the field and as an atonement for their error, they offer part of the gold that they took as plunder, 16,750 shekels worth, which is brought into the Tabernacle as a memorial (v48-54).

This is a very different attitude than we have previously seen throughout this journey. It began as a journey marked by failure after failure on the part of a selfish, self-absorbed people who were unwilling to press on to the reward the Lord had in store for them. It has ended in this moment of victory over the adversary and celebration between God and His people. In dividing the plunder we truly see God as King of His people and their deepening identity with Him. Even though the officers failed in bringing the women back to camp, their free will offering was an acknowledgment not just of their own error, but also of the Lord's power, provision, and protection. They have, in a sense, reached a moment of Sabbath oneness with Him and attained a taste of peace and rest. What a magnificent step in spiritual maturity.

This war with the Midianites is the last event recorded in the book of Numbers and, as fitting for the end of the journey, it is overflowing with End Times imagery. The prophetic picture actually extends from Balaam's prophecies through the end of the book. Let's lay out that prophetic picture now.

	Total (soldiers' half)	Lord's Tribute
Sheep	337, 500	675
Cattle	36,000	72
Donkeys	30, 500	61
Captives	16,000	16
	Total (camp's half)	Lord's Tribute
Sheep	337, 500	6,750
Cattle	36,000	720
Donkeys	30, 500	610
Captives	16,000	160

The Prophetic Picture of the End Times

When we were in the Wilderness of Zin, we saw wave after wave of prophetic imagery speaking of Christ in His first coming—His sacrificial death and resurrection. Now we are in the second generation of that picture, and this time we will see waves of imagery speaking of Christ in His second coming as King to claim His Kingdom.

This picture begins with Balaam's prophecy in Numbers 24 of a scepter rising in Israel. A king is coming. *"I see him but not now."* The picture continues all the way through chapter 31 (war with Midian). Beyond chapter 31, instructions are given for entering the Land and claiming the inheritance.

Numbers 24-31 tracks well with the book of Revelation in regards to these events, even foreshadowing its structure to a certain extent. There is a basic timeline of events, but then there are the parenthetical chapters that give details or sweeping overviews of events. Mixed into these events are a number of people who are types of characters in the End Times. I will present the types and basic timeline first, which include:

- Israel's harlotry with Moab (Chapter 25). I will pair this with the "falling away" described in 2 Thessalonians 2.
- Zimri and Cozbi (Chapter 25) as types of the Man of Sin and the Harlot of Babylon (2 Thes. 2, Rev. 17-18) who come into view at the height of the falling away and embody it in its fullness.
- Phinehas as a type of Christ. In Chapter 31 Phinehas and the 12,000 are a parallel picture of Christ and the 144,000. In the war with Midian, Phinehas and his army correspond to Christ and the armies in heaven at war with the Beast and world alliance of nations (Rev. 19)

In terms of the timeline, Numbers 25 and 31 track closely with chapters 17-19 of Revelation. Once we establish the timeline, then I will come back with the parenthetical chapters that include:

- The second census, inheritance laws for daughters, and commissioning of Joshua (Chapters 26-27). These are paired with a series of pictures in Revelation 7 and 14.
- The overview of the Sabbaths and Feasts with their emphasis on grain and wine offerings being poured out, which I pair with Revelation 14 and the reaping of the earth and the treading of the winepress of the grapes of wrath.

Types and Timeline

My purpose in this section is simply to present picture elements that I see in the Numbers' narrative that correspond to what I see in the book of Revelation's narrative. It is not to intrepret the book of Revelation, but to examine the structure and typography they share that may shed light on the inclusion and order of the parenthetical chapters in Numbers.

Balaam as a Type of False Prophet

Earlier in this lesson, I discussed the challenge of recognizing the counterfeit, which led into a discussion of the deception of false prophets and teachers in 2 Peter 2. Peter specifically mentions Balaam. His tactics of drawing believers into idolatry and sexual immorality are something that the Enemy continues to use through history.

The deception and doctrine of Balaam are so far reaching as to infect the churches mentioned in Revelation 2. The compromising church at Pergamos will be lured astray into eating meat sacrificed to idols and committing sexual immorality (Rev. 2:14). The same is true of the church at Thyatira, only they will give way to a prophetess whom John calls Jezebel, who perpetuates Balaam's tactics (Rev. 2:20-21). Just as Cozbi and the Moabite women were Balaam's tool, so this woman Jezebel will be the Enemy's tool.

Israel's Harlotry with Moab (Numbers 25)
Falling Away (2 Thessalonians 2, Revelation 2)

From the false prophets described in 2 Peter 2 we segue into the falling away and great apostasy described in 2 Thessalonians 2.

Many of the children of Israel have been led away into idolatry because they went after the counterfeit. The New Testament also talks about a future time when people will give themselves over to a lie, which will be in conjunction with the coming of the lawless one.

> *"The coming of the lawless one is according to the working of Satan, with all power, signs, and lying wonders, and with all unrighteous deception among those who perish, because they did not receive the love of the truth, that they might be saved. And for this reason God will send them strong delusion, that they should believe the lie, that they all may be condemned who did not believe the truth but had pleasure in unrighteousness."* 2 Thessalonians 2:9-12

In essence, that is what happened in Numbers 25 and will happen again in the future. A group of believers have failed to discern the truth from the counterfeit and have given themselves over to the Lie, the deception of the counterfeit. They have given up believing in the truth and chosen to pursue pleasure in unrighteousness.

God knows the spiritual condition of their heart to be unfaithful but instead of just letting their unfaithfulness play out as it will, He is going to do something that pushes their behavior to its fullest extent. He sends them a "strong delusion," and it will harden their hearts to the point where they are blind to what is happening, past feeling and having seared consciences—just like Zimri (and just like Pharaoh). The day is coming when there will be no more delay and God will shorten the time to their destruction by forcing the issue to a crisis point.

> *"Let no one deceive you by any means; for that Day will not come unless the falling away comes first, and the man of sin is revealed, the son of perdition, who opposes and exalts himself above all that is called God or*

that is worshiped, so that he sits as God in the temple of God, showing himself that he is God." 2 Thessalonians 2:3-4

In 2 Thessalonians 2-3 Paul exhorts us to stand fast (I will add, with the company of Caleb and Joshua). Remember, God chose us from the beginning for salvation through sanctification by the Spirit and belief in the truth. We are called to be glorified with God's glory, not our own. When Christ is glorified, we are glorified with Him and through our identification with Him. We are to hold to what we have been taught and withdraw from every brother who walks disorderly and not according to sound teaching. We are also warned against idleness in 2 Thessalonians 3:6-15. Remember, this incident in Numbers happens at a time where Israel is resting on the plains of Moab after defeating the Amorites. Idleness has overtaken them and they have let their guard down.

Zimri (Numbers 25) / Man of Sin (2 Thessalonians 2, Revelation 17)

2 Thessalonians 2:3 tells us that at the time of the falling away, the man of sin is revealed. Here in Numbers 25, in the midst of our falling away to the deception of the Moabite women, Zimri appears on the scene with Cozbi in tow. Zimri is a type of the man of sin, who is also called the son of perdition or the lawless one. In John 17:12, Jesus calls Judas the son of perdition. Judas and Zimri are both types of this character.

The man of sin exalts himself rather than God. Here in Numbers, we see Zimri exalting himself against God and Moses. In the Numbers text, it is not clear whether Zimri took Cozbi into his own tent or into the Tabernacle of meeting. It only says that he presented her before Moses and the congregation who were weeping in front of the Tabernacle and then Phinehas goes into "the tent" after Zimri and Cozbi. Tradition says that Zimri took Cozbi into his own tent, but if Zimri did indeed enter the Tabernacle with Cozbi, then he most certainly has flaunted himself as God in keeping with the description of the man of sin in 2 Thessalonians 2:4.

> *"For the mystery of lawlessness is already at work; only He who now restrains will do so until He is taken out of the way. And then the lawless one will be revealed, whom the Lord will consume with the breath of His mouth and destroy with the brightness of His coming."*
> *2 Thessalonians 2:7-8*

The man of sin will come at a time when the restraint that the Lord has put in place is lifted. Here in Numbers, Zimri comes to the forefront just as the children of Israel have thrown off the restraints they had been under to seek the pleasure of the Moabite women. In our own times, we are seeing a concerted effort, particularly in our younger generations, toward throwing off restraint, causing a tremendous escalation in violence, crime, licentious living, and addictions to everything from drugs to cellphones. I believe this is the beginning, but it isn't yet as bad as it is going to get, for the Spirit is still with us. When all restraint is lifted, this world will begin to fall apart in an unprecedented way.

> *"The coming of the lawless one is according to the working of Satan, with all power, signs, and lying wonders, and with all unrighteous deception among those who perish, because they did not receive the love of the truth, that they might be saved. And for this reason God will send them strong delusion, that they should believe the lie, that they all may be condemned who did not believe the truth but had pleasure in unrighteousness."*
> 2 Thessalonians 2:9-12

I already mentioned the spiritual Enemy who gives power to our human enemy, and how the Enemy is the one really at work in Zimri because the events that play out in Numbers aren't something that Balak could have orchestrated. The man of sin comes with unrighteous deception among those who perish and is himself given over to the lie. "Those who perish" easily describes the children of Israel who committed harlotry with Moab and suffer the plague as a result. They know the truth but don't love the truth. They are unfaithful and will be condemned for unfaithfulness. They will be given over to strong delusion to believe the lie, and they will choose to pursue pleasure in unrighteousness.

Zimri is a type of the man of sin to come. He is associated with a harlot princess.

Cozbi (Numbers 25) / Harlot of Babylon (Revelation 17-18)

Let's sketch a profile of the Harlot of Babylon from Revelation 17-18, and then draw some parallels to Cozbi.

> *"Then one of the seven angels who had the seven bowls came and talked with me, saying to me, 'Come, I will show you the judgment of the great harlot who sits on many waters, with whom the kings of the earth committed fornication, and the inhabitants of the earth were made drunk with the wine of her fornication.' So he carried me away in the Spirit into the wilderness. And I saw a woman sitting on a scarlet beast which was full of names of blasphemy, having seven heads and ten horns. The woman was arrayed in purple and scarlet, and adorned with gold and precious stones and pearls, having in her hand a golden cup full of abominations and the filthiness of her fornication. . . . I saw the woman, drunk with the blood of the saints and with the blood of the martyrs of Jesus. And when I saw her, I marveled with great amazement."* Revelation 17:1-4, 6

It is interesting that the angel takes John to the wilderness to show him this picture. We are still on our wilderness journey as this picture in Numbers unfolds. We have come into the land that some of the tribes will take as an inheritance, but it is still referred to as the wilderness. We have not yet entered the Land proper by crossing the Jordan River.

The Harlot of Babylon described in Revelation embodies a prevailing world economy based on power, wealth, luxury, and sensuality. She is associated with the Beast who is a political power. She sits on the scarlet beast which is filled with blasphemy and has seven heads. An interpretation of this picture is given farther on in Revelation 17.

> *"Here is the mind which has wisdom: The seven heads are seven mountains on which the woman sits. There are also seven kings. Five have fallen, one is, and the other has not yet come . . ." Revelation 17:9-10a*

The Harlot sits on seven mountains which also represent seven kings. Five of these kings will fall early, one is, and one is to come. She is dressed in a fashion associated with royalty and in her hand is a gold cup overflowing with abomination and fornication. The kings of the earth commit fornication with her and live in luxury with her, and she is drunk with the blood of God's people.

Cozbi represents the apex of the Moabite attack to draw Israel into idolatry and licentious living. She is fully representative of that lifestyle and worldview, as is the Harlot of Babylon.

Cozbi is a princess of Midian, associated with its royalty. There are seven kings of Midian mentioned in Scripture, Midian representing a type of world power and alliance. Five kings fall to Phinehas, and two will be destroyed by Gideon in the time of the judges. Five have fallen. Two are to come. While the parallel to the seven kings associated with the Beast is not quite exact, I think it presents an interesting symmetry.

Cozbi has joined herself with Zimri, a prince of Israel and a parallel to the kings of the earth. She is a harlot fully engaged in the filthiness of fornication with him. They revel together in their own sensual pleasure while all around them the people of God are dying because of the plague.

> *"And I heard another voice from heaven saying, 'Come out of her, my people, lest you share in her sins, and lest you receive of her plagues. For her sins have reached to heaven, and God has remembered her iniquities. Render to her just as she rendered to you . . .'" Revelation 18:4-6a*

Just as the Harlot of Babylon brings plagues upon the people who share in her sin, so Cozbi and Zimri bring plague on the camp.

> *"Therefore her plagues will come in one day—death and mourning and famine. And she will be utterly burned with fire, for strong is the Lord God who judges her. The kings of the earth who committed fornication and lived luxuriously with her will weep and lament for her..."*
> Revelation 18:8-9a

The Harlot's destruction is described as her plagues coming upon her and the kings of the earth leave her desolate and naked (17:16). Her destruction comes in one day and in one hour, then the sounds of musicians and flutes will not be heard in her anymore, nor will the voice of the bride and bridegroom (18:22-23).

Just as the Harlot loses her life to God because of her sins with the kings of the earth, Cozbi loses her life to Phinehas because of her sin with Zimri. She dies, naked and desolate, in the act of fornication with him, in one day and in one hour. With her death comes an end to the "flute-playing" by which Moab enticed Israel to join with Ba'al, their husband-god (a perverse bride and bridegroom imagery). Midian itself is left bereft of brides and grooms as every male is put to death along with every woman who has known a man.

The parallels between Cozbi and the Harlot of Babylon are striking.

Phinehas and the 12,000 (Numbers 31)
Christ and 144,000/Christ and the Armies of Heaven (Revelation 14/19)

In the book of Numbers, this is the second picture where the son of the High Priest does something significant. The first time was Eleazar performing the Red Heifer sacrifice (Numbers 19). We talked about how that was a picture of Christ, the Son of God, who went outside the camp to facilitate that atonement with His own body, to become the sacrifice that cleansed us from death.

Now we see the second generation of that son in Phinehas. This time, the son is not facilitating the sacrifice. He comes to judge and make war. He comes with sword in hand to deal with Zimri and Cozbi, first. For this act of faithfulness, the Lord gives Phinehas a covenant of peace and the covenant of an everlasting priesthood, for his zealousness for God and for the atonement he made for the children of Israel. It is Phinehas, not Joshua, who is called to lead Israel's armies into battle against the Midianites, because the prophetic picture being built here is the comparison between the two pictures of the sons of High Priests.

The first is a picture of Christ in His first coming. The second is a picture of His final coming.

There are two pictures of Christ—one in Revelation 14 of Christ and the 144,000 and the other in Revelation 19 of Christ and the armies of heaven engaged in battle—that are blended together into the picture of Phineas and the 12,000 in Numbers 31. Let's look at the Revelation 19 parallel first, and then talk about the 144,000 in the next section.

In Revelation 19, we see Christ coming on a white horse with the armies of heaven to battle the Beast and his armies. Christ is called Faithful and True and "in righteousness He judges and makes war" (v11). Phinehas is characterized by the same faithfulness, being made a priest forever because he was jealous on the Lord's behalf. Like Christ, he goes to war against the Lord's enemies.

Out of Christ's mouth comes a sharp sword to strike the nations (v15). The name, Phinehas, in Hebrew means "mouth of brass," and it is a sword-wielding Phinehas who strikes down the Midianite nation.

Revelation 19:19-21 details the capture of the Beast (the political power who stands against Christ) and the false prophet, and then the kings of the earth are killed by the sword. In the Numbers parallel, not only does the Midianite alliance fall, but Balaam the false prophet is also captured and killed.

Numbers 31 is the shadow picture of Revelation 19 in many of its elements.

Preceding the battle in Revelation 19, there is another picture of Christ, this time with the 144,000 in Revelation 14. This picture also is foreshadowed in chapter 31, but the picture of the 144,000 is further developed out of chapters 26-27. Chapters 26-27 fill in prophetic details found in Revelation 7 and 14.

The Second Census, Inheritance of Daughters, and Commissioning of Joshua (Numbers 26-27)
Sealed of Israel, the Multitudes and Vision of the Lamb (Revelation 7, 14)

In Numbers 26, the second census of Israel is taken after the plague for harlotry has ended. From these men will be chosen 12,000 (1,000 from each tribe) to go to war with Phinehas against Midian. The 12,000 have kept themselves from the women of Moab and are not associated with the Midianite "Lie." In Revelation 7 we see the same ratio—12,000 out of every tribe are chosen to join the Lamb, for a total of 144,000. The 144,000 have not been defiled by women and no deceit is found in them (Rev. 14:4).

In Numbers 27, after the second census, there is the issue of who can claim inheritance in the Land, and it is established that the daughters can inherit the Land as well as the sons. Just as inheritance in the Land can fall to relatives of the patriarch (even distant relatives), so the inheritance in the spiritual Kingdom is open to anyone of any nation or tongue so long as their kinship ties are to the Son of God. This tracks with Revelation 7:9-16, where we see a vision of the multitude of every nation, tribe, and tongue praising God before the throne.

Numbers 27 ends with the commissioning of Joshua, after the census and inheritance laws. This establishes Joshua as the new leader to replace Moses, but it is not a role he takes immediately. It is the role he is going to play in the future as Israel's shepherd after he has brought them into the Land. Likewise, Revelation 7 ends with a picture of Christ the Lamb who will shepherd His people.

> *"for the Lamb who is in the midst of the throne will shepherd them and lead them to living fountains of waters. And God will wipe away every tear from their eyes." Revelation 7:17*

The Lamb will be their shepherd, but it is a role He will play after He has come into His Kingdom, just as it is a future role that Joshua will play when He brings them into the Land.

Numbers 26 and 27 follow a similar structure to Revelation 7. They are parenthetical chapters from the narrative timeline that fills in details for us.

- The census of those men not given to women and the Lie corresponds to the 144,000 sealed of Israel.
- The inheritance of Zelophehad's daughters translates into the vision of the multitudes in the kingdom and the final "census" of believers after the Tribulation whose place in the kingdom is by right of kinship to the Son born through the woman's lineage.
- The commissioning of Joshua gives the shadow picture of a shepherd to come, paralleling the vision of the Lamb as shepherd at the end of Revelation 7.

Numbers 26–27 prefigures the pictures in Revelation 7 (with a few details added from Revelation 14) down to their order of revelation. Numbers 28-29 will pick up the vision of Revelation 14.

The Grain and Wine Offerings of Sabbaths and Feasts (Numbers 28-29) Harvest of the Earth and Treading of Grapes (Revelation 14)

In these interim chapters between our harlotry with Moab and war with Midian, we are given a reminder of these feasts which actually provides a brief but sweeping overview of the eschatological timeline. The Sabbaths and Feasts of Israel have eschatological significance, which I will outline briefly.

We have discussed the placement of the Sabbaths on the timeline in regards to entering into the Land and into the Lord's rest. On this journey we have been celebrating the Sabbath days only, but that experience will take on a new dimension when we enter the Land and begin celebrating Sabbath years. We should be working toward the Jubilee experience, however, we will not reach that goal until Christ's second coming. That rest—the Lord's rest—remains. Everything about the Sabbaths is focused on reaching that final fulfillment.

Interwoven with the Sabbaths are the Feasts of Israel in this order:

- Passover, Feast of Unleavened Bread, and Feast of First Fruits (barley harvest) in first month
- Feast of Weeks (wheat harvest), aka Pentecost, in third month
- Feast of Trumpets, Day of Atonement, and Feast of Tabernacles in the seventh month

The first three feasts (in the spring) represent Christ at His first advent—His death, His burial, and His resurrection (Passover through the Feast of First Fruits). The fourth, Feast of Weeks, also known as Pentecost, marks the physical harvest of wheat, and the spiritual harvest of believers and the giving of the Spirit.

The last three feasts (in the fall) represent the events of Christ's second advent—the sounding of the trumpet at the Feast of Trumpets and the Day of Atonement (prophetically cast as Judgment Day and the Day of the Lord), when Christ the King comes for battle and to claim His Kingdom. The sounding of the Jubilee will coincide with that future fulfillment of the Day of Atonement. The Feast of Tabernacles represents the time of rest and rejoicing in the Land when the full harvest has been brought in to the storehouses—a picture of the Millennial Kingdom.

This reminder of the eschatological timeline is brought to our attention in these interim chapters of Numbers 28–29. The narrative timeline between Numbers 25 and 31 is momentarily broken to present a broader overview of events to come. The structure is similar to the book of Revelation where we also see the narrative timeline broken in various places to present a broader overview of future events. One of those places is Revelation 14.

The feasts of Israel in Numbers 28–29 and the reaping of the harvest and grapes in Revelation 14 both carry the theme of harvest. Numbers 28–29 focuses on the very specific offerings of grain and wine to be made with each sacrifice. Revelation 14 speaks about the harvesting of the earth and the gathering of the grapes of wrath. Again, the focus on grain and wine.

The points that stand out in Numbers 28–29 are 1) the timeline of the feasts which represents a timeline of physical and spiritual harvest; and 2) the emphasis on grain and wine as part of the offerings. The grain and wine had not been detailed before because they can only be practiced once we enter the Land (so this is a view of something yet to come).

The grain harvest happens midyear in the physical harvest season, celebrated by the Feast of First Fruits and the Feast of Weeks, but the harvest is ongoing in the spiritual sense as Jesus indicates in His parable of the wheat and tares (Matt. 13). This parable is resolved in Revelation 14 with the reaping of the earth. The Parable of the Wheat and Tares connects the physical harvest represented in Numbers 28–29 with the spiritual harvest of Revelation 14.

The grape harvest happens in the days leading up to and during the fall festivals, namely, the Feast of Trumpets and Day of Atonement. These same feasts also focus on the spiritual separation of believer from unbelievers and judgment on the wicked, which translate to the End Times events of the Tribulation and Judgment Day. So pair the gathering and treading of the grapes to this time of spiritual judgment.

The focus on grain and wine offerings in Numbers 28-29 now connects to the working out of the wheat and tares and the gathering of grapes in the time of judgment in Revelation 14.

Once the harvest is in and the judgment is over, only then do we celebrate the Feast of Tabernacles, which is a picture of the Millennial Kingdom of Christ.

The placement of chapers 28–29 in the Numbers narrative seems like an interruption of the timeline of events. Why give this overview now and then pick up again where chapter 25 left off? We must assume it is placed there because it is relevant thematically to the events going on in the chapters adjacent to it. This overview of the feasts does not seem to have the same relevance in regards to the immediate physical journey, but it is *very* relevant to the prophetic pictures that the Lord is building.

Summary

From Numbers 25 to 31, we can see these parallel pictures in Revelation:

Numbers 25: The falling away of God's people, Zimri and Cozbi
    Revelation 5: Judgment of the churches
    Revelation 13: Rise of the Beast and his government
    Revelation 17: Harlot of Babylon

Numbers 26: The census of men not given to the Moabite women or the "Lie"
    Revelation 7 and 14: Picture of the 144,000 sealed of Israel

Numbers 27: The inheritance laws extended to daughters and distant relatives
    Revelation 7: Vision of the multitudes coming out of the Tribulation (whose inclusion is based on their spiritual relationship to the Son)

Numbers 27: Commissioning of Joshua
    Revelation 7: Vision of the Lamb as the coming shepherd of His people

Numbers 28-29: Sabbath/Feast overview; Pouring out of drink offerings and burning of grain offerings in concert with judgment for sin
    Revelation 8: Trumpet judgments that strike the earth
    Revelation 14: Reaping of the earth's harvest and grapes of wrath
    Revelation 16: Pouring out of the bowl judgments
    Revelation 18: Fall of Babylon (likened to pouring out a cup of wine)

Numbers 31: Phineas and the army go to battle with Midian, Balaam killed
    Revelation 19: Christ and the armies of heaven in battle with the Beast and his government, capture of the Beast and False Prophet

In the next lesson we will study chapters 31b-34 which focus on setting up the Kingdom in the Land. These chapters continue the parallel with Revelation, corresponding to Revelation 20 and the setting up the Millennial Kingdom.

These final chapters of Numbers give us a bare-bones sketch of the Revelation timeline with just enough detail to make it a very tantalizing study. The end goal of the Numbers narrative is not just to bring the children of Israel on a physical journey to the Land, but to bring believers on a spiritual journey ending with a vision of a glorious, future Millennial Kingdom. That is the goal for which we strive.

This brings us to the end of this lesson. The war with Midian is the final event recorded in the book of Numbers. All the chapters after this will contain instructions for dividing the inheritance and building the nation of Israel in the Promised Land.

LESSON TWELVE

The Plains of Moab by the Jordan

CHAPTERS 26–36

"The plains of Moab by the Jordan across from Jericho" is very specific phrase mentioned eight times in the book of Numbers between chapters 21 and 36.

- It is the final place where we camp before we enter the Land (Numbers 22:1, recorded again in Numbers 33:48-49).
- It is the place where the second census reveals who will enter the Land (Numbers 26 is bookended, beginning and end, by this phrase).
- It is the place where the plunder was divided after the war with Midian, and where the last of the Midianite women and male children are put to death (Numbers 31:12).
- It is the place where Moses gives us the last set of instructions. In the book of Numbers, that phrase marks two commands in regards to taking the Land and dividing the inheritance (Numbers 33:50-52 and Numbers 35:1-2).
- The book of Numbers ends in Chapter 36:13 with this verse: *"These are the commandments and the judgments which the LORD commanded the children of Israel by the hand of Moses in the plains of Moab by the Jordan, across from Jericho."* Looking at the book of Numbers, there don't seem to be many commandments given here relative to the rest of the journey, compared to (for instance) the time we spent at Mount Sinai receiving the Law and Leviticus. But when you consider that the entire book of Deuteronomy is given on the plains of Moab by the Jordan, across from Jericho (Deut. 1:1), and it is also the staging area for Israel to enter the Promised Land under Joshua, it becomes a highly significant location.

Numbers 22:1 opens with a reference to this place. Numbers 36:13 ends with a reference to it. Between these two bookends are the trials, victories and failings that the second generation experienced after their parents died in the wilderness. We have walked along with them in chapters 22-31, but there are a few more issues to iron out in these last chapters. For this last lesson I am going to make a high level pass through chapters 32-36 and pull out a few points as follows:

- Numbers 32 deals with the issue of inheritance for Reuben, Gad, and Manasseh east of the Jordan. I want to go through this in some depth because it contains some particular applications for the spiritual journey.
- Numbers 33:1-49 is an overview of the journey which I will not go into. There are forty-one campsites mentioned, but most cannot be found on modern maps. Chapter 33:50-56 contains one of the *"plains of Moab by the Jordan, across from Jericho"* markers and details Moses' commandment concerning the taking of the Land and dividing the inheritance. I will go through that briefly.
- Numbers 34:1-15 details the boundary lines for the inheritance of each tribe, which I will skim over. Verses 16-29 give another list of leaders, similar to the first census, and as we have been looking at name meanings in Numbers, I will draw a picture out of that list.
- Numbers 35 details the commandment concerning the cities for the Levites and the cities of refuge. These instructions have a spiritual as well as prophetic significance.
- Numbers 36 returns to the issue of the inheritance passing to Zelophehad's daughters and a clarification of that.

The Inheritance of Reuben, Gad, and Manasseh (Numbers 32)

Over the course of this journey, the tribes of Reuben and Gad have accumulated a large herd of livestock, and livestock require large areas of grassland. The plains of Moab extending up through Gilead and Bashan are the perfect place for them.

The Reubenites and Gadites have come into this pleasant place and they are ready to end their journey at this point, even though it means not crossing into the Land. In verse 5 they ask Moses not to take them across the Jordan, but let them stay here on the plains.

Moses responds to this with an exceedingly strong rebuff.

> *"And Moses said to the children of Gad and to the children of Reuben: 'Shall your brethren go to war while you sit here? Now why will you discourage the heart of the children of Israel from going over into the land which the LORD has given them? Thus your fathers did when I sent them away from Kadesh Barnea to see the land.'" Numbers 32:6-8*

Everyone helped take the land that Reuben and Gad now want to settle on, but from Moses' reaction it appears Reuben and Gad are ready to settle here rather than help their brethren in return. The rest of the tribes still have years of wars ahead of them before they can claim their inheritance.

Moses storms at them about acting just like their parents. Remember, the spies from Gad and Reuben were among those brought the bad report of the Land, discouraged the people, and turned them away from the Land. Their discouragement caused everyone to wander the wilderness for forty years. Moses warns this generation that if they discourage the people and turn them back at this point, God will leave them all in this wilderness where they will all perish (v8-15).

We are standing with Caleb and Joshua, watching history begin to repeat itself. Caleb and Joshua were the only ones who gave a good report of the Land and were allowed to enter it, while the rest of our generation died in the wilderness. We learned pretty quickly that just because we were found faithful didn't exempt us from continuing the journey and its trials. We have been walking these forty years with that unfaithful generation, enduring the wilderness, the failings, and deaths. Now we have come alongside this new generation, walked with them, battled with them, and encouraged them.

We are all supposed to be walking with the Lord and lifting one another up on this journey. Our goal is for everyone to enter the glory of the Land God has promised us. We have all come to this resting place and without a doubt we would all like our journey to be over. It is very tempting just to settle in this moment, but this is still the wilderness. We haven't entered the Land. We haven't entered into our inheritance. More battles are looming in the Land, but that is also where our reward lies.

Apathy, a New Form Discouragement

While Gad and Reuben agree with Moses to enter the Land and fight on behalf of their brethren, Moses' response in this moment warns us of a potential pitfall in the journey. That pitfall is apathy.

We are all called to help one another on this journey. Apathy and a desire to "settle" in a comfortable place in our journey can bring discouragement to those who still need help with their own continuing battles. There is nothing worse that being left to battle alone by fellow believers who have settled for second best because they lack the heart to press on to the final reward.

It is the same kind of apathy that settles for the least glorious manna-and-water Sabbath-day level of experience with God instead of pressing on to the more glorious, fruitful Sabbath-year level of experience in the Land. The first generation who settled for the least glorious experience were the same ones who fell into discouragement at the end of a fruitless journey.

Apathy is self-centered at heart. It takes what it wants for itself, but does not give in return. We helped the Reubenites and Gadites when they were fighting battles. We helped them come to a place of peace and rest in their life, but now they will not do the same for us. That was one of the greatest sins of the first generation. It led to their wandering in the wilderness for the rest of their lives to learn how to be others-focused.

Apathy is very difficult to overcome because it is like an inertia that takes over a people and withstands any effort to overcome it. Apathy is one of the worst of communicable diseases that can infect our camp. As it begins to take over, those who are doing the work begin to labor harder and harder to accomplish the tasks that would have been easy if many had been helping. Eventually the few that carry on to the end become worn out and stop altogether. The inertia of the rest drags them to a stand-still as well, and with it comes disillusionment and discouragement.

So how does a leader overcome apathy in their congregation? Pastors have been asking themselves that for years. Moses does a couple things.

First, there is the verbal rebuke and a reminder of what happened to others who carried the same heart attitude. Moses calls attention to the sinful heart attitude.

> *"Shall your brethren go to war while you sit here? Now why will you discourage the heart of the children of Israel . . .?" Numbers 32:6-7*

> *"Thus your fathers did when I sent them away from Kadesh Barnea to see the land. . . . And look! You have risen in your fathers' place, a brood of sinful men, to increase still more the fierce anger of the LORD against Israel." Numbers 32:8, 14*

Not only does Moses say they are following in their fathers' footsteps, but he points out that it is sinful behavior. It is selfish behavior. Being a discouragement to a brother on this journey is a sin against that brother. Camp Rule #2 reminds us that sin against a brother is equal to unfaithfulness to God.

Our apathy makes the Lord angry, for which there are consequences.

> *"For if you turn away from following Him, He will once again leave them in the wilderness, and you will destroy all these people." Numbers 32:15*

People who are engaged in apathetic behavior don't always realize that they have ceased to follow the Lord. The Lord is still moving forward. The Lord is still leading believers through personal struggles and spiritual battles, and even if we ourselves have come to a place of peace and rest in our lives, we are still expected to help others in their endeavor. We are still called to be burden-bearing Kohathites.

Giving in to apathy is equal to not following the Lord. It is a destructive behavior that affects not just the individual but the corporate body as a whole. If we persist in apathy, God will leave us in the wilderness of that least-glorious relationship with Him and we will waste away in unfruitfulness in this life and also the life to come.

The Vow (Numbers 32:16-24)

Having given them the verbal harangue, Moses requires a formal agreement from the tribes who wish to settle east of the Jordan. They may settle their families and livestock in the land they wish to take as their inheritance, so long as they agree to cross over into the Land and go to war alongside their kinsmen until their inheritance has been secured also. That is their vow.

Vows are serious things. Once made, vows must be carried through or else they are counted as sin and the repercussions can be devastating. Think about what these men have vowed. They have committed to battling for the Land until it is subdued, but they don't have any idea how long it will take. The battles before them may take the rest of their life. They may die in battle and never return. They will be held blameless so long as they keep their vow until they are released, but if they do not follow through from this point on, they will have sinned against their brothers and the Lord. It is a noble vow, but a bit scary, too.

Moses warns them strongly, *"do what has proceeded from your mouth."*

In light of their vow, Moses relents and gives instructions to Eleazar and Joshua to award the Reubenites and Gadites the land east of the Jordan, on condition.

> *"And Moses said to them: 'If the children of Gad and the children of Reuben cross over the Jordan with you, every man armed for battle before the LORD, and the land is subdued before you, then you shall give them the land of Gilead as a possession. But if they do not cross over armed with you, they shall have possessions among you in the land of Canaan.'"*
> Numbers 32:29-30

If they don't fight on behalf of their brothers, then they will not get the land they want. They will get what the Lord gives them on the other side of the Jordan with the rest of their brethren. If they don't fight on behalf of their brothers, then they will fight for their own inheritance. They will fight one way or another.

So the children of Reuben and Gad fought and received the land east of the Jordan, as did the tribe of Manasseh. Manasseh had not asked for the land with the other two, but is given the land of Gilead in addition to an allotment within the Land. This is where Zelophehad's daughters came to stay, being descended of Machir, son of Manasseh.

Instructions for the Conquest of Canaan (Numbers 33)

The Campsites (Numbers 33:1-49)

The first forty-nine verses of chapter 33 detail every site where the children of Israel camped along the journey. There are forty-one campsites mentioned by name in this section. Not much detail is given of any the campsites, although four are given a brief note:

1) From the third campsite near Migdol, we passed through the midst of the sea into the wilderness.
2) The fifth campsite, Elim, had twelve springs of water and seventy palms.
3) The tenth campsite, Rephidim, had no water to drink. Here water was given from the rock that Moses struck.
4) The thirty-third campsite, Mount Hor, is where the High Priest died. From this point we turned away from the Land to camp at Zalmonah because of King Arad of Canaan.

Consider these four notable highlights in regards to the spiritual journey, because there is a relationship between them.

The first highlight notes a passage through water and represents baptism— our physical passing through the sea and beginning of that spiritual relationship marked by a passage through water.

In the second, we are given life from physical springs of living water; in the third, we are given living water given from the Rock, which we know is a prefigured Christ (1 Cor. 10:4).

At the fourth, our High Priest dies—again, a picture of Christ.

Considering these four references together, we have two main pictures of water associated with the death—a passage through water (baptism) and the giving of living water. The association between a passage through water and death of Christ are well understood in New Testament doctrine. Baptism is an act of identification with the death of Christ, our High Priest.

The giving of living water takes on a spiritual significance in the prophetic Scriptures where it becomes associated with the Feast of Tabernacles:

> *"Therefore with joy you will draw water from the wells of salvation." Isaiah 12:3* (This is recited as part of the water-drawing ceremony of the Feast of Tabernacles.)

Joel speaks of the Spirit being poured out like water in the Messianic Era:

> *"And it shall come to pass afterward that I will pour out My Spirit on all flesh; Your sons and your daughters shall prophesy, Your old men shall dream dreams, Your young men shall see visions. And also on My menservants and on My maidservants I will pour out My Spirit in those days." Joel 2:28-29*

Jesus draws on the imagery of living water when He speaks to the woman at the well of a never-ending fountain of life that springs from within a believer (John 4). He again connects the giving of the living water and the giving of the Spirit to those who believe:

> *"On the last day, that great day of the feast, Jesus stood and cried out, saying, 'If anyone thirsts, let him come to Me and drink. He who believes in Me, as the Scripture has said, out of his heart will flow rivers of living water.' But this He spoke concerning the Spirit, whom those believing in Him would receive; for the Holy Spirit was not yet given, because Jesus was not yet glorified." John 7:37-39*

Jesus makes this statement at the Feast of Tabernacles, just as the priest is pouring out the water in an appeal to God to provide water to the people. The Apostle John adds the further understanding that Jesus was speaking of the pouring out of the Spirit that would come after Jesus' death to those who believed.

These little details highlighted in Numbers 33 lay a foundational picture for salvation, eternal life, and the giving of the Spirit. A tremendous amount of doctrine springs from this understanding, and yet, when studying the grand sweep of the Exodus and wilderness journey, the picture is easily lost. Numbers 33 highlights these for us, that we might consider the connection between them and what it teaches.

Instructions for the Conquest of Canaan (Numbers 33:50-56)

Following the campsite list, we receive instructions for the conquest of Canaan. We were looking back at where we have been. Now we are looking forward. Our instructions are as follows:

1) Drive out the inhabitants. Dispossess them.
2) Destroy all trappings of idolatry (engraved stones, molded images, and high places).
3) Divide the Land by lot among our families. Larger families get a larger lot. Smaller families get a smaller lot. All are to have as much room as they need. The Land is to be divided by tribal boundaries to keep families together geographically.

There is a warning of what will happen if we don't accomplish goal #1. If we fail to drive out the inhabitants, then they will become irritants in our eyes and thorns in our sides to harass us. In addition to that, the Lord will add His own judgment on us, as He says, *"Moreover it shall be that I will do to you as I thought to do to them." Numbers 33:56*

The Canaanites will become irritants and thorns. Both words stem from Hebrew words referring to thorny hedges that create unwanted barriers in our fertile fields. They will become something we have to continually beat back and battle with in life—battles which we would not have had if we had just been obedient to the Lord and done the job thoroughly.

Moreover, the Lord says if we are not obedient in doing these things, not only will we suffer harassment from enemies, we will also suffer the punishment the Lord planned to visit on our enemies. We need to understand what the Lord is saying here.

God is a glorious God, and He will be acknowledged as a glorious God by all people, either by praise of His people or by demonstrating His sovereignty by putting down His enemies. When we are unfaithful, we are, in essence, defecting to the opposition and making ourselves enemies of God. When we choose to be disobedient, God will treat us the same way He treats His enemies. He will do to us as He planned to do to them.

This has been the Lord's mode of operation throughout this journey. When we have been disobedient, we have suffered defeat at the hands of the enemies rather than having our enemies defeated. We have suffered the fear of our enemy that our enemy should have suffered on account of us. When we prove ourselves unfaithful in what He gives us to do, we suffer the consequences.

Leaders Appointed to Divide the Land (Numbers 34:16-29)

I will not go into the first part of this chapter, which traces the borders of the land of Canaan. The second half of the chapter lists the names of the leaders appointed to apportion the Land. Joshua and Eleazar are appointed to divide the Land among the tribes.

Eleazar was the one who officiated the Red Heifer sacrifice back in Numbers 19, which was a foreshadowing of Christ offering Himself as the sacrifice outside the camp. Now Eleazar is appointed to oversee the division of the inheritance. In Eleazar, there is a shadow picture of the future prophecy of Isaiah 53:12.

> *"Therefore I will divide Him a portion with the great, and He shall divide the spoil with the strong, because He poured out His soul unto death, and He was numbered with the transgressors, and He bore the sin of many, and made intercession for the transgressors." Isaiah 53:12*

Once the tribal lands are apportioned, then a leader from each tribe is appointed to divide their portion among their kin. Since we have been studying names throughout our lessons, I thought I would list them here.

Caleb, son of Jephunneh	One pressing forward, for whom a way is prepared
Shemuel, son of Ammihud	His name is El, our majestic kinsman
Elidad, son of Chislon	One whom God loves, his confidence
Bukki, son of Jogli	Wasting away, in exile
Hanniel, son of Ephod	Has been shown favor, a priestly garment
Kemuel, son of Shiphtan	Raised up by God, to be judge
Elizaphan, son of Parnach	My God has protected, one who is weak
Paltiel, son of Azzan	God has delivered, one who is very strong
Ahihud, son of Shelomi	Brother of the Jews, one of peace
Pedahel, son of Ammihud	Whom God preserved, our majestic kinsman

Again, these names are not in order of tribal ranking or birth order, or even in the same order as previous lists of names by tribe. They are placed in such an order that their meanings tell something of a story.

> He who presses forward, for whom the way is prepared, His name is El. Our majestic kinsman, whom God loves, His confidence, who wastes away in exile, has been shown favor and grace,

> A priestly garment raised up by God to be judge.
> God has protected the weak. God has delivered the very strong.
> Brother of the Jews, one of peace, whom God preserved,
> Our majestic kinsman.

I think it is interesting how the meanings of these names also echo Isaiah 53. Our majestic kinsman, lowered and then lifted up on our behalf, brings us peace. What a glorious picture of a Messiah to come!

New Environment, New Rules (Numbers 35)

Numbers 35 talks about the cities of Levites, cities of refuge and the laws concerning man-slayers (those who are guilty of accidentally killing a man). The cities mark a significant change in the relational dynamic that we have been used to in camp. This new living arrangement is going to have a similar layout to the camp but with some significant alterations in setup and rules. The greatest change is going to involve the Levite placement and role of the Levites in this new environment.

In this section, I want to walk through the physical changes that will happen in the Levite living arrangements and discuss the implications of those. Then I will go more deeply into the purpose of the cities of refuge, the issue of manslaughter and the newly-added role of the avenger of blood.

Outside the Gates

As we move into the Land, the first rule to be altered is Camp Rule #1, which defines who gets put out of camp and where they are put. Those who defile the camp are the leper, the one defiled by discharges, and the one defiled by death. The solution is to put the defiled people outside of camp until they are cleansed and atonement made for them.

The change affects where these people are put. In the Land, they will be put outside the gates of the city. Outside the gates of the city is equivalent to being outside the camp. It's the place where the defiled will be sent to prevent them from defiling the city. "Outside the gates" is a place relative to the city but in a state of separation from it.

An individual will be put outside the gates for ritual defilement, but when the entire nation defiles itself, then the nation gets put outside the Land.

Outside the Land

The conditions that get us put out of the Land run along similar lines to Camp Rule #1 and being put outside the gates, except we are dealing with defilement at the national level. The Lord warns us the whole reason the Canaanites are being ejected from the Land is because they have defiled it with bloodshed, idolatry and sexual immorality. If we follow their practices and defile the Land, the Land will vomit us out as well, just as it did the nations before us (Lev. 18:24-28). This is a much more serious level of defilement than temporary ritual defilement.

Cities of Levites (Numbers 35:1-8)

We are moving into a new environment, so rules and boundaries are changing, particularly the living arrangement of the Levites.

In the camp environment, the Tabernacle compound was marked by a walled courtyard, and the Levites worked within that boundary wall and camped outside around its perimeter. The tribes camped outside of the Levite perimeter. Beyond their boundary was designated as "outside the camp."

The Levitical domain was sacrosanct. No one except a Levite was allowed to cross into the Levitical domain, let alone dwell there, except by marriage covenant to a Levite. To do so merited death.

Once we come into the Land, the Levites' living arrangement will change dramatically. Instead of being centrally located around the Tabernacle, the Levites will be scattered across the territory and given their own walled cities in which to live and work. Every tribe is commanded to allot a proportion of their cities to the Levites along with the common land around the cities for keeping their livestock. The Levite common lands extend from the wall of the city outward, two thousand cubits (1,000 yards, or just over half a mile) to the north, south, east, and west.

The layout of the Levite cities is very much like the layout of the camp,

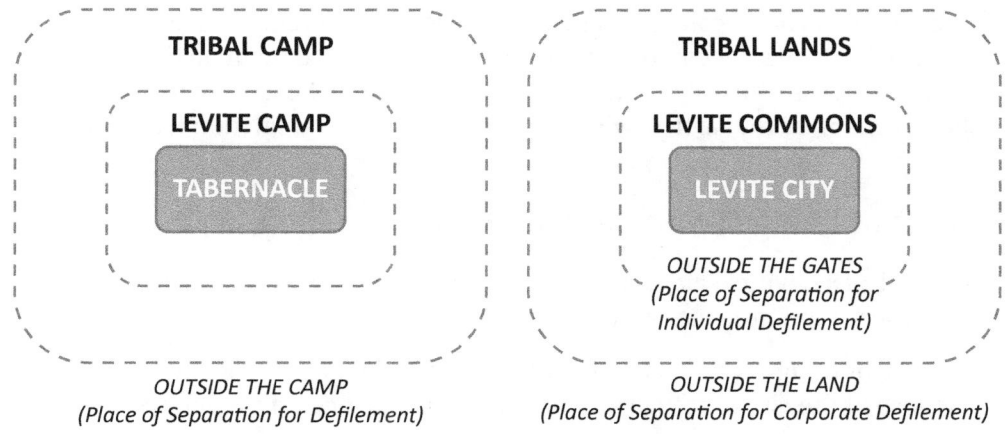

except the Tabernacle is missing where you would expect to see it. The walls of the Tabernacle courtyard have been replaced with the walls of the city, and the Levites are now within those walls, and representative of God in place of the Tabernacle. So we have lost one element in this new layout—the Tabernacle. The Tabernacle itself will come to rest at Shiloh in the tribal lands of Ephraim (Joshua's tribe) during the conquest of Canaan.

There is an important point in all this. Do you remember when we talked about the appointing of the elders at Kibroth Hatta'avah back in Lesson 4? We saw the leaders of the tribes being brought into the realm of the Levites to be commissioned for service under Moses, and then they were sent back out to minister to the tribes. Now the Levites themselves have followed suit. They are the representatives of the Law and still called to serve the Lord and the Tabernacle, but they are no longer rooted to that place around the Tabernacle. Now they minister in the midst of the tribes.

If we root our identity to a physical place in this journey, we will lose our identity at some point. Not even the Levites are exempt from this.

Even so, each Levite city retains the pattern of the camp layout, with the separation of the Levite dwellings from the rest of the tribes by the common lands around their cities.

Forty-eight cities are given to the Levites from among the tribal lands, and the placement of the different clans is detailed in Joshua 21:3-7.

- The sons of Aaron will settle in Judah, Simeon and Benjamin.
- The Kohathites will settle in Ephraim, Dan and Manasseh.
- The Gershonites will settle in Issachar, Asher, Naphtali, and Manasseh.
- The Merarites will settle in Reuben, Gad, and Zebulun.

Once the Tabernacle comes to a rest, the roles of the Gershonites and Merarites are dissolved in regards to the duties assigned them on this leg of the journey. Only the roles of the Kohathites remain as bearers of the Ark of the Covenant, as that article will continue to move in conjunction with battles.

Cities of Refuge (Numbers 35:9-34)

Six of the 48 Levitical cities are designated as cities of refuge. Three cities of refuge are appointed east of the Jordan and three west of the Jordan.

The city of refuge is a special kind of Levite city. I want to talk about the purpose of the city of refuge and the rules that govern it first and then make an observation on the change to the physical boundaries and relational dynamics that result.

Taking Vengeance

The city of refuge is a safeguard that the Lord establishes in the Land to ensure that the execution of judgement between murder and manslaughter is handled correctly, as the taking of life is involved.

We have not been concerned with defilement of the wilderness land so far on this journey, but as we prepare to enter the Land, defilement of the Land by bloodshed becomes a particular issue. Any time a man's blood is shed in the Land, it defiles the Land. The only atonement that can be made for the Land is to shed the murderer's blood.

> *"So you shall not pollute the land where you are; for blood defiles the land, and no atonement can be made for the land, for the blood that is shed on it, except by the blood of him who shed it. Therefore do not defile the land which you inhabit, in the midst of which I dwell; for I the LORD dwell among the children of Israel." Numbers 35:33-34*

When a man's life is taken, the right is given to one of his kin to perform the necessary atonement in taking the life of his kinsman's murderer. He is called the *ga'al*, the kinsman-redeemer or the avenger of blood.

Back in Lesson 6, we went through the names of those spies sent into the Land, and one of the spies name was Igal. Igal comes from this word, *ga'al*, meaning to redeem or avenge. In that lesson I talked about how the decisions we make reveal the nature of our actions, whether they are meant to bring glory to God or to ourselves. The taking of vengeance is another one of those issues we face in our walk, and we must be discerning of how vengeance should be carried out because it can be done in a way that is glorifying to God or in a way that glorifies man.

We have a perfect example of both sides of vengeance in Genesis 4. When Cain killed Abel, the Lord cuts off Cain's relationship with the land. It will no longer yield fruit to him, so Cain becomes a wanderer. Cain is afraid that in his wanderings, someone would find him and kill him. That would have been a fitting end for a murderer in accordance with this law, but the Lord offers grace in putting a mark on Cain for protection and declares Himself to be Cain's avenger.

> *"... Therefore, whoever kills Cain, vengeance shall be taken on him sevenfold.'" Genesis 4:15a*

That is God in a *ga'al* role. Any vengeance on Cain will be recompensed sevenfold by God to His glory.

Five generations later, we hear Lamech, the great-great-great-grandson of Cain, declare, *". . . I have killed a man for wounding me, even a young man for hurting me. If Cain shall be avenged sevenfold, then Lamech seventy-sevenfold." Genesis 4:23a-24* .

Lamech, by contrast, took vengeance for himself and for his own glory, killing for even a small slight. He exalted himself in the act of taking vengeance, not just sevenfold as the Lord would have done for Cain, but seventy-seven fold.

Vengeance can be a righteous act when done in accordance with the Lord's direction and with the understanding that the Lord Himself is the ultimate judge of the issue. We just studied an example of this in chapter 31, where the Lord tells Moses, *"Take vengeance on the Midianites for the children of Israel."* (Num. 31:2) When vengeance becomes a means of personal glorification according to the judgment of man, as in Lamech's case, then it becomes sin.

If any of the children of Israel take on the role of kinsman-redeemer and avenger of blood, they had better know how to discern between intentional murder and accident death, lest they themselves become murderers like Lamech.

Numbers 35:16-23 defines the difference between the murderer and the man-slayer, and the difference falls along the same lines as the laws concerning presumptuous sin and unintentional sin that we studied in Lesson 7. What we do in executing vengeance had better be for the glory of God and not our own glory.

When the killer flees to the city of refuge, the Levite congregation is called to judge whether the killing was intentional or not. If it was intentional, then the man is put to death as a murderer, but if unintentional, then the man-slayer will be allowed to remain in the city of refuge. He must remain within the city of refuge until the death of the High Priest sets him free. No ransom can purchase his freedom (v32).

Consider for a moment what it would be like to have to flee to a city of refuge.

> On any given day, you might be involved in an accident for which you are at fault, though you did not cause the accident intentionally. Nevertheless, a death occurs because of something you did. In that moment, your life ends for all intents and purposes. You must flee to a city of refuge because

the person's husband, brother, uncle, whoever, is coming after you to kill you. You become a hunted person.

You flee. You don't go home and pack your things. You don't say goodbye to loved ones. You flee with whatever you are carrying at that moment. With luck you will make it to the city of refuge before the avenger overtakes you.

You come into this city of Levites, but you are not a Levite. You are a stranger. Everyone knows why you have come here.

You are put on trial to determine your guilt or innocence. Being found not guilty, you are released—to the city. You cannot leave. This place is not your home and you cannot go home. You have no possessions except those you brought with you.

The Law has bound you to this place on pain of death, and so you remain in this protective custody for the rest of your life. The only way you can be released is by the death of the High Priest. So you wait and wait and wait for that event. It may be years before you can return home, or it may not happen in your lifetime. Meanwhile you must find a way to make a life here where you are, among the Levites and others like yourself who have found refuge in this city.

Sounds like a pretty bleak existence, right? You have entered a wilderness moment that, while unpleasant for a time, is necessary to preserve your life. Once you enter that city of refuge, life is about looking forward to that future hope of release and reclaiming of your inheritance.

Taking vengeance is a very emotionally charged act, and as we have seen, it can easily become an act of glorifying ourselves. For this reason, the Lord puts in place a safeguard to help keep the act of vengeance in check in cases where the death was unintentional. That safeguard is the city of refuge.

That is the purpose of the city of refuge. Now let's look at this new layout and its implications.

Shifting Boundaries

In the special case of the city of refuge, the boundary between life and death has shifted. Death and defilement used to reign outside the camp (that is, outside the tribal camp), but now death will reign outside the gates of the cities of refuge, within tribal land. So we have lost a level of separation. Anywhere outside the gates will become the domain of the avenger of blood. If the man-slayer goes outside the limits of his city of refuge, the avenger of blood can take his life with impunity.

So this is a flip. Where once a man would die for entering the Levite domain and Tabernacle compound, now the man dies if he goes outside it. The only way to preserve his life is to remain inside the boundary of the Levites and the Law until the death of the High Priest.

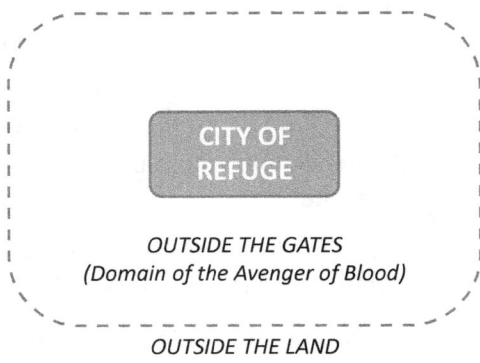

In this there is a glimpse of that picture from Numbers 16 of Aaron standing between the living and the dead. When Aaron made atonement of the people, he did not do it by going to the Tabernacle and making atonement there. Instead he went out among the tribes and established a spiritual wall that death could not cross, much like that city of refuge with its wall. All those who were found within that wall behind Aaron were granted life, as are those found within the city of refuge.

The Prophetic Picture

The basic elements of the prophetic picture are a man who faces death for unintentional bloodshed and has to remain within the confines of the city of refuge until released by the death of the High Priest. He takes refuge not just within any city but within a Levitical city.

The High Priest, of course, is a type of Christ. His death becomes the substitutionary payment for sin that releases us from the penalty of death.

The city of refuge represents the Law. Until the death of Christ, the Law preserved us, spiritually, from death so long as we remained within the boundaries of the Law. The penalty of death was executed on those going outside the confines of the Law until we were released from the Law by Christ's death. The Law is no longer our keeper in regards to the penalty of death.

There is a good bit of doctrine to be taught from that picture.

A Final Word on Zelophehad's Daughters (Numbers 36)

Chapter 36 ends the book of Numbers with these last instructions on the marriage of female heirs.

For the sake of maintaining a tribe's boundaries in the kingdom, a further stipulation is made that, should the inheritance pass to the daughter, she must marry within her tribe. Not within her family, not even within her clan, but within her tribe. The inheritance must remain in the lineage of the patriarch who originated it.

For Israel, this was a practical problem in preserving their tribal boundaries that the Lord had established. For us as believers, I think it simply translates into the requirement that those of the faith and Kingdom marry others of the faith and Kingdom. Believers should take believing spouses.

Bethabara

The last verse of the book of Numbers ends with these words:

> *"These are the commandments and the judgments which the LORD commanded the children of Israel by the hand of Moses in the plains of Moab by the Jordan, across from Jericho." Numbers 36:13*

Much has happened while we have been camped on the plains of Moab by the Jordan, across from Jericho. We have had battles, victories, and some signature failures. We have been assembled, counted, and our inheritance has been apportioned to us though it has yet to be claimed.

Here the Lord is preparing us for entering the Land with the instructions given through His prophet, Moses. In addition to the Laws we have studied here in Numbers, the entire book of Deuteronomy will be delivered while we are camped here. Moses will also speak of another Prophet to come after him, who will be the Word of the Lord to us (Deut. 18:15-19). From this place, after Moses' death, Israel will pass through the waters of the Jordan with Joshua to enter the Promised Land.

In this same place, some 1,400 years from now, another prophet will appear out of the wilderness again. He comes to the plains of Moab by the Jordan and begins to prophesy of a coming King and Kingdom and instruct the Jewish people as to what they need to do to enter that Kingdom.

The timing of this prophet may well have coincided with the fall feasts. They have tremendous eschatological significance for the Jewish people, which adds to the gravity of this prophet's message and actions and explains the people's reaction to him. At this time of year, there is an anticipation of the sounding of that last trumpet signaling them to rise, assemble, and follow the King when He comes to reign over His people. That is the message and theme of the Feast of Trumpets. There is an expectation for the fulfillment of the Day of Atonement, which the prophets likened to the Day of the Lord, when He comes to execute judgment on the nations and proclaim the Jubilee for His people and Land. There is a yearning for the final fulfillment of the Feast of Tabernacles, when they will have rest and peace and abundance in the Land, and everyone will reclaim the land of their inheritance.

In the month before these feasts, the rabbis in the synagogue begin the festival readings from Law and Prophets which will include the Deuteronomy passage about the Prophet who would come after Moses and Isaiah's prophecy of the voice crying in the wilderness (Isa. 40:3).[1]

This prophet who appears out of the wilderness is a Levite with a ministry of mikveh (the Jewish practice of water immersion we call baptism). Mikveh is practiced as an act of repentance before the Day of Atonement, but unlike the rest of the Levites who perform mikvehs at the Temple, this Levite is baptizing people at the banks of the Jordan. He exhorts them to repent (in keeping with the message of the Day of Atonement), and pass through the waters of the Jordan in preparation for entering the Kingdom.

This prophet appears at the right physical place. He appears at a significant moment in time with the message and actions the people expect. The synagogue readings have placed this prophetic figure foremost in their minds. Seeing this ancient picture returning to life before their eyes, multitudes of Israel will flock to him and ask, "Are you the Prophet?" Are you the one of whom Moses prophesied?

This man is not the Prophet but John the Baptist. This place on the plains of Moab by the Jordan, across from Jericho where he is prophesying will be known at that time as Bethabara (John 1:28).

I have never heard a pastor or Bible teacher make the connection between Bethabara and the plains of Moab by the Jordan across from Jericho. I really don't know how I stumbled upon the fact, but in researching this, the geographic description of Bethabara fit this place exactly—even in its being east of Jericho. When we lay all that we have studied about the events on the plains of Moab and the significance it had to the children of Israel on top of the picture of John the Baptist, then many details of Israel's reaction to the man, his message, and his ministry fall into place.

In John's day, the people think they will be entering a physical kingdom under a physical king who will make war with the Romans and throw them out of the Land, in accordance with the prophetic imagery of the fall feasts. It is true that the Messianic King begins His ministry at this time, but He is only laying the foundation for the coming spiritual kingdom.

---

1   A series of passages from Isaiah called the Seven of Consolation are the traditional readings for the fall feasts. The first in this series is Isaiah 40, which includes the prophecy of the voice crying in the wilderness.

No one, even the King, enters into the Kingdom without first identifying with the Passover. We left Egypt in the wake of the Passover. We began this leg of the journey in Numbers with a memorial celebration of Passover. No one was allowed to start this journey without that identification being accomplished. The first feast we will celebrate coming into the Land with Joshua will be the Passover memorial (Jos. 4:10).

Christ the King cannot come into His Kingdom without celebrating that Passover, although for Him it will mean His death just as it did for Passover Lambs. We cannot enter His glorious Kingdom without our own acceptance and identification with His death, of which Passover is symbolic. We have come full circle.

This brings us to the end of this study of the book of Numbers.

CONCLUSION

Glorification

Having come through this study of Numbers, I want to revisit the theme of glorification that runs through this leg of the wilderness journey. The purpose of this study was to learn from the example of the children of Israel what are the pitfalls and obstacles along the journey that get us off track and keep us from fully realizing God's glory in our lives.

At the beginning of the study, I explained that if we are going to navigate this journey successfully, we need to establish these things in our mind:

1. What a glorious God looks like
2. What our own glorification looks like
3. What God's definition of glorious life is

I want to revisit these in light of what we have learned.

What a Glorious God Looks Like

Walking with the children of Israel in the physical journey, we have seen Him in His physical glory in the cloud and fire that has been leading us all these years. We have seen His glory in putting our enemies under our feet in battle, and in His terrifying judgments against those in our own camp who were rebellious and unfaithful. We have seen Him glorified by a few faithful people like Joshua, Caleb, and Moses, and even an unfaithful heathen, Balaam. He has established His sovereignty and glory either by the praise of His people or by vengeance against His enemies.

Walking the spiritual journey today, we don't have the physical representations of Him, but the physical proofs aren't necessarily effective or even needed. Even with physical proofs the children of Israel still fell into unfaithfulness and rebellion. The real glory of God has to be an internalized picture of His power to take life and His love in the preserving of life, even giving eternal life. Understanding that balance of power and love is one key to understanding the glory of God. If you forget one or the other, you will get off the path in your spiritual journey.

Another key to keeping on the path is knowing His promises and plan, believing He will be faithful to keep them, and pursuing those ends. That is what separated Joshua and Caleb from the rest of Israel in terms of faithfulness. They remembered God's promises and they stayed on track with His plan, even when it took a 40 year detour.

He is a sovereign, almighty, powerful God who visits unspeakable judgment against His enemies.

He is a loving God who tempers His power with grace and mercy toward His people.

He is a faithful God—faithful to keep His promises and faithful to us even when we are unfaithful to Him.

Sovereign, powerful, loving, merciful, gracious, faithful. That is what a glorious God looks like.

What Our Glorification Looks Like

From the beginning of this Numbers journey, we have been experiencing God's "lifting up." In the taking of the census, He identifies us as individuals by "lifting our heads," which is as much a psychological act as a physical one. He identifies us with Himself by putting His name on us with the Aaronic blessing. Even in the midst of our failings and our wanderings, He invests us with greater and greater responsibilities to Himself and each other and begins molding us into the image of a royal priesthood. He writes His own message of hope into our lives at every stage. For the children of Israel, He wrote the prophetic images of Christ even into their worst moments of failings. Talk about the glory of God in earthen vessels!

Our identity is linked to God's identity and our glory is linked to His glory. The goal we are pursuing is an oneness with Him.

When the Enemy tries to get us off the path to that glorious oneness, one of the main things he attacks is our identification with God. He tries to uproot us or get us rooted in other places. We talked about some of the things we become rooted in that undermine our relationship with God, most of which were physical things. On this journey, many of us were rooted in a physical place, like Egypt, and our desire to return there warred with our pursuit of the glorious Land. We can be rooted in physical places such as our home, our church, the place where we grew up, or even our country, to the point that we refuse to move when the Lord asks us to minister in a new place. Even in the realm of our congregation, we can root ourselves in a particular place or denomination, or even a particular ministry. We can make superficial cliques for ourselves as Miriam did, which caused the Lord to have to uproot her and put her in another less glorious place for a while. Even in our faith we can become very earthbound when we should be heaven-bound.

We can become rooted in physical relationships and physical roles. The roles of parents and spouses are a couple examples of physical relationships that must change over time. We can root ourselves to a particular leader as Joshua did with Moses, or with those who have made an identity out of being a victim as the mixed multitude did.

Those who root themselves in wrong places spring up quickly but languish just as quickly when the trials of life overtake them. That is what the Parable of the Sower in Matthew 13 teaches us. This whole journey has been one of constant change and that, in itself, is part of the trials.

Leadership changes. If we root ourselves in certain leaders, we will fail when they fail—and they will fail on this journey. If Joshua had rooted his identity in Moses, he would not have entered the Land either.

Relationships and places change. God puts people in our lives that we consider out of place simply to be a catalyst in our lives and effect change.

Circumstances change. If your happiness stems from the circumstances you find yourself in, then this entire journey will be without the slightest taste of peace, rest, or well-being. The physical things of life are the wrong place to root ourselves in our life journey.

Only God never changes. We must root ourselves in a spiritual relationship with God and pursue that in whatever place or role or circumstance He puts us at any given time. If we root ourselves in the physical things, we will lose our identity at some point on this journey.

A servant is not greater than his master. Our identity is linked to God's identity, and our glory is linked to His glory. When our identity with Him becomes derailed, our own glory diminishes as a result. When we take glory from God by setting ourselves or others up in rivalry to Him, it is also an undermining of that identity with Him. Our own glory diminishes when God is diminished.

Throughout this journey, many of us have tried to do our own lifting up and take glory for ourselves in various ways. Some notable examples have been Miriam, the unfaithful spies, Zimri, Korah, Dathan, and Abiram—even Moses in one devastating moment. We talked about ways we take glory from God, mostly by not giving Him His rightful place in our lives. Some cut God out of the picture entirely. Some set themselves up as rivals in kingship and authority, while others challenged authority and boundaries God had put in place. All these challenge the Lord's place in our life and His authority and sovereignty as King over us. It isn't just important that we identify with God, but how we identify with God.

Those of us who remained rooted in our identity to Him didn't always experience fruitfulness as a result. The first generation certainly didn't experience fruitfulness in the journey. They griped about the lack of fruit in their lives until the end, not realizing that the fruitfulness they should have been pursuing was a spiritual fruitfulness and not a physical fruitfulness. .

We can be rooted and yet not fruitful. Fruitfulness has a direct relationship to faithfulness, and faithfulness is the outworking of trust. This is also something that the Parable of the Sower teaches. The parable describes those who were rooted yet not fruitful as those who received seed on thorny ground.

> *"Now he who received seed among the thorns is he who hears the word, and the cares of this world and the deceitfulness of riches choke the word, and he becomes unfruitful." Matthew 13:22*

For the most part, the first generation were poorly rooted and unfruited, but even some of the second generation were poorly fruited. Both generations failed in faithfulness, but for different reasons. While focus on the cares of this world and failing to trust the Lord marked the failing of the first generation, falling for the deceitfulness of this world's offerings most certainly marked the failing of the second. The second generation had success and victories that the first generation didn't, but those victories brought a sense of false security, self-empowerment, self-determination, and laxity that sucked many into that pursuit of worldly lusts and idolatry with Moab. They failed to remain faithful to the Lord, went after the counterfeit, and as a result, failed to enter the Land.

Following the harlotry of Moab incident, Reuben and Gad were content to remain east of the Jordan. They didn't care to enter the Land at all because they considered the plains of Moab as good enough for their families and flocks. They had come into a place of relative rest and peace, and were content to quit the journey while their brothers still hadn't come into their inheritance. A lack of understanding God's big picture and a lack of heart to pursue the final reward are the failings of the second generation.

Following the parable to its conclusion, there would be those who experienced the fruitfulness of the good land, and increased that fruitfulness in varying degrees. There were those who entered the Land to claim their inheritance with Joshua, but we don't read about them in the book of Numbers. Numbers is really about those who go through this journey unrooted and un-fruited, and that is what makes it an admonition to us, as Paul tell us in 1 Corinthians 10.

What God's Definition of Glorious Living Is

God's glorious living is embodied in the Sabbath experience in the Land. The ultimate experience of glorious living is pictured in the Jubilee which is defined as an experience of rest, peace, joy, well-being, freedom, fruitfulness, oneness with Himself, and harmony with each other. The final fulfillment of God's glorious living is something that remains for believers in the future, but we can get tastes of that glorious life as we walk on this journey of life. In fact, having those brief experiences of peace, or joy, or well-being are what carry us through this journey at time when we want to give up.

On this journey in Numbers, we spent most of the time in the least glorious Sabbath experience with God. He fed us, but not what we wanted to eat. He led us, but not where we wanted to go. We slept when we needed sleep, but it wasn't restful. He kept us from enemies, and yet we had no peace. He let death and enemies overtake us when we rebelled so that we would understand the corruption within us and the protection and preservation He so mercifully offers. Only a few of us got a taste of the fruitfulness awaiting us in the Land, but most rejected it as a reward not worth pursuing. By the end of the journey, those same people ached for fruit in their lives and fell away in discouragement.

The first generation coming out of Egypt covered much ground in life but never progressed in their relationship with God. They were forever rooted in the unrealistic expectation of what they could get from Egypt and a desire to return there. They were forever demanding their own way in pursuit of worldly desires and cravings. Their lives were marked by a resistance to authority, poor decision-making, and a lack of trust. Their example is meant as an admonition to us and yet so many of us follow their path in our own spiritual life.

I think there are a lot of Christians who settle for the least glorious experience with God. They live in a spiritual wilderness like the first generation did, walking through life with one foot still in Egypt. They believe in God, they go through the motions of walking the walk, but when decisions have to be made in life, they let their own judgment and physical desires dictate the path they take. When strength is needed, they look to their own resources, their human leadership, and whatever support they have in life rather than to God. They walk and walk, and yet are not at rest or peace, or experiencing any fruitfulness in life. For them the walk of faith becomes like an unendurable slogging through deep sand, and many will end up leaving the faith because it has been an unfulfilling experience. But when asked why it was unfulfilling, they won't know why.

The reason this happens is because, when the moment comes where they have to step up in trust and faith that would take them to the next level, they drop back instead and settle for the less demanding relationship. They think they will be satisfied with simply walking and being fed and having God's protection and provision, but what they will be missing is fruitfulness. The fruitfulness that comes out of that next level of relationship with God is what makes this journey of life bearable. Without it, there remains only this vague sense of aimlessness and wasting away.

Fruitfulness comes with giving up something to God and reaping a return from it. I am *not* endorsing the "prosperity" doctrine in this, which promises a physical return on a physical sacrifice and focuses largely on giving money. No, that is not what I mean at all. When I talk about the act of giving up something, it is a relational act such as the one James describes.

> *"Humble yourselves in the sight of the Lord, and He will lift you up."*
> James 4:10

Maybe it is an act of submission to authority. Maybe it's an act of letting go of something in life—letting go of your Egypt or a craving. Maybe it is deliberate decision to trust God to handle a situation instead of relying on yourself. It is a giving-up moment that engages God and gives Him His place in our lives. In doing this, we glorify God, and He in return lifts us up and rewards us with glorification. So how do you get to that next level?

Making Progress in the Journey

This is a journey for all of us, and it is vital that we keep progressing toward that reward and a fullness of relationship with God. If you feel like you are not making progress, it may be that somewhere along the way you ceased giving glory to God or living in a way that brings glory to Him. Maybe you are reacting to a situation in a way that is not glorifying to God. Maybe you are trying to remedy the situation by your own power, will, or wisdom, instead of submitting to God's will or wisdom, or trying to control the situation instead of letting God have control. Maybe you have simply retreated to that least glorious level of relationship with God. At this level, you are taking from God but not stepping up of your own volition to engage in the journey with Him.

Getting to the next level of relationship with God is going to require that step of faithfulness and trust. Whatever your circumstances are or whatever conflicts you are dealing with, approach them with these questions:

- What does a glorious God looks like to me?
- What do I know of God's power and love from past experience? Has He been faithful to me in the past?
- If I give my situation over to Him, do I believe He has the power to deal with it?
- If He has the power to deal with it, do I trust Him to deal with it? Am I willing to let go of my own control and give control to Him?
- Do I trust Him enough to be at peace with His handling of the situation?

The best strategy for successfully navigating our spiritual journey is to become sensitive to the ways we give glory to God or take glory from God. We don't always realize what we are doing when we are doing it, so self-reflection has to be a continual habit. Here are some questions to ask for self-assessment.

- How am I handling my situation or circumstance?
    - What is driving my decision-making? Am I making decisions based on my estimation of myself, my abilities, and resources, or God's? When we studied the names of the spies in Lesson 6, we saw a number of ways we give glory to God or take glory from Him in the decisions we make.
    - Where or to whom do I turn for lifting up? Am I trying to promote myself, justify myself, vindicate myself, or otherwise take glory for myself? Is personal vengeance involved?
    - Have I fallen into self-pity over this circumstance? Self-pity is a means of self-glorification because it demands people lift you up as a victim. We talked about that in Lessons 3 and 4.
    - Am I resorting to old ways of coping? We talked about that in Lesson 4.
- How am I pursuing the end goals of peace, love, joy, and my own well-being? By what source or what means am I trying to achieve these?
- What things do I fear? Is God more powerful than the things I fear? We give power to things we fear and their power rivals God's place in our life. We talked about this in Lesson 6.

- Where is my security (my job, my family, retirement savings, or insurance policies)? Am I so dependent on these things that God will have to take them away from me before I learn to rely on Him? That is what He had to do to teach the children of Israel to rely on Him. As Moses said, *"So He humbled you, allowed you to hunger, and fed you with manna which you did not know nor did your fathers know, that He might make you know that man shall not live by bread alone; but man lives by every word that proceeds from the mouth of the LORD." Deuteronomy 8:3*
- Am I being inflexible over some issue?
  - Is my inflexibility because I am standing firm in alignment with God or is it for self-serving reasons, such as not submitting to authority or just not liking to be uprooted?
  - Is my inflexibility inhibiting my ministry? We talked about how extremes in living, character traits, or sensibilities can prevent us from fully entering into ministry or cause conflict in the congregation. This is what the Corinthian church suffered from.
- How do I react when God puts me in extreme circumstances?
  - Can I give Him glory by looking to Him when I am abased and in need?
  - Do I forget to give Him glory when I am abounding?

Consider what conflicts you have in your life. As we have seen in this study, conflicts often arise when relationship boundaries are being crossed or are not in alignment with what God has defined. We talked about these in Lessons 4 and 5.

- Do you know your relational boundaries with the people in your life? Consider the relationships you have in life and how God says those relationships should work. This should include Kohathite-type roles that we talked about in Lesson 2.
- Are relationship boundaries being challenged?
  - Have you taken responsibility for unrealistic expectations people have put on you?
  - If someone else is challenging your boundaries, what have you done to re-establish those boundaries and correct the relationship? Have you made use of your Kohathite- and priest-level supports?
  - If you are the one challenging boundaries, what do you need to do to correct that relationship?
- Is there disunity in your family or congregation? Disunity is one of the symptoms that an old-man nature may still be at work.

- Are there tearing-down behaviors in your relationships (criticism, back-biting, etc.)?
- Are superficial boundaries and rules causing conflict and division in your relationships?

That's a lot to work on. It takes a lifetime of work, and even if you come to a place of rest and peace, you aren't exempt from continuing the journey. So long as you have fellow believers still on their journey, you are called to help them as well. Lift your head and press on.

Our glory is linked to God's glory. The more glory we give Him in our lives, the more His glory will reflect on us and lift us up. The goal is to reach that oneness with Him.

I send you on with this blessing:

> *"The LORD bless you and keep you; The LORD make His face shine upon you, and be gracious to you; The LORD lift up His countenance upon you, and give you peace." Numbers 6:24-26*

www.ingramcontent.com/pod-product-compliance
Lightning Source LLC
Chambersburg PA
CBHW060418010526
44118CB00017B/2269